The Road Going

A Mother,
A Daughter,
An Extraordinary
Journey

Suzanne Bobo

Suzanne Bobo
and
Brittany Tregarthen

BRittanyTregarthen

HUNTER LEE Studies in Language, Literacy and Culture
Kodiak, Alaska

The names of Brittany's peers have been changed for their privacy, as have the names of birthparents and social workers involved in the adoption proceedings described in Chapters One and Two.

THE ROAD GOING
A Mother, a Daughter, an Extraordinary Journey

Copyright © 2011 HUNTER LEE Studies in Language, Literacy and Culture. Except for brief quotations in critical publications or reviews, no part of this book may be reproduced in any manner without prior written permission from the publisher. Write: Permissions, Hunter Lee Studies, P.O. Box 264, Kodiak, AK 99615.

HUNTER LEE Studies in Language, Literacy and Culture
Post Office Box 264
Kodiak, AK 99615

ISBN: 978-0-615-44158-0

Cover photography and design by Annjannette Larsen

The Road Going

Contents

To Bo, who made it happen — Suzanne
To my best friend, Aharon — Brittany

Acknowledgements

So many people have encouraged us to write this book. We are grateful to them all. We thank LeeAnn Schmelzenbach, Leslie Leyland Fields, Deb Robson, Stephen Lesko, Sara Loewen and Gennifer Moreau, who reviewed early drafts of the manuscript and made valuable comments. Priscilla Gibson-Roberts gave us much-needed advice on the creative and the business aspects of our project. Victor Downing, Bob Borchardt, Jane McBee and Annjannette Larsen took wonderful photographs. Kitty Deal wrote the fantastic discussion questions. We thank them all for their work and their friendship. Thomas Hutton and John Leavitt, public relations officials at the University of Colorado at Colorado Springs and the City of Colorado Springs, respectively, helped us with fact checking. Attorney Ernest Schlereth, staff at Hope Community Resources, and members of the Stone Soup Group actively supported Brittany's goal to pursue writing as a career. We thank them. And we thank our family and friends who have supported us, encouraged us and prayed for us as we have worked on this project. We give thanks above all to our God. It is a great blessing indeed that He crafted us both into writers and then gave us the gift of one another.

Foreword

When Suzanne Bobo approached me to write this Foreword, my reactions were mixed: amazed, thrilled, excited, honored, and a little nervous. Why did she ask me? Was it because we had connected so well when we first met in 2005? At the time Suzanne contracted with me to customize The Visions System, a computerized independent living system, for Brittany to help her move forward. I remember the first letter I wrote to her when I expressed my feelings about her and her daughter: "You have such a wonderful attitude, and you have done so much to build Brittany's independence."

I loved Suzanne's wonderful laid-back temperament and her determination to continue to see everything through, no matter what. Even though I was only a minute piece of her existence in her very complex life (as I have learned from this book), I could see that she was always trying to make independence happen in the best way for Brittany and for others as well.

As I read this compelling memoir, I reflected on many important times in my own life. Suzanne must have known how I could relate. One day that came to mind was when my 5-year-old son was being rolled into the operating room for open-heart surgery and my eyes were welling up with tears. The man standing next to me was watching his daughter being rolled into the operating room at the same time. I said to him, "what is she going in for?" and his response was "Brain surgery." Brain surgery! It was at that moment that I realized I wasn't the only parent suffering for her children.

Suzanne and I are both parents of young ladies with developmental disabilities. We also have a passion that our daughters be independent and a part of their community. My daughter, Stacie, lives in her own townhome and has belonged to the Jaycees, a regular bowling league and softball league, and goes to church with her own friends. She has had several dynamite jobs in the community over the years. However, Stacie can't read or write and can only articulate about 150 words.

Similarly, Brittany is enjoying the many community activities such as movies, bowling, and lunch dates with her many church friends. She has such a wonderful network. And even beyond that is where I totally commend Suzanne. She has taken all of Brittany's gifts and utilized them to the fullest. To see them writing a book together is absolutely outstanding. For Suzanne to encourage Brittany to expand her talents to song writing is, without a doubt, the ultimate. To read the lyrics just sends chills up my spine. What disability? Brittany will definitely change the way people think!

The Road Going is a great title. This memoir takes you down many roads, most of them quite unexpected. There are sudden turns, there are times when you feel you might fly off a hairpin curve or that you might be approaching a dead end. But the authors keep going. Most of the of the time you will be surprised at the outcome. The authors write with an honesty and a truthfulness that keeps you believing in every word.

I loved the tone of the book. Suzanne's deep-seated love for taking care of her children, her husband, her faith. I loved when she had time to sit back and have a cup of tea. She always made life feel low-key but, at the same time, got things to happen.

There is no doubt that the most important aspect of this memoir is how Suzanne and Brittany shared their thoughts and brought them together as one in this book. To see mother and daughter working alongside each other and compiling their work in the same book will bring tears to your eyes in the same fashion as the story itself does. I loved every word, every page, and every chapter. The anticipation kept me turning pages as fast as I could.

Do you have struggles in your life? This book is the friend you need. What a great opportunity for parents, parents of children with disabilities, and parents of children who are adopted to see another family work it out. What a great opportunity for professionals in education, health care, ministry and social services to peek inside the world as it experienced by so many of their clients. Anyone and everyone will be challenged, comforted, and encouraged to become a better person by reading *The Road Going*.

Nancy Baesman
Vice President
Visions for Independent Living, Inc.
Littleton, Colorado

Chapter One

The Journey Begins

I am standing at the sink washing dishes and watching my children play in our back yard. A concrete walkway meanders through dense patches of lilac shrubs, and my five-year old son Doran cautiously navigates this sidewalk on his Big Wheels. He sports a Superman cape, pajama pants, a helmet and a mischievous grin.

When I looked out a moment ago, four-year old Brittany was riding her tricycle behind her brother, trying to work up speed to pass him, but now I see only Doran.

I notice something moving near the leftmost part of the yard, and I crane my neck to take a look. I see a shiny pink object over by the Little Tikes toddler slide and realize it is the top of a bicycle helmet. After a few seconds I can see Brittany's head and shoulders. She is struggling to get up the Little Tikes stairs and I have difficulty understanding why: she's reached the top of this slide countless times. Finally, I catch on: she's attempting to drag her tricycle behind her!

My first impulse is to rush outside and stop her, for I can already see what is about to transpire. But I stop myself. She has it in her head to ride the tricycle down the slide. If I divert her from the task now, she will certainly attempt it later. I tell myself it is better for her to learn the hard way that riding down the slide is a bad idea. I know it will cause a scrape, and some tears will certainly fall. But I also know this is the way she learns. So I bite my lip and watch as she positions the tricycle at the top of the short slide and mounts.

As I expected, she crashes. The tricycle makes it to the bottom but tips over, and Brittany tumbles off. I wince and wait for her to wail. She does not. Instead, she takes the trike around and ascends the staircase again. Once again, she crashes, and I wait for the wail. I wait in vain. A third time she drags the trike up the stairs and mounts it at the top of the slide.

This time when she falls I hear her scream, but not in pain. Rather, she screams in anger. "Stupid, stupid bike!" Her face is red with rage. She finishes her tantrum and lugs the trike once more to the top of the slide. This time, she completes her ride without tumbling. She pauses, brushes the grass off her shorts, and pedals to rejoin her brother on the raceway.

I CHOOSE THIS STORY whenever I want to describe my relationship with my daughter Brittany, who is now 23 years old. The story illustrates how, as a parent, I have walked the fine line between the impulse to protect my child and the desire to let her grow, even when I know that growth may be painful. There is a universal quality to it. When I tell this story, other parents smile and nod; likewise, when I say that the scene on the slide has re-peated itself—with different props and different outcomes—at nearly every stage in my daughter's development.

The story also illustrates specific information about my daugh-ter. When I tell this story I mean to convey something about Britta-ny's athleticism, her competitiveness, her persistence and her ten-dency to get angry at someone else (in this case, her trike) when something goes wrong. My audience can quickly grasp the traits that are so deeply ingrained in Brittany's personality.

The story says nothing about the fact that Brittany has Down Syndrome, a genetic condition that has caused delays in her intel-lectual, emotional, social and physical development. Nor does it suggest how my role as her parent has been shaped by the challenges of raising a child with Down Syndrome. The diagnosis is not the central feature of Brittany's existence, nor is it the focus of my relationship with her. She is my daughter; I am her mother; these features define us with respect to one another. She is quick-tempered, athletic and ambitious; I am reflective, deliberate and stoical. These traits often place our individual personalities at cross-purposes.

We share a love of adventure, though, and this brings me back to the story on the slide. Today, Brittany's prop is her bicycle; "the slide" is the steep driveway connecting our house to the gravel road below. Brittany loves the freedom of riding her bike from our house to our church, and she promises to stop and look before she heads down the gravel drive and into the road. I have taught her how to ride her bike safely. I wouldn't worry if it was one of my other children riding. But when Brittany mounts her bike at the top of the drive, I cannot tear myself away from the window, where I stand and watch and pray.

The truth is Brittany has watched and waited, too, as I have taken joy-rides down the slide. My adventures have had a different character than hers, of course, and her response to them is that of a daughter and not a mother. But she has watched me when I have experienced triumph, and she has seen me crash and burn. We have prayed for each other, laughed at one another, comforted one another. She has stories she tells, too, when she wants to communicate the nature of our relationship and her perspective on my personality.

Brittany and I share a fondness for story-telling. I am a newspaper columnist, feature writer and former reporter. Brittany writes poetry, song lyrics and, sometimes, fiction. Her creative style differs from mine, her subject matter is more reflective of her age, but we have this in common: sometimes we hurry that bike faster down the slide just so we can run into the house and write about the ride.

The Road Going is the story of one ride we have yet to finish, our journey through what we call "Brittany's launching years," this

sometimes uneasy period that will end when she has reached ma-
turity. We have come a long way; Brittany has her own apartment
and can cook all of her own meals. But the road stretches out before
us yet; her apartment is in the basement of her parents' home, and
as a young woman confronting the challenges of an intellectual disability, she is beginning to recognize that a life of quasi-indepen-
dence is a more likely outcome for her than a life in a home of her
own. The place she lands, once these launching years are done, will
look quite different from the place awaiting her siblings, and that is
part of the thrill of the journey for Brittany. But it will be somewhere other than my home; I have come to accept this. And that is
part of the terror of the trip for me.

As stories go, this one is more like a mutual travelogue than an
auto-biography. It is a very personal story about a mother and a
daughter traveling to a destination that is yet unknown. It includes
my reflections on the journey and Brittany's. How the story ends is
anybody's guess. Like all fantastic adventures, however, this story
does have a very definite beginning.

WHEN BRITTANY ENTERED my life, I was 24 years old,
married to the young chairman of the university economics department, and writing for a profession. Tim and I had a comfortable
mountain home poised grandly over the city of Colorado Springs
on a ridge between the summit of Eagle Mountain and Sunrise
Peak. When Tim was home, we worked on a joint publishing project, a monthly journal used nationally in college classrooms. When
Tim was teaching at the university I worked on my independent
writing, took long walks through woods dense with ponderosa
pine and scrub oak and developed my skills in black-and-white
photography and photo finishing.

And I delighted in our son Doran. At sixteen months old, Doran
was a meteor of happy activity. He toted building blocks and dish
towels around the house in a bright orange wagon with plastic tires
that made a funny sound on our hardwood floors. He giggled in

delight as he tumbled with Buffy, our energetic greyhound/golden lab mix, who was only a puppy but who would have trampled a toddler any less stout than Doran. He loved his outdoor time, and every day after lunch he would grab a bucket of toys I kept for him by the front door and head outside—with me in tow—to dig with a spoon in his sandbox or to pick wildflowers in our alpine meadows.

Doran had been physically placed in our care at birth, a private arrangement between his birthmother Teresa and us, but he was not yet, officially, ours. Due to the extraordinary difficulty of finalizing a private adoption that involved parties in two different states, we had been obliged to get an agency involved when Doran was about fourteen months old. The Colorado Court would not recognize the letters of relinquishment from Connecticut, so to proceed with the adoption Teresa would have to relinquish her rights to him in Colorado, which by some miracle she agreed to do. However, Colorado had just recently made private adoptions illegal, so she would have to relinquish Doran to the adoption agency, which would then officially place him with us. To call the process an ordeal would be a gross understatement, but with Doran now at sixteen months old, and the relinquishment hearing on the Court docket, Tim and I finally saw tangible signs that the adoption would, some day, be final.

Teresa flew in from Connecticut to appear at the relinquishment hearing which took place in the El Paso County Courthouse at one o'clock on Friday, November 13, 1987. A separate hearing, in which the legal parental rights of the "absentee" birth father had been terminated, had taken place two hours earlier. Teresa had asked the agency to arrange a meeting between her and our family and she wanted the meeting to occur after the hearing. We had decided to meet at a playground area in Monument Valley Park on Colorado Springs' north end.

Tim and I were already there pushing Doran on a swing when Teresa arrived accompanied by two representatives from the agency, Gloria, the social worker, and Sharon, who worked as an assistant. The two women kept a respectful distance while Teresa sat on a bench and watched our family play. Tim sat next to Teresa for a short while and talked with her but she never took her eyes off our son. After about thirty minutes Teresa got up and approached me and Doran near the slide. "I can see," she said, "who his parents really are, and I wish you all the best." Then she turned and walked away.

Gloria walked with her, but Sharon held back. "Can you wait here for just a minute?" she asked us. "I need to get something from my car and talk to you."

NO TWO ADOPTIONS ARE alike, but with the exception of those that occur within families or certain social groups, such as tribes, most adoptions involve several Court hearings, a home study completed by a psychologist or social worker, agonizing periods of waiting and wishing, thousands of dollars, and reams of paperwork. When, through our attorney, we secured the assistance of a private adoption agency, Tim and I weren't sure what, exactly, to expect.

We had already completed several steps in the adoption process, though new laws in Colorado had made some of them mute. Teresa's original relinquishment of her rights and placement of Doran in our home, for example, were invalid as far as the Colorado Court was concerned; hence the requirement that Teresa appear before a Colorado judge. However, the fact that Tim and I had already completed a home study worked in our favor. We were very relieved when Gloria told us that the existing home study met all of the agency's requirements.

There was the paperwork, however. Before the agency could even petition the Court for the relinquishment hearing, Tim and I had been required to complete an enormous application for adoption. Although this was a time-consuming process, for the most part, it was simple. The sections asking information about personal background were a cinch. We weren't sure, however, how to complete some sections because the paperwork didn't really fit the circumstances, particularly where we were instructed to indicate what category of child we would adopt. Doran was male, white, less than a month old at placement, had no known birth defects—should we check only the boxes next to those criteria, or should we check the boxes we would mark if we were answering in the abstract?

After some discussion, we decided to check the boxes as if we were starting the process from scratch. What gender would we accept? We checked both female and male. What race would we accept? We checked all. Would we consider siblings? We checked yes. How many siblings? The list went on and on.

The medical part exhausted us. Every manner of birth defect and illness was listed, and the form had a yes and no box for each one of them. We referred frequently to our medical dictionary as we navigated our way through this section, because many of the conditions listed were things we had never heard of, and we wanted to answer truthfully. Could we adopt a child who had a cleft palate? Yes. Cushing's syndrome? Yes. Heart disease? We lived at a very high elevation, so here we thought it would be best to say No.

DORAN AND I WERE sitting on the bench sharing a snack when Sharon returned from her car with a file, presumably ours, in her hand. "Everything went fine today," she said as she took a seat next to Doran. "We're working with your attorney to prepare the paperwork requesting a hearing to finalize. We're looking at January... maybe February."

"That's a great relief," said Tim, finally able to relax and join us on the bench. "When you said you had something to talk to us about, we thought..."

"No, no," she said, smiling. "Everything went fine." She paused, then she opened the folder on her lap and pulled out our adoption application. She leafed through several pages, then stopped and looked up at us.

"When you filled this out, you said you would be willing to adopt a child with Down Syndrome. Is that still the case?"

We looked at each other. "Yes..." said Tim. He looked at Sharon. "Why?"

Her eyes met his and she smiled, "We have a six-week-old girl. We need to place her by Monday or she goes into the County system." Sharon looked at me. "This baby has a little bit of Down's, but she's a nice clean baby."

DOWN SYNDROME IS A congenital condition in which a person has extra genetic material, an additional chromosome at the twenty-first pair. The anomaly, also known as Trisomy 21, is exhibited in a set of physical traits frequently seen together in persons with the extra chromosome. This set of traits includes: a small, abnormally shaped head; decreased muscle tone; flattened nose; a single, deep crease in the palms of the hands; small ears, mouth and hands; upward slanting eyes; white spots on the colored part of the eyes; a tendency of tongue protrusion; and short stature.

Occurring in about 1 out of every 800 live births, Down Syndrome is the most common chromosomal disorder in humans and the most common and best-known cause of intellectual disability. Intellectual disability is but one Down Syndrome symptom; others are hypotomia (low muscle tone); delays in physical growth, maturation, bone development and dental eruption; delays in emotional, physical and social development; heart defects; hypothyroidism and other autoimmune disorders; diabetes; Alzheimer disease and cataracts. While it is true that these symptoms vary in severity from person to person, ranging from mild to severe, no person with Down Syndrome may be said to have only a "little bit of Down's."

When Sharon used these words to describe the baby known to the agency as "Brittany," Tim and I interpreted it to mean that, overall, the baby was healthy. Sharon told us what little she knew about Brittany; that her Apgar scores at birth were good and that she had a tiny hole in heart but that the opinion of the cardiologist

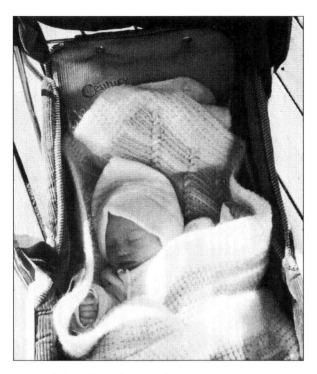

Brittany's first day in her new home.

was that the hole would close on its own. She wrote the name of Brittany's cardiologist on a piece of notebook paper, gave it to us, and closed the file, encouraging us to think about it over the weekend. She needed our answer by Monday, she said, then she got up and left us sitting, speechless, at the park.

WHEN PARENTS LEARN that their baby has a disability, they may experience a tangled knot of emotions that includes fear, elation, doubt, sadness, guilt, excitement, uncertainty, grief. Of course, as parents we know that none of our children will live a life free of challenge, but we can expect a disabled child to encounter obstacles each and every day. It is a sobering thing, to ponder the future of this child, even though a baby's arrival is usually an occasion for celebration.

When Tim and I called Sharon at the agency on Monday morning and told her that we wanted to adopt Brittany, we thought we had a good idea what to expect. Before we went home late Friday afternoon we stopped at the library and checked out every book we could find on raising children with developmental delays. Using our connections through our church we got the cardiologist's home telephone number and we called him to hear for ourselves his assurances on the heart issue. We also called several parents referred to us by the local Down Syndrome society. When Brittany arrived in our home one week later, the fact that she had Down Syndrome was neither a surprise nor a shock to us. We had no reason to grieve over her diagnosis.

Or so we thought.

Grief found us three weeks later when Brittany's health took a nose dive. I was home with her, scrambling to meet a deadline for an article. Tim had taken Doran to town to run errands and to do some research at the university library. Since Brittany's placement, she had seemed weak and listless, certainly not the bundle of energy Doran had been at two months old. We didn't have her established at our own pediatrician's office yet, but several times I took her to see the pediatrician who attended her at birth, and he said that most likely Brittany was exhibiting the lower level of physical activity one could expect from a baby with Down Syndrome. By the morning of Brittany's nineteenth day in our home, my concern turned into dread. Brittany had no fever, but in the previous 24 hours she had spit up all of her milk. She was uncomfortable being held. Her skin had a grey cast and purple splotches. I called her pediatrician's office again. When the doctor returned my call he asked only a few questions then said: "It sounds like your baby is in heart failure. Get her to Memorial immediately. They will be expecting you."

BY THE GRACE OF GOD, it was our own pediatrician who was pulling duty in the ER the day I carried Brittany's limp little body into Memorial Hospital. Within moments, he was summoned to her bedside, where the pediatric cardiologist soon joined him. Brittany had already been placed under an oxygen tent and on an IV solution for hydration, a heart monitor, and a machine that measured her oxygen saturation. Before the end of the hour, chest X-rays had been ordered, blood drawn, an echocardiogram performed, various meds added to Brittany's IV. I stayed by her the entire time, holding her fragile hand in my own and pleading with God for her comfort. At one point, one of the nurses started to ask me to leave then thought the better of it. Instead, she told me that preparations were being made for Brittany to be admitted to the pediatric intensive care unit. Our pediatrician, who by now was tending to another child in the ER, caught my attention from across the room and promised to catch up with us in the pediatric ICU.

Hours later, while Tim sat with Doran on his lap, on one side of Brittany's bed and I sat on the other, the pediatrician and cardiologist came in to Brittany's room together. The pediatrician told us that Brittany had experienced RSV respiratory distress. RSV, or respiratory syncytial virus, can affect the lower and upper respiratory tracts, is prevalent in respiratory illnesses such as pneumonia and can be extremely dangerous in infants and others with compromised cardio-respiratory systems. The prognosis for Brittany's recovery from RSV was good, but we would need to keep her in the hospital until her health status improved. I had questions—a lot of questions—but somehow I couldn't find the voice for them, so I nodded dumbly as the pediatrician spoke.

Finally, the cardiologist chimed in. The reason the RSV had affected Brittany so profoundly was due to an underlying heart condition. The echocardiogram revealed that Brittany had a massive hole, approximately the size of a nickel, in the wall between the atrial chambers of her heart. The hole, known as an atrial septal defect, would need to be closed surgically. Brittany would need to remain on oxygen until her situation improved. We could expect this initial hospitalization to last about ten days.

It was Tim who managed to speak first. "But you told us on the phone that the hole in Brittany's heart was small and that it would close on its own."

"You called me at home," the cardiologist answered. "When I spoke to you I had this child confused with another that I also am treating. That child, who also has Downs, will heal on her own." He pointed at Brittany. "This child has a massive hole in her heart, and it will not close without surgery."

WITHIN 24 HOURS OF Brittany's hospitalization, Tim and I had become conversant in a new language. We could diagram the heart with all its chambers, valves and septa. We could describe the normal functioning of the human heart and explain why the hole in Brittany's resulted in an increased flow of blood to the lungs, causing a swishing sound known as a heart murmur. We understood the dynamics of respiratory syncytial virus. We knew what "respiratory distress" meant, along with a host of other terms, such as mottling, heaving, bronchiolitis, nebulizer and pulmonary hypertension. We tossed around codes (ASD, RSV, CBC, O2 sat) like medical insiders.

I stayed at the hospital with Brittany, snatching sleep in an upholstered chair that converted into a small bed. I learned where the housekeeping staff stored sheets and towels, and I helped myself to them as I needed. I knew which nurses made coffee and I became their regular visitor. I discovered that Brittany's morning respiratory treatments lasted just long enough for me to walk down the hall and take a shower.

Brittany was improving; I could see that. The oxygen especially perked her up. The oxygen "tent," positioned so that it covered her face, resembled a clear glass serving bowl placed upside down. When she peered out of it she looked like a tiny astronaut. Her curious eyes danced as she took in the scene around her. She kicked her legs energetically. She reached for a blue penguin toy Tim had brought her. She had more of a grip when she squeezed my finger.

I was allowed to hold her only when she needed to be fed, because she did so much better under the oxygen tent than she did just wearing a oxygen cannula under her nose. But I ached to hold her more. I noticed that some of the older children in the pediatric ward had oxygen tents large enough for them to sit up in, so I pestered the nurses to give Brittany a similar tent and, after two days, my request was granted. I watched how the nurses tucked the plastic sheeting under the mattress. When they left the room I undid one corner, crawled under and secured the edges behind me. I sat under the tent, held Brittany close to my chest and sang to her. She watched my face from clear blue eyes that grew heavy with sleep. I hummed softly while she rested.

WHILE BRITTANY GREW stronger and I kept a bedside vigil, Tim and Doran dealt with the ramifications of Brittany's diagnosis. Brittany had recovered from the dangerous effects of the RSV, but she had pulmonary hypertension, a condition related to her heart defect. Our Eagle Mountain house was built at an elevation of 9,000 feet above sea level. Neither the cardiologist nor the pediatrician would authorize Brittany returning to that altitude—and Tim and I didn't want to take her there—so she would remain in the hospital until she could be released elsewhere. Colorado Springs is at an elevation of about 6,500 feet above sea level, which the doctors thought would be acceptable. Tim and Doran scoured the city for a rental that would be suitable for our family and our dog. With a stroke of luck, they located a split-level house in an older suburban neighborhood within walking distance of the university.

Gloria, the social worker from the adoption agency, stopped by the hospital and I brought her up to date, encouraging her to visit the new house, if she felt it was necessary. A cardiac catheterization had been scheduled for Brittany on January 12. It was a routine procedure that would shed more light on Brittany's cardiopulmonary condition, but it did carry a risk of infection and death. If Brittany dies in that procedure, I told Gloria, I don't want her to die without a family of her own. I begged Gloria to pull whatever strings she had to pull to get our adoption finalized before January 12.

Meanwhile, a team of friends and fellow faculty members gathered on the mountain and packed our belongings into a huge truck Tim had rented. Before packing the extension ladder, Tim leaned it against the house and climbed up to pull down the Christmas lights he had strung just a month earlier. Our neighbor Don came over and called up to him. Tim couldn't hear, so he climbed part-way down. "The adoption isn't final, Tim," Don shouted up to him. "Why don't you just give her back?"

I heard this story when one of Brittany's nurses came into her room to tell me my husband had been admitted to the ER. In a fit of rage over Don's comment, Tim had slammed the cargo door on the moving van, catching his own hand in the act. By the time I got to the ER, Tim had learned that his hand was not broken—just badly bruised—but not so bruised as his spirit, which still reeled from the impact of our neighbor's insensitivity.

IN ORDER TO GET THE January issue of our magazine to subscribers on time, Tim and I had to have the page proofs to the printer by December 15, a deadline we missed because neither of us was capable of stringing words together to make sentences, let alone pages. We sent our subscribers and our advertisers a postcard apologizing for the delay and promising a double issue for February. When the moving van brought our household goods to the Applewood Drive house, Tim unloaded the computer right away and got busy setting up the cumbersome system that would allow him to write his articles. His second priority was Doran's bed, followed by the ladder and the box that held Christmas lights.

The lights blinked cheerfully when we brought Brittany home. Our new house seemed delighted to shelter us—all of us—in one place for the celebration of Christ's birth. Gloria called us on Christmas Eve and gave us the wonderful news that the juvenile magistrate had agreed to a hearing for the finalization of adoption on Friday, January 8, and had said she would hear the case for finalization for both Brittany and Doran at the same hearing. The day after Christmas Tim called our priest and made arrangements to have Brittany baptized on Monday, January 11. Whatever the outcome of the cardiac catheterization on January 12, our bonds to her would be sealed by the stamp of the Court and the waters of Holy Baptism. Tim and I would be relieved from the fear of losing Doran in the adoption labyrinth. Eighteen months after his birth, he too, would be ours at last.

Chapter Two

Stop That Baby!

It was the kind of telephone call that people conjure up in their worst nightmare.

Her pregnancy had been a difficult one, with unexplained bleeding early on and extraordinary fatigue. She was a young woman, she had that in her favor, but she was overwhelmed. She and her husband had a sixteen-month old toddler who had been having medical problems. After months of wondering and testing, they had discovered the little girl had a disability she would never outgrow. They were delighted with the second pregnancy, but scared, too. If this baby had problems, how would they ever cope?

The obstetrician recommended an amniocentesis, and an appointment was scheduled at a hospital in nearby Denver. An amniocentesis is an analysis of the amniotic fluid that surrounds a fetus. The test is performed by inserting a needle through a woman's belly and into the uterus. About 2 tablespoons of amniotic fluid are removed and examined. The fluid reveals important information about the baby's health, such as the presence of certain genetic conditions like Down Syndrome.

The amniocentesis came back normal, indicating that to the extent possible by the test, several potential disabilities were ruled out. When the young mother experienced premature labor several weeks later, she went on bed rest and endured.

Two weeks before the scheduled birth date of the baby they now knew was a daughter, the phone rang. A hospital administrator explained that there had been a mix-up in the lab on the day the amniocentesis was done. Another woman, whose fetus had been diagnosed with Down Syndrome had just delivered a baby who did not have Down Syndrome. The other women who had had tests the same day were all being notified. Could she please return to the hospital for further testing?

With only a week remaining until her due date, the young woman learned that indeed it was her lab sample that had been switched with that of the other woman. The baby she was expecting was confirmed to have Down Syndrome. She had been expecting the news and had already located a private adoption agency that was prepared to find a home for the baby she knew she could not keep. A month later she and her husband relinquished "Brittany" to the agency that would subsequently place her with us. I have thought about this couple often, prayed for them, wished for their happiness. And I have wondered: does my love for Brittany diminish at all the loss they must have felt the day they let her go?

IN THE LATE AFTERNOON on January 8, 1988 our house bustled with joyful activity. Tim and I hosted a festive open house, a sort of post-Christmas, house-warming, thank-you party to express our gratitude to all of those good friends who had supported our family during the recent crisis. The staff from the adoption agency, colleagues from the university, neighbors, friends from church, and family members filed in at different times to see our new place and to express congratulations for the adoptions, now final, of our two precious children.

Tim and I had been prepared for a long Court session earlier that morning, but the hearing before the magistrate took less than twenty minutes. Our attorney was present, of course, as was Gloria, the social worker from the adoption agency. Doran went to the hearing. He sat on Tim's lap. Brittany was there, asleep, in her car seat. The magistrate summarized the report submitted to the Court by the adoption agency and asked if Tim and I were in agreement with it. We were. Did we understand that as of the end of this hearing, we would be fully accountable for the children? We did. Did we understand that we would be responsible for the children until they reached the age of emancipation? We did. Were we aware of any reason we would be unable to fulfill our obligation to the children? We were not. The petition for the adoption of the children, Doran and Brittany, by Timothy and Suzanne Tregarthen was granted. Just like that. It was done.

Now it was time to get ready for a party!

Tim dropped the children and me at the house to decorate, and then he left to pick up deli trays. Doran handed me green and red balloons to fill from a rented helium tank, while a home-care respiratory therapist gave Brittany a nebulizer treatment in the family room downstairs. When her therapy session was done, Brittany was exhausted but very hungry, so I gave her some formula and then she slept soundly. Doran put little candies on frosted gingerbread men, and I poured wassail into the crock pot for warming. When Tim got home around three o'clock, I woke Brittany so we would have plenty of time to bathe the children and get them dressed for the open-house which was to start at four.

It was a full day. Merry. Warm. I couldn't have been happier. Or more exhausted. By the time the last guests filtered out at seven, all I could think about was climbing into my bed. I would stay there, I mused, until Valentine's Day. But one of my unspoken rules was that I never went to bed with a dirty kitchen, so while Tim took Doran upstairs to get him ready for bed I scraped food off of plates and filled the sink with hot, soapy water. Brittany was sleeping in a playpen I kept for her in the living room. From the kitchen I could see the color of the Christmas lights reflecting off the balloons and realized that the balloons were slowly inching along the ceiling, the way they do when they start to run out of gas. By the time I finished cleaning the kitchen the balloons had congregated, all of them, in a single spot above the play pen.

I leaned against the wall and took in the sight of the red and green bouquet. I wanted Tim and Doran to see the balloons, but I didn't want to disturb their bedtime routine. The balloons would still be there in the morning, I told myself. But on this night, the balloons hovering above Brittany, and the added effect of the Christmas lights—this was something worth seeing.

The piercing sound of the doorbell startled me out of my reverie. I glanced at the clock: 7:25. Who…? I didn't want the bell to ring a second time, so I hustled to the door and opened it.

Salesman, was my immediate assessment. But at this hour? I felt cold suddenly and very alert. The man removed his hat and held it in his gloved hand. His heavy overcoat was draped over one arm, as if he expected to be invited in. He wore gray slacks and a tweed blazer, all made of fine wool. He was too polished and formal to be someone from the university. The only people in Colorado Springs who dressed like this man were the people who worked in the banks or in the Court house.

In fact, he was a lawyer. He presented a card, bearing his name and a Denver address, and asked if he could come in. I said no, I didn't think so. He said he was aware that our adoption of the baby girl was final this day and said, "Congratulations, that makes it a special day." I said nothing.

He cleared his throat and finally got straight with me. "You and your husband are aware certainly of the negligence that resulted in the birth mother being told by the hospital that the baby would be a normal birth. The birth parents are in a position to win a sizeable claim against the hospital because of the error," he said. "I came to talk to you and your husband about a separate claim that should be filed on behalf of the child."

He paused, waiting for me to say something, but I said nothing. He cleared his throat and continued. "A wrongful life claim, made on behalf of the child, could secure sufficient financial resources for that child to be comfortable and well-provided for. There will be expenses far and above ordinary expenses to care for this child. I am proposing a claim that could guarantee that funds would be available to meet those expenses."

"You are talking to the wrong person," I said. "If you want someone to seek compensation because of the incorrect diagnosis, you should be talking to the birth parents."

"They are making their own claim," he said. "I am proposing an action on behalf of the baby. As of 11:45 today, you and your husband are the baby's legal parents, and it is the legal parents who must make a claim on behalf of a child." He paused. "Now if I could come in and discuss this with you and your husband..." I remained in the doorway.

"How would this work?" I asked. "What sort of 'claim' would we be making?"

"A wrongful life claim is basically a medical malpractice suit," he explained, "with the hospital as the defendant. We would argue that if the hospital had not been negligent and mixed up the test results, that the birth mother would have known about the baby's diagnosis of Down Syndrome and would have had an abortion. But, because of the negligence, the baby was born—wrongfully. As a result of being born disabled, the child will have extraordinary expenses for which compensation is due."

"You want me to say that my baby's birth was wrongful?" I asked.

"Yes, that's the gist of it...that the baby would be better off not having been born than to live a life with medical disabilities."

My knees felt weak. I was having trouble getting enough air. "I want you to leave," I said, my voice sounding to me like it came from some place far away.

"You have my card..." His voice dissolved as I did what I had never done before: I slammed the door in the face of another human being.

ON JANUARY 11, 1988, the eve of her cardiac catheterization procedure, Brittany was baptized with water in the name of the Father and the Son and the Holy Spirit. She then was anointed with oil and clothed in white garments. Born into physical life on September 28 and then passed immediately into the care of foster parents, she found her way to our home on November 12. A civic hearing on January 8 formalized our legal bond to her. On January 11, Tim and I sealed our bond to Brittany, spiritually, in the waters of her Holy Baptism.

By the evening of the next day we had another reminder of how tenuous her life on earth might be. Brittany sailed through the catheterization procedure with no difficulties, but the test indicated that the heart defect was far worse than we had anticipated. The diagnosis of pulmonary hypertension was confirmed. An infection of the upper airway appeared to have developed. She was already receiving supplementary oxygen through a nasal cannula 24 hours a day; we were told to increase the flow to 1 liter of oxygen per minute and to follow up with her cardiologist the following day. Brittany was released with two prescriptions—an antibiotic to treat the infection, and a diuretic to treat the hypertension.

We left the hospital late in the afternoon. Tim took Brittany to the house and I drove with Doran to the supermarket to get the prescriptions filled and to buy a few groceries. After dinner I laid Brittany in her playpen, got the bag containing her prescriptions out of the refrigerator and dug through my first aid drawer for some dispensers. The diuretic, a liquid called Lasix, required my smallest medicine dropper. At a dose of only .3 cc every six hours, the Lasix was intended to help Brittany's body slough off unneeded water and salt through her urine. Brittany needed one-half teaspoon, or 2.5 cc, of the antibiotic, also a liquid. Although Brittany had received both the antibiotic and the Lasix when she had been hospitalized a month earlier, the medicines had been dispensed through her IV, so I was unfamiliar with both of them.

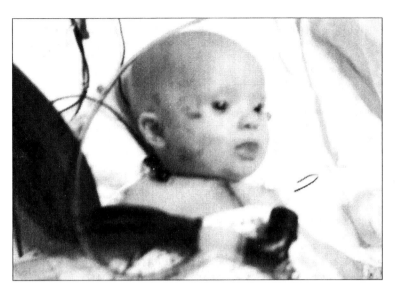

Brittany's first day post-op at Children's Hospital in Denver.

It was extremely difficult for me to measure the appropriate dose of Lasix. The milky white liquid seemed too frothy to dispense at such a small quantity. I thought I might be able to get at the medicine better if first I put it into a measuring cup. As I poured it, I understood why it had been so difficult to measure at only .3 cc. It was heavy and sticky, the consistency was like that of an antibiotic. I set the bottle down and took a deep breath. I picked up the amber glass bottle and removed the pharmacy label that said "Augmentin." Underneath it was a manufacturer's label: Lasix.

Clearly, the pharmacist had mixed up the bottles. The one labeled Augmentin was really Lasix. The one labeled Lasix, was...I couldn't be sure. There was no manufacturer label on that one. I set the bottles down and took a deep breath. Couldn't anyone get it right? I wondered. The cardiologist mixed up patients in his mind; somebody mixed up samples at the hospital laboratory; now this? Was there some chaos principle in effect where this little baby was concerned? Would I spend the rest of my life double and triple checking every single thing? What if I wasn't there to do that for her? I grabbed both bottles and the keys to the car and headed to the store, ready to rip the pharmacist's head right off his shoulders. By that time, 7:35 p.m., however, the pharmacy had been closed up tight. I would have to return in the morning to get the correct medications and to find out what the pharmacist had to say for himself.

I CALLED THE CARDIOLOGIST'S office the following day. When I told him about the mix up with the medicines, he explained that giving Brittany a half teaspoon versus .3 cc of Lasix probably would not have killed her—as I had feared—but, over time, it would have caused her to become seriously dehydrated, draining her body of the water she needed and upsetting the balance of electrolytes. He then told me that, based on his review of her case, he was recommending open heart surgery but wanted to wait until she weighed at least twelve pounds, or until she was a year old, to do the procedure.

At almost four months old, Brittany weighed seven pounds one half ounce, only ten ounces more than she had weighed at birth. We had moved her from an elevation of 9,000 feet to an elevation of 6,500 feet. Brittany got supplemental oxygen through a cannula and received respiratory therapy treatments in our home every week. Still, she ate little, slept a lot and seemed terribly weak most of the time. She loved to play with her brother and listen while Tim and I read stories, but the effort exhausted her. When I called Tim at the university and told him that the cardiologist wanted to wait to intervene, he fell silent and then asked what I thought. My heart spoke for me: "She won't make it, Tim."

Within the hour Tim had called the head of the department of cardiology at Denver's Children's Hospital and had arranged for him to evaluate Brittany the following Monday. Then he called our doctors' offices and the hospital and requested copies of Brittany's records. When we drove to Denver we had copies of reports from Brittany's EKGs, echocardiograms and the cardiac catheterization. We also had the films from all of her previous chest X-rays. The Denver cardiologist said he would use these reports for a baseline and sent us down the hall for a fresh EKG and echocardiogram. When we returned to his office two hours later he told us what we had expected to hear all along: "Your daughter is in serious need of surgery. The repair is absolutely necessary and should have been done already. To wait for her to reach 12 pounds is to open the door for pneumonia and other complications to develop. Your daughter will die before she will ever reach 12 pounds."

Brittany was admitted at Children's Hospital on February 11, 1988; her open heart surgery scheduled for the following morning. Laboratory staff in fresh white uniforms came into her room early on the 12th to draw blood samples, and Brittany, the surgery nurses, Tim and I stopped at the radiology department on our way to surgery so the hospital could take baseline chest X-rays. A nurse pushed Brittany's bed down the long corridor leading to the operating room; Tim and I walked alongside, each of us holding one of Brittany's small hands. We all stopped and turned when we heard a shout behind us. "Stop! Stop that baby!" The radiology technician sprinted to catch up to us. He waved the huge envelope containing Brittany's X-rays while he caught his breath. "You can't go to surgery. That baby," he said, still breathing heavily, "that baby has pneumonia."

BRITTANY RECOVERED from pneumonia, had surgery and returned to our home by the 20th of that month. Once the ASD was repaired, she gained weight and grew healthier, although she continued to need supplemental oxygen until she was about a year old, and had mild pulmonary hypertension until she was three. She also remained extremely susceptible to respiratory viruses. When she caught a cold, which happened frequently, she often became dangerously sick, a situation complicated by the fact that she rarely got fevers or developed a cough, so two of the principal signals of serious illness were missing.

Still, she developed a sinewy strength coupled with a deep reservoir of energy. She made huge developmental gains when she

Doran, happy to see his sister as her hospitalization for heart surgery came to an end, late February 1988.

should have been waning, often reaching the most significant developmental milestones from her hospital bed. She learned to roll over in a hospital bed and taught herself to sit up in a hospital bed. Once, her pediatrician admitted her to Penrose Community Hospital to treat a particularly recalcitrant bout of RSV. The pediatrician was making his hospital rounds and was reviewing patient files at the nurses' station. Brittany's vital signs plummeted while a CNA was in her room; the CNA pushed the emergency button and called desperately for the doctor. Brittany used the crib bars and pulled herself into a standing position to smile and wave at the party of doctors and nurses who burst into her room expecting to find a catastrophe. One of the pediatrician's notes from her medical file relates drily: "I saw Brittany today in the office. I basically had to chase her around to get a listen to her."

IN THE MID-1990'S AN editor asked me to write an article on wrongful life lawsuits. It had been years since I had thought about the well-heeled, poorly-mannered lawyer who had intruded on my brightest day. In researching the article I learned that the lawyer had triumphed in a wrongful life action. His client was a couple filing on behalf of their eight-year-old son who had been born blind. His blindness was caused by a hereditary condition that a geneticist failed to diagnose. Had the parents known about the genetic flaw they would have aborted the pregnancy, according to testimony heard by the Court. As a result of being born with a disability, the boy would have significant financial need for his entire life. He deserved appropriate monetary compensation. The parents testified that the boy would have been better off not having been born than being born with the disability of blindness.

Their logic prevailed in a lower Court, but the lawyer's victory was overturned by the Colorado Supreme Court. The justices wrote that the notion of wrongful life was "too metaphysical" an issue for the Court to recognize. The State of Colorado does recognize wrongful birth actions, such as the action supposedly filed by Brittany's birth parents. Like 19 other states where such actions have been overturned, however, the State of Colorado is not prepared to honor the argument that some lives are not worth living at all.

Chapter Three
Riding in Circles

The landlord gave us permission to dig a 4'x4'x8" hole for a sandbox, and we finished digging and bolting together the boards for it on Mother's Day. Tim took Doran to Home Depot to buy bags of sand while I lined the inside of the hole with chicken wire. Still having fun with the digging part, Brittany scooped spoonfuls of dirt out of the hole, and I worked around her, attaching the liner to the wood with a heavy-duty stapler.

Brittany and I were waiting with a wheelbarrow when the boys pulled into the driveway. Tim and I took turns wheeling bags of sand from the back of our SUV, through the garage and into the back yard. The children galloped after us, giggling and clamoring for rides on our return trips. Tim retrieved the last bag and slammed the double back doors to the Suburban closed. He left his load alongside the sandbox and then went inside for a drink. Doran and I ripped open the bags and dumped sand into the box, scrunching up our faces so the dust wouldn't get in our eyes.

I was watching Doran dig up sand with a Tonka toy when Tim came back outside. He handed me a glass of ice water. "Where's Brittany?" he asked.

My legs went cold. "I thought she was with you." At the same moment we turned our heads and saw that the back door to the garage was open. We realized that the front door of the garage must be open as well!

Brittany had not wandered far. Using an empty five-gallon container and a fishing tackle box, treasures she had found in the garage, she had made two stairs to help her climb onto the back bumper of the Suburban. She had a long thick rope, and she had looped one end of it through the handle of a can of white paint. By the time we found her, she had already looped the other end of the rope though the top rung of a ladder that was mounted on one of the Suburban's back doors. From her position on the back bumper, she was trying to use this pulley system to hoist the paint can to the top of the ladder.

It was Doran who finally interpreted the scene. "Sissy don't like a brown truck. Sissy wants a white truck."

SHE WAS THREE YEARS old and so tiny we easily could have carried her in that five-gallon bucket, but Brittany was determined to be as big as her brother. Like him, she brushed her own teeth—the few she had. She used the potty, not a diaper. She fed herself with a fork and a spoon. And she could scale anything that didn't move. The side of her crib was no longer any challenge for her, and she could work her way to the top of any jungle gym. She frequently shimmied over the six-foot fence separating our backyard from that of our neighbors.

The one thing Brittany couldn't do was climb mountains. Although she had very mild pulmonary hypertension when she was tested in Colorado Springs, she couldn't tolerate being at an elevation any higher than about 7,000 feet. Her skin took on a grey pallor whenever we drove over the mountain passes between us and my family in western Colorado. She got mottled, grey, and sleepy the few times we tried taking her up to Eagle Mountain.

In 1992, four years after putting the Eagle Mountain house on the market, we finally got an offer on it. The offer fell $20,000 short of paying off the second mortgage, and the holder of the second

Doran and Brittany, Christmas 1990.

blocked the sale. Eventually, we got another offer, this time for even less than we had been offered before. The holder of the second mortgage grudgingly approved the sale, and Tim and I assumed the obligation of paying the balance. The Eagle Mountain house became the property of the couple who owned the company that had supplied Brittany's home oxygen for the first two years of her life.

IT WAS TIME FOR US to buy our own house in town. Tim and I made a list of ten things we wanted in a home. Then we set out to visit the listings from the real estate ads, often taking long drives around town with the kids sitting in the backseat and munching on cookies or French fries. We really liked a small two-level rancher we found in an older neighborhood near the university. With the realtor but without the children, Tim and I toured it twice.

For our third tour of the Anitra Circle house we brought the children. Tim and I walked through the vacant rooms quickly, and then we stood in the kitchen making small talk with the realtor. The children took their time exploring all the rooms. We could hear them laugh when the floors squeaked under their feet. Suddenly Brittany's voice went quiet, but it was easy to discern her location. As she went through each bedroom, we could hear the sound of closet doors opening and slamming shut. We heard all the drawers opened and shut in the bathroom. Finally she came into the kitchen. She pulled out every drawer and opened every cupboard door, shutting each one more vigorously than she had done the last. When she exhausted all options for drawers and doors, she turned on her heels, crossed her arms in front of her, and stared us down. "There is no food in this house!" she said. The realtor laughed but she held her ground, her eyes narrowing with contempt.

As far as Tim and I were concerned, the house met all of our criteria except two—a laundry room on the same floor as the living area and a front door level with the walkway. Despite these drawbacks—and the deficiency Brittany observed—the house had everything we really wanted in a home and in a neighborhood. Tim and I asked the realtor to draw up an offer for our signatures that night. Six weeks later, we moved in. We had been in the house for less than an hour when we heard the clang of the doorbell. Tim answered. From Doran's new bedroom I could hear the muffled sounds of Tim's brief conversation, and then I heard the screen door creak as it closed. Tim came into the bedroom with a Cheshire-cat smile. "I am going to love this place," he said. Our visitor had been a thirteen-year old girl from two houses up who had offered her services for babysitting. Within minutes, the doorbell clanged again. Doran rushed to the door and was nearly trampled by a herd of children excited that new friends had moved onto the block. Tim and I looked out Doran's window and saw bikes, tricycles, skateboards and wagons parked higgledy-piggledy in our driveway.

The same band of children played together for years, sometimes depositing their bicycles in our driveway, sometimes in the driveways of other families. Tim, Doran and I built another sandbox, slightly larger, but this time we put it in the front yard. Every

day children played in it with plastic army men, Barbies, Trans-
formers, trucks, or tablespoons stolen from my kitchen. Our side-
walks were dusty from artwork drawn with fat pieces of chalk,
my roses trampled in twilight games of kick-the-can, the garage
cluttered with baseball bats, ramps for bicycle stunts and portable
goals for street hockey.

Most days I took a "tea tray" out front and Doran and Brittany,
their friends and I would take a breather to share a snack and conversation. Often, one of the other moms joined in, and we conjured
up plans for pet parades, Halloween parties and white elephant gift
exchanges over pots of tea. Sometimes on hot summer afternoons
our senior neighbor Janet whipped up a pitcher of wicked margari-
tas. We moms made the natural progression from my front step to
Janet's driveway, where lawn chairs waited for us under the shade
of a massive elm tree.

JANET'S DRIVEWAY HAD a special kind of magic for Brittany, too. Years later I bought a special notebook for Brittany to use
as a journal. In it she asked me to write her memories of Anitra
Circle. She dictated:

> I remember how we had so much fun on Anitra Circle. We liked
> to ride our bikes around in circles at our neighbor's house, Curtis
> and Janet's driveway. Then we were having a Fourth of July race
> on our bikes. I believe I made the shortcut to be the fastest one
> to win the race.

> In our backyard we had a pulley. I borrowed a blue harness—from
> the Halls—with a lock for a seatbelt and I used it on the pulley for
> safety. I miss that old bedroom, my Pocahontas wallpaper and my
> big Barbie house.

> We always went raspberry hunting along the ditch. My best friend
> Stephanie's mother let her sleep over. It made me so happy. I still
> have a photo of that.

TIM HAD A CONTRACT with a Manhattan textbook publisher for a comprehensive book on the principles of economics. He had completed the first draft of four dozen chapters and was deep in the throes of the revision process, having received the comments of two development editors and nine economists who had reviewed each chapter. I contributed numerous editorial pieces to the book, including biographical essays on great economists and newsy features applying economic concepts to contemporary events.

While Doran and Brittany were in school I worked out of an office at the university where I managed a small staff, wrote feature articles, and coordinated the efforts of a dozen freelance contributors to the economics magazine. I also prodded Tim to get his articles done. With each issue, it grew increasingly difficult to get him to finish his work on time to have it adequately handled by our editorial and production people. Tim was our chief writer: none of the other economists contributing to the magazine had his genius for writing, and I did not have his command of economic theory. The last three days before a press run became a time of such tremendous stress that I was relieved when the university halted production of the magazine during a statewide sweep of so-called auxiliary departments. Even though the magazine was at the height of its popularity and was financially self-sustaining, like many other operations not crucial to the education of local students, it was eliminated.

I found a half-time research support position at Colorado College, a small liberal arts institution in downtown Colorado Springs. I worked mornings at the college and devoted a lot of time to my independent work. I got a contract to write a book on the lives of men and women important to the development of economic theory, and I started working on a children's book with one of my neighbors, who was an illustrator. I continued to build my library of photographs, which I marketed and sold for use as stock photography. My collection was rich with photographs of the American West, images of landscapes, animals and the sun-creased faces of everyday people—ranchers, truckers, miners, skiers—that collectively contributed to my understanding of my own culture. Brittany got in the habit of sneaking my camera for her own creative use. Each time I took canisters of film to the photo shop for processing, the envelopes I picked up would include photos of Barbies riding on Brittany's pulleys.

A small corner upstairs served as my home work space. Each day I sat at my desk with the afternoon sun spilling over my shoulders. Sometimes I wrote. Sometimes I organized my photographs and negatives. Sometimes I just daydreamed. After I picked the children up from school we would have our tea-time; then I would work in my garden or sit on the front step with another mom and laugh while our children played.

ONE DAY IN EARLY FALL I walked to the school to meet the kids, carrying Doran's skateboard in my backpack and Brittany's hard plastic four-wheeler under my arm. They rode away im-

Brittany, Doran, and Tim, December 1996.

mediately, but as they had been taught, they stopped and waited for me at the one intersection we had to cross. After we crossed the street Brittany straddled her "bike" and took off. Doran walked alongside me in silence, carrying his skateboard and staring at his feet. "Mom," he said and then he paused. I waited. "They didn't let Sissy have lunch today."

I stopped. "What?"

"They didn't let Sissy have lunch today or yesterday either."

Since Doran had lunch with the other fifth graders and the third graders ate at a different time, I asked him how he knew this.

"Sissy told me," Doran said, and he started walking again. "Mom, I went to the office. The lady asked the lunch lady. They said Sissy's lunch wasn't paid for."

How could that be? Every two weeks I gave Doran a check to pay for the lunches of both children in advance. As if he understood my thoughts, Doran said, "I told them I paid, but Mom, they said Sissy has no lunches left."

"Why didn't she say anything to me?"

"She thinks maybe you don't have money for her lunches."

When Doran and I reached the house, Brittany's four-wheeler lay sideways on the lawn. She was in the house, sitting cross-legged in the middle of the kitchen floor and eating Fritos like there was no tomorrow.

The next morning I discovered that the money I had sent with Doran to school had been applied—all of it—to Doran's account, leaving Brittany with a zero balance at the beginning of the week. It was Thursday when Doran talked to me; by then, Brittany had been denied lunch four days in a row. I couldn't decide what angered me the most: that a developmentally disabled child had been denied food for reasons she couldn't understand or articulate; that the lunch room staff did not transfer funds from Doran's to Brittany's account; that no one from the school alerted me to Brittany's so-called account deficiency; or that it was the policy of the district to deny any child a warm lunch when there was a surplus of food right there in the kitchen! When our family gathered at the table for supper on Friday, Doran watched wide-eyed while I fussed and fumed.

When I finally ran out of steam he cleared his throat. "You know what I want to do when I grow up?" We all looked up at him, and he cleared his throat again. "I'm going to live in the house of the Lord! I am going to find shelter for the homeless! Feed the hungry!"

Tim and I were stunned, but Brittany took another bite. "I be a pirate!" she said before she swallowed her beans.

JUST WEEKS AFTER THE lunch fiasco, Doran told me that Brittany was having trouble with a bully on the lower-grades' playground. Brittany confirmed that a particular boy kept teasing her and she pointed to a place on her arm where she said he had pinched her. I talked to Brittany's teacher, and she referred me to the assistant principal, who asked me to come back and see the principal. After talking with me and collecting observations of Brittany's playground activities over the next five days, the principal sent me a letter on district letterhead. Teachers observed no problems on the playground, he said, and he indicated that he "had no idea at all of any circumstances that would cause Brittany to make such a report to you."

By then Doran had begun to struggle academically. He had always had difficulty with phonetic spelling and word pronunciation, issues stemming from a history of ear infections that often muffled his hearing. He had compensated visually; he read voraciously and had an advanced ability to comprehend written text. But a lingering problem, known as a central auditory processing delay, made it difficult for him to hear and concentrate in a situation where there were distractions. The fifth-grade classes were arranged in a quad: four groups of 28 students each in a large room separated only by five-foot partitions. Doran often seemed exhausted and discouraged at the end of the school day.

Tim and I met with the principal of a private Missouri Synod Lutheran school. The principal called Doran and invited him to sit in the 5th/6th grade classroom for a few days and see what he thought. After his third day as a visitor Doran asked to be transferred.

At the supper table that evening I gave Tim the enrollment papers that needed his signature. "The principal told me that he spoke to the other teachers at a staff meeting," I said, while Tim reviewed the paperwork. "The Lutheran school welcomes Brittany, too. I think we should enroll her."

"So…Sissy is going to the new school, too?" Doran asked. He poked at his meat with a fork, while I cut Brittany's steak and Tim signed documents.

ONE OF THE UNMET criteria from our house-hunting list came back to haunt us.

Prior to our marriage, Tim had been diagnosed with multiple sclerosis (MS), a neurological condition that results in "scrambled messages" between the brain and other parts of the body. For the fifteen years I had known him, Tim's disease had followed an exacerbate-remit pattern; every six to eight weeks he had a flare-up, and he would experience dizziness, fatigue, slurred speech, blurred vision and involuntary twitching for a period of two to three days. When he recovered from these exacerbations the disease went into remission and he was able to function as normal. There was always a chance the disease could become progressive: we knew MS patients who could no longer walk. Although Tim was convinced that the likelihood of progression was remote, we had wanted a house with the front door level with the front walkway just in case, someday, he would need to use a wheelchair.

As he wrapped up the revision process on his book, Tim began to experience flare-ups that were more severe and occurred more frequently than in the past. During periods of remission he threw himself into fitness. He became serious about long-distance run-

Brittany, so happy at Redeemer Lutheran School.

ning and began training for a marathon. During the summers he frequented an outdoor neighborhood pool, where he followed a swimming regime that would enable him to be the first MS patient to swim the English Channel. He drank protein drinks to build muscle mass and maintain his weight and insisted that the family adhere to a low-fat diet, which he believed would help reduce the number of MS-related lesions in his body.

When he ran in local races, the children and I got up early so we could cheer him on when he reached the finish, but we watched in sadness as Tim's reservoir of energy dropped. Every time he went out for a long training run he came back drained. If he didn't come back when we expected him, the children and I loaded up in the car and followed his training routes. We sometimes found find him sitting along the sidewalk or on a bus bench. After we found him one day lying in a ditch, I begged him to stop running, but my pleas fell on deaf ears.

DORAN WAS EATING at a friend's house when I told Tim and Brittany at dinner that the dean at the liberal arts college had offered me a promotion. "It'll be full time even during the summer, which is the big drawback," I said, "but I'll be reporting directly to Timothy Fuller, the dean."

"This is what I was afraid of," he said. "Full time at that place and in no time you'll be wearing Birkenstocks and refusing to shave under your arms."

"Right. Well, after five years it'll mean free tuition for Doran," I said.

"Doran would have to be accepted first," Tim said, "and Doran is not exactly college material."

As I lay awake in bed that night I thought of the things I wished I would have said, but there at the supper table I was too stunned to respond, and I finished my meal in silence.

BRITTANY AND I WERE running errands after school and didn't get home until twilight. As we rounded the curve at the top of Anitra Circle, Brittany said, "There's Daddy sleeping on the grass." I pulled into the driveway and rushed over to Tim. He was alert and trembling from the combined effects of the chilly air and his MS-related twitches. "I fell after playing catch with Doran," he said. "I called, but Doran was already in the house and he didn't come out." I covered Tim with my coat and went into the house to get Doran, who was lying on his bed listening to music. We managed to get Tim seated on a lawn chair, and then we lifted Tim's arms over our shoulders and hoisted him into a standing position. We half-helped/half-dragged him up the front stairs while Brittany held open the door. We got Tim situated on the couch, and Doran went outside to retrieve my coat. He quietly asked me if I needed any more help. I told him I was fine, and he walked down the hall to his room. I helped Brittany lay a blanket over Tim and then I followed after my boy. He was sitting on the edge of his bed with his hands clasped between his knees, his head hanging low and the weight of world on his bony shoulders.

On a winter day several months later Tim took a similar fall at the university. He lay on his back on a wide sidewalk; his briefcase lay beside him. Students walked by and he called to them, but no one stopped. He was keeping himself awake by counting the number of dead leaves clinging to the tree branches above him, when Art Torrenos, the supervisor of the university's grounds department found him. I heard the story from Art when he brought Tim home. He eased Tim out of his pickup and up the walkway using a wheelchair that had belonged to his mother. Then he supported Tim's weight and helped him climb the front steps. Art suggested to Tim that he keep the wheelchair, and, to my surprise, Tim agreed.

A PHYSICAL THERAPIST came to the house and showed me and Doran how to assist Tim in and out of the wheelchair and how to lift him if he fell. At twelve years old, Doran outweighed me and, at 5'8", he was almost as tall. Our height and weight, relative to Tim's, worked to our advantage, but there was a lot to learn about lifting that had nothing to do with size. The therapist showed us how to use a transfer board to assist Tim into the wheelchair from a chair, a bed, a car and a shower bench.

Our neighbor Curtis, who had built nearly 100 wheelchair ramps through his civic service organization, grudgingly conceded that constructing a ramp to our front door was not feasible. Without a ramp, the front steps were too difficult for Tim to climb even with Doran and me assisting, and too steep for us to maneuver Tim up in the wheelchair. The physical therapist recommended that we install a chair elevator which would run along a track mounted to our inside stairs, themselves accessible from the garage.

The staircase topped out at a 40"-square landing that was level with the back deck. At the top right of the stairs was the doorway to the kitchen, distinguished from the landing by a six-inch rise. When Tim rode the chair elevator to the top, he would make the transfer from the elevator chair to a bench we had rigged up in the landing. Then, using grab bars we had installed, he would pull himself up the riser and into a wheelchair we kept upstairs. As his legs and arms grew weaker he could no longer make the transfer without help. Eventually, his legs could not support him at all, so we would lift him onto the bench; then, using a strap wrapped snug around his chest, we would pull him up, make a 180° pivot, and lift him six inches higher and into his wheelchair, supporting his weight all the while.

I was home alone with Tim, helping him make the transfer from the kitchen down to the landing the first time I dropped him. As soon as I was certain that Tim wasn't injured, I called my neighbor Dwight who, in turn, called our neighbor John. The elevator chair had effectively blocked Tim from toppling down the stairs, but he was wedged hard in the landing, and it took Dwight and John over an hour to get Tim up and onto the elevator chair. I prayed that I would never have to ask our neighbors to lift Tim this way again. When Doran came home later that day, I told him that he was never, ever to attempt to assist Tim with a transfer up or down the landing.

I was lifting Tim up into the kitchen the second time I dropped him. I had made the assist to the bench, had supported his weight and made the pivot when I lost my balance and fell backwards into the wall. My body completely cushioned his fall, so Tim had not been injured, but I was pinned in the landing and I could feel a sharp pain in my right hip and knee. I wriggled out from under Tim and called 911. Three firemen exchanged puzzled glances as they discussed the best strategy for getting Tim out of his predicament. Finally, they removed the back door off its hinges, giving themselves more space, and carried Tim into the top floor of the house on a stretcher.

Curtis came over to help me re-hang the door. After he left, I went through the recycling bins and found the real estate supplement to the previous Sunday's newspaper.

THE PRINCIPAL AT THE Lutheran school told me about a program that offered group support for children in homes like ours. The program, called Support for Kids with Ill Parents, met once a week over a period of five weeks. I made a few phone calls and enrolled Doran and Brittany in an upcoming SKIP class which would be held at one of the "big-box" churches on the northeast side of town. A friendly middle-aged lady sitting behind a reception table greeted us when we walked into the building. She wrote out name tags for Doran and Brittany and led us down a long hallway to a gymnasium where about seventy kids gathered in small groups with college-aged counselors. "You can leave them here with us; they'll be fine," our hostess told me.

"Is there a lounge or waiting room or something?" I asked.

"Nope. You go on. Come back at 8:30. We'll take it from here."

She was not so cheerful when I returned. "Your daughter, she, uh, well she has issues of her own, and she's a distraction for the group as a whole. The children here all have problems they need to work through; they don't need to deal with her issues too. I'm sure you understand."

I didn't say a word.

"Well, we really can't do anything for her," she said. Then she rubbed Doran's shoulder and said perkily, "But we'll see...Dorian, is it? Yes, we'll see Dorian next week."

Brittany sang songs on the ride home and Doran sat in silence. When we pulled into the driveway, Brittany hopped out of the car and scampered through the open garage door and into basement. Doran held back.

"What happened, Doran?" I asked. "Did she swing from the rafters? Hide in a closet? Burp the ABCs?"

Doran smiled and shook his head. "Nothing like that," he said. Then he got serious again. "We had a little thing we had to do. Wrap a Christmas present—an imaginary Christmas present of the One-Thing-We-Wish-We-Could-Give to our sick parent."

"What did you wrap?"

"I wrapped a box and called it 'The Gift of Bladder Control.'" I smiled, happy to see my intelligent, funny son peeking through the cracks.

"That's a good one, Doran. Dare I ask—what did Brittany wrap?"

"She wrapped herself. What was so wrong about that, Mom?"

Later, when I went into his room to kiss him goodnight he told me he didn't want to return to SKIP. "What's happening to us is happening to us as a family. I won't go without Brittany."

Chapter Four

Light of Day

We found a one-story ranch house in May 1999. As soon as school let out, Doran flew with Tim to California, where Tim would stay for six weeks with his family and finish the second edition of his book, and Doran would join fifty other adolescent boys and girls in a junior lifeguard training course that met daily on a sandy beach north of Los Angeles. Brittany and I stayed in Colorado Springs. It was our job to close two real estate transactions and move the household into the new place on Flintridge Drive.

Using a financial instrument known as a "bridge loan," I closed on the new house in June, before completing the sale of the Anitra house, signing for Tim on both transactions as his "attorney-in-fact." The Flintridge house would require a facelift before we could move—the carpets reeked of cigarette smoke and pet odors; wallpaper was peeling off the walls in the kitchen and bedrooms; yew bushes and dense weeds had overtaken the expansive lawn—so I equipped Brittany and two of her eager friends with scrapers, hammers and a CD boom box, and our team went to work.

The girls joined hands and danced in large rooms vacant of furniture. They donned protective eye goggles and took turns whacking at a flimsy wall I wanted removed between the kitchen and the dining room.

They screeched in delight as they ripped layers of paper off the walls and shrieked in horror when I rolled back the carpet in Brittany's new bedroom and found the hardwood floor underneath stained white in large patches from dog urine.

I forbade the girls from playing inside the kitchen, where tobacco juice and cooking grease streamed down my arms as I steamed and scraped off wallpaper and where, even underneath the paper, residual tobacco still showed the outlines of the copper Jello molds that had once hung on the walls. When all the paper was removed I sent Brittany to a friend's house, covered my mouth and nose, and sprayed all the inside walls with KILZ. The next day, when Brittany and I returned to the Flintridge house we could see tobacco beading through the primer in every room.

A week later after the soiled carpet had been hauled to the dump, the stain on Brittany's floor sanded out, and the tobacco foiled with three coats of KILZ, Brittany and I took a Sunday off. We got out of bed too late for church, stayed in our pajamas until after lunch and sat lazily together on the front step of the Anitra house. She drank a soda and I sipped my tea. I thought about Isak Dinesen's observation that the cure for anything is salt water—sweat, tears, or the sea. I wondered idly what Dinesen would have said about tobacco juice, KILZ and Irish tea.

BY THE END OF JULY we had closed on the sale of our home on Anitra Circle and all of our belongings had been moved to the Flintridge house. To this day I have no recollection of how our things were moved. I have no photographs, journal entries, notes on calendars, or cancelled checks to help me retrieve a memory. Surprisingly, Brittany, also, has no recall. Friends from church and from the neighborhood must have helped, but hard as I try, I cannot picture it. All I know is that one summer morning Brittany and I awoke at the Anitra house and later that night we went to bed on Flintridge Drive.

Before we did anything else Brittany and I set up the bedrooms. The insurance company had approved the lease of a hospital bed equipped with an adjustable base that would allow Tim to push a button to sit up or to raise his legs, and a special mattress that would reduce the risk of his developing bed sores during long periods of bed rest. The mattress sat higher off the ground than most, which made it easier for the person who was helping Tim with his bathing or dressing, but more difficult for Tim to get in and out of safely, so the insurance company also approved the lease of a hoist that could be used to help him transfer between the bed and his wheelchair. Brittany and I set up Tim's bed in the master bedroom suite, where he would have his own bathroom. I installed grab bars on the walls and put a new plastic bench in the shower. We went shopping and Brittany picked out a new blanket, a comforter and some cheery bed pillows for Tim's bed. When he and Doran returned from California, Brittany was more excited to show Tim his bedroom than she was to show off her own.

"Do you like it, Daddy?" She asked, taking command of his wheelchair and whipping him through the house on the shiny wood floors. "It was sooooo funny, Daddy. Andrea and Stephanie and me had soooo much fun, and look, Daddy," she pointed to her cat, "Lady likes to sleep on my new bed, and, wait, Lady and Hector have a new kitty box ..." She wheeled Tim's chair into the newly expanded kitchen. "There was a wall here, Daddy, but now there isn't. It was so much fun." Tim smiled and told Brittany that everything looked nice.

"You got a lot done," he said to me, smiling vaguely. He wheeled himself to the bay window in the living room and looked out at the street with a dreamy expression. "It was a good trip." He closed his eyes. "I'm just—it was really a good trip."

I HAD LEFT MY JOB AT the college and accepted a teaching position at a private Christian high school. Although I had a lot of preps to do over the summer I could schedule my work according to my own needs, so I had a lot of time that summer to take care of things at home. After making several phone calls, I found a private-hire CNA who could come over each morning to get Tim out of bed and dressed, a process that took two to three hours. A neighbor agreed to come over each day during the week to take care of the meal and any other needs Tim might have over the lunch hour. Both women started work in early August, giving us all time to iron out any problems before I had to start leaving the house daily at 7:15 a.m.

The house, too, got a lot of attention. Doran and I built a ramp over the single step in the front entryway. I hired a contractor to lay tile on the floor in the kitchen, Tim's shower and the living room bay. An electrician repaired the wiring on some outlets that hadn't been grounded properly. A neighbor and I replaced the chain link fencing with wood slats tall enough to keep our dog in the yard, and I hired a landscaping company to remove yew bushes and repair the sprinkler system. Brittany badgered me to re-hang her pulley, and I had to keep showing her that the new yard didn't have trees or posts to anchor it. I asked her if she wanted me to build a sandbox and she said it was "too baby-ish." I made a few stabs at tilling some ground for a flower garden but gave up. The conditions just weren't right for getting anything to grow.

I was sitting out back wondering how long we could go before we replaced the wood on the floor on the deck, and the phone rang. I went inside to answer it, letting my eyes adjust first to the change in light, so I could read the number on the caller ID. It was a California phone number. I answered and the female caller asked for Tim. "He's at a luncheon meeting," I said. "I don't expect him back until about 1:30. Do you want to leave a message?"

"No," she said tentatively. "I am the nurse who took care of him in Pasadena. I just wondered how he is doing."

I brought her up to date. "That is all good," she said. "Please tell Tim I called."

She called several times over the next few months, but whenever I answered the phone she would hang up as soon I said hello.

DORAN STARTED HELPING me with Tim's bedtime routine. If Tim had been too weak to get up, I would set a wash basin up on a hospital table, and Tim would take what the kids called a "bird bath." If he was up, I would wheel him in his chair to the bathroom, where he would brush his teeth and wash up in the vanity sink. He wore a bag hooked to a catheter, so he didn't use the toilet unless he needed to have a bowel movement, which rarely happened at bedtime. After Tim was done washing, I would take him to the side of the bed where Doran and I, working together, would slip a sling behind his back, under his bum and through his legs. Then, we would align the hydraulic lift alongside the bed, attach the sling to the lift and hoist Tim vertically. After I moved the wheelchair, Doran would turn the lift to position Tim over the bed, waiting until I was on the other side before lowering him onto the mattress and removing the sling.

Once he was in bed, Doran and I would remove Tim's overshirt, socks and denim jeans, lightly wash and dry his legs, and look closely for sores that might have been caused by sitting too long in the chair or in bed. While I got Tim's nighttime meds ready, Doran would share the highlights of his day. As time went by, he grew more selective, it seemed, with the events he would share.

"Why didn't you tell your dad what the dermatologist said today about the new treatment for your skin?" I asked Doran one night after Doran told his dad goodnight and he and I left Tim's room.

"Because it didn't even dawn on him to ask," Doran replied. "Good night, Mom," he said, and he headed downstairs to his bedroom.

"I love you, Sweet Pea." I said after him. He stopped.

"Love you, too, Mom."

BRITTANY BEGAN HAVING difficulty sleeping through the night, and most mornings she woke tired and grouchy as if she hadn't slept at all. During the day she complained of headaches, an

Brittany, Lady, and Hector.

effect, I thought, of her lack of sleep. We tried rearranging the furniture in her room, playing music softly at night, and saying additional prayers before bed, but the problem worsened. She asked if she could sleep with me. I thought it might help, so I allowed it. The first night was uneventful, but the second night she kept me awake with her flailing about. She would roll from one side to the other, beat her pillows into a shape to support her head in a quasi-upright position and occasionally sit bolt upright in bed, legs crossed, and attempt to sleep in that position. None of these antics seemed to wake her, but they robbed her of any bona fide rest.

There were other problems. Her physical development had halted. At 12 years old, she weighed 60 pounds and hadn't gained any weight in over a year. She still didn't have all of her primary teeth. When she got a cold or a lesion, such as a skinned knee or a cut on her lip, she was slow to heal. The skin on her hands and feet dried severely, leaving deep and painful cracks. She was still living life at full throttle: running, skipping, jumping, riding her bike. But it was as if her body didn't have the energy it needed to be fully well.

As her symptoms worsened, she and I went to the pediatrician's office frequently. He tried many different types of treatment. We tried eliminating milk, thinking lactose might be the problem. We tried counseling, thinking the problems might be a result of depression. Concerned that her heart problem had returned, I took Brittany several times to the cardiologist. After extensive tests, some of which were done at Children's Hospital in Denver, doctors ruled out lactose intolerance, heart problems, a host of gastro-intestinal disturbances and even clinical depression. Still, she experienced crushing headaches and frequently said she wished that she were dead.

AS BRITTANY'S DOCTORS and I continued to seek explanations for her headaches and fatigue, we became aware of a problem we could fix. X-rays revealed huge knots commonly called bunions developing on the lower joint of her big toes; her toes were being shoved inward at a sharp angle and the fourth toe on each side was curling under the others. She complained that her feet looked like "little old lady feet," but the frequent, burning pain in her feet bothered her far more than did their appearance. We were reluctant to perform bunion surgeries while Brittany was still growing, because of the likelihood of recurrence, but in December 2001, when Brittany was 14 years old and stood 4'8" tall, X-rays done at the orthopedic specialist's office showed that Brittany's growth plates had closed. Brittany would have surgery on both feet at Children's Hospital at the end of January.

By then, we were, for the sixth time, looking for a CNA to assist Tim in the mornings. The first one had been hired by a hospital; the second by a nursing home. The third quit to take care of problems with her own family. The fourth quit with no explanation. The fifth seemed to be working out fine but suddenly began insisting that her husband or adult-age daughter accompany her when she came to the house. They would arrive just after the kids and I had left in the mornings, so I didn't know that Angie had been bringing an escort until a couple of days when Doran had stayed home with a cold. We were talking about it on the drive home from school one day and Brittany piped up from the back seat: "Angie don't like to be at the house alone with Daddy."

"Did she tell you this?" I asked, looking in the rear view mirror for a peek at her face.

"No," she said, absentmindedly staring out the window. "I just know it."

Before long Angie stopped coming. With the new year around the corner we had Brittany's surgery on the horizon, my teaching schedule to work around and no CNA.

BRITTANY AND I STAYED at Children's Hospital in Denver for five days. When we left she had casts on both legs and long pins driven into her feet to hold her bones—which had been cut, shaved and repositioned—in place. I lifted her into our station wagon and covered her snugly with the zebra stripe fleece blanket my mother had given her. It was a cold February day, blustery white. The wipers struggled to keep pace with the fat flakes of snow that converged on the windshield. "I want just one thing," Brittany said as I pulled out of the hospital parking lot and onto Colorado Boulevard. "McDonalds."

She had a few sips of her soda but when we pulled into our driveway in Colorado Springs 90 minutes later, her meal was yet untouched. I waved at Doran who stood in the bay window, and then I got out of the car. Doran watched soberly as I opened the hatch, pulled out a pediatric wheelchair and wheeled it to the side of the car. I opened the door, lifted Brittany into the chair and wheeled her up the front ramp. Doran waited in the entryway holding a "Welcome Home" sign in one hand and his cat Hector in the other.

Brittany would be non-weight bearing for six weeks. Since Brittany's school had no accessible facilities, I had notified the teachers there that I would homeschool Brittany during that six-week period. I had taken a leave from my teaching position at my school. David, one of Tim's previous CNAs, had decided he could work at the nursing home and take care of Tim, so he came over most mornings. Tim's parents were planning to visit for an indefinite period to help.

On Brittany's first night back home, I wheeled her into the bathroom to help her wash up before bed. She said her head felt dirty and she wanted a real bath, so I lifted her onto my lap, sat on the edge of the tub and ran the shower gently to get her body as wet as possible without dampening her casts. I turned the water off, wrapped her in a towel and shampooed her hair, rinsing it under the tub faucet. She patted her hair dry and brushed it. I helped her get into her pajamas, wheeled her into the living room where she said goodnight to Tim and Doran, and then carried her into my bed. I wrapped ice packs in towels, laid them over her casts and covered her with her zebra blanket. "It hurts, Mommy," she said and she pinched back tears.

"I know it does, Baby. I know it does."

IT WAS GREAT LENT, that long period of reflection and prayer that prepares us spiritually for the annual celebration of one of the greatest mysteries known to man: the resurrection from the dead of Jesus Christ, the Son of God. Through our baptism, Christians symbolically join Christ in the tragedy of death and the triumph of resurrection, as we die to the "old self" and are born anew into a life with Christ as its center. Great Lent reminds us annually that the new life is a difficult life, that doubts may assail us, friends may abandon us, evil may befall us, but that with Christ we triumph ultimately over every evil indeed, over death itself.

During Lent we attended worship services more frequently. In addition to our usual Saturday vespers and Sunday worship services we went to evening services every Wednesday, followed by a meal and study in the fellowship hall. As the calendar brought Easter into view, the number of church services increased, until Holy Week, when there were services every day as communally the members of the parish recalled the tragic events leading to Christ's crucifixion.

Although the children and I couldn't attend every service, we did our best to help Tim participate. Taking sizeable draws from our retirement accounts, we had purchased a conversion van with an automatic door, a hydraulic ramp, and room for both Tim and Brittany to sit in the center in their wheelchairs. The days of lifting them in and out of the car were over.

By Holy Week Brittany had graduated from her wheelchair and had walking casts, one in black and one in red, her favorite colors. She had asked me to continue homeschooling her, because she was excited with the things that she was learning. I told her I was happy to be her teacher, not telling her that the person who had taken over my classes at the school had been hired for the entire semester anyway. We were sitting at the dining room table, working together on a lesson about snow crystals when I realized that we had only two-and-a-half hours to get ready for the Holy Thursday service and I hadn't set anything out for dinner.

I gave Brittany permission to watch one of her movies and asked Doran to come with me to the grocery store. During our absence Brittany experienced one of her headaches. She remembered the day clearly as she asked me to write, nine years later, in the notebook we used for her journaling.

> My mom and Doran were grocery shopping. I was watching a movie and I had something to eat—Ramen noodles. Then I got a bad headache. I paused my movie. I went to my dad's room to ask him did he have any Tylenol. He said he did have Tylenol, but he couldn't get up to show me which one I could take. I took the medicine from my dad's bathroom, top shelf. I took seven of them.

When my mother and my older brother Doran got home, then my mom noticed something. She noticed I had both of my hands on my head. I felt very, very, very weak and feeling like I was going to die. I told her I took some medicine and she asked me to show her the bottle and how many did I take. I said I took seven.

Mom ordered my brother to call for the ambulance. Doran was so scared about his sister. Doran was calling the ambulance, and my mom picked me up and carried me to the couch because I was feeling so very weak.

Then the ambulance and the fireman and the police came to the house very fast. I could tell they knew what was going on because Doran called them. They put me in a gurney and put the IV in and put me in the ambulance and talked to my mom about my health—everything. They let my mom come in the ambulance. Then that's all I remember.

IT WASN'T TYLENOL that Brittany had ingested, but Baclofen. A prescription muscle relaxer, Baclofen had been prescribed to help treat Tim's MS-related twitches, a condition known as spasticity. Tim's dose was one 20 mg tablet three times a day; Brittany had taken seven tablets at one time. Before the ambulance made it to Memorial Hospital, Brittany had slipped into unconsciousness, and I could tell from the heaving of her chest that she was in trouble. As the paramedics lowered Brittany out of the ambulance, I reached for the cold metal frame of the gurney and held on fast, staying close to my daughter as she was rushed into the treatment bay. There, they went to work immediately: two nurses transferred Brittany to a bed and hooked her up to machines to read her vital signs while a doctor prepared to administer activated charcoal intended to absorb the toxins in Brittany's body.

I watched as the medical team worked in tandem to push a tube through Brittany's mouth and down her esophagus, and then I watched them struggle as the tube seemed to hit a roadblock. One of the nurses held Brittany's body tight and the doctor shoved the tube, but still it wouldn't move. Instead, a volcano of charcoal erupted out of the other end. Brittany's body heaved as the doctor removed the tube and began to prepare another.

"Stop!" I yelled. "Look at her!" I pointed to my child. "Look! She cannot breathe!"

"You need to move out of our way," the doctor barked, getting ready to shove a tube, once again, in Brittany's mouth.

"No! Look at her!"

"Her vitals are fine," she snapped. Then she yelled over to the ER management station, "Get security over here; get her out of here!"

God's mercy is great, because at that moment our pediatrician David Hoover passed through the doors of the ER making his way to the elevator to begin his hospital rounds. I saw him and cried out to him. Without hesitating he came into the treatment bay and took over.

"Forget the gastric tube," he said pulling it from Brittany's mouth as the offended junior doctor looked on in disbelief. Dr. Hoover looked sternly at the young woman. "This patient is in heart failure. We need to intubate her immediately."

"That's what I thought, too," said the ER doctor who only seconds ago was telling me that Brittany's vitals were "fine."

"I DON'T UNDERSTAND why it made Brittany so sick, Mom." With Brittany stabilized on a ventilator I was finally able to call Doran from the payphone at the ER.

"Because Baclofen is a muscle relaxer. It relaxes everything—her heart, her lungs—slows them way down to where she can't use them to breathe."

"Dad called Pam; she's going to drive us over. Can we see Brittany?"

"You'll be able to see her by the time you get here, but, Doran..."

"Yeah, Mom?" he asked.

"It may be a while before she can see you."

She spent eighteen hours hooked up to the ventilator and three days in a coma. During that time I was interviewed three times by caseworkers from the hospital's social services department. It was routine procedure, Dr. Hoover later told me, when a teenage patient is admitted and a drug overdose is confirmed. In other parts of the country there were groups of teens using Baclofen to play some sort of dangerous game and the social workers were responsible for ruling out Brittany's involvement. They were evaluating the situation also as a possible attempted suicide, a routine evaluation with a drug overdose, Dr. Hoover assured me.

I often have wondered if Brittany could hear the questions being asked in the room; what images she saw and what she dreamed during her three-day coma, but these things remain mysteries to me. I only know that when she awoke she seemed terribly frightened but also very grateful to see the light of day. She later wrote:

> I can feel that my mom stayed with me the whole time. I think she was standing on my right side when I woke up, and my Uncle George came to see me. I felt weak still—sore everywhere, my whole body and my head and my heart and my chest. I felt so not well. I didn't want to die. I wanted to do great things.

For several nights after we got her home, Brittany cried to herself quietly and then fell into a fitful sleep. When she woke she would reach for me and ask for water, which she would gulp down. "So thirsty," she would say, and then she would rearrange the reading pillow I had bought her, lean against it and drift into sleep again.

I SAT AT THE DINING room table nursing a pot of tea and putting some lessons together for Brittany, completely unaware of the passage of time until a growing ache in my lower back caused me to go to the kitchen for the lockbox that now contained all of the family medicines including aspirin. One fifteen a.m. I put the kettle on for more tea, and then switched it off again. I filled a glass with cold water, switched off the lights and trundled down the hallway to my room.

Brittany slept soundly so I groped in the dark to find the telephone and move it to the floor to make room on the nightstand for my water. I slipped gingerly into bed. I tried several positions, hoping to eliminate the throbbing in my lower back, but I couldn't make myself comfortable. By now the pain made my breath short and I could feel warm tears streaming down my face. I thought about calling out, but I knew there was nothing Tim could do for me, and Doran wouldn't be able to hear me. What I need is an ambulance, I told myself. I slowly rolled onto my left side and started to reach out my arm for the phone. Pain squeezed my mid-section. I pulled my arm back, remembering that the phone was on the floor. There was no way I could ever, ever reach the phone, and I told myself it was better that way: an ambulance arriving at the house would terrify Brittany, who, finally, was getting some sleep.

I lay on my side, my knees pulled up slightly, my face and hair soaked with my tears, and I prayed for relief. Brittany's cat Lady announced herself with a meow in the doorway and padded softly into the room. She leapt expertly onto the bed, curled herself into a ball in the small of my back and started purring. The next thing I heard was the raucous morning song of the birds who nested in the blue spruce outside my bedroom window and the sound of Brittany mumbling, "Fly south, why don't ya," as she buried her head under her pillow.

For the next two days I distributed my time between my bed and the couch. The CNA pulled double duty, returning in the evenings to help Tim at bedtime. Doran found a ride to school with the mother of one of the other freshmen, and Brittany sat near me and played with her Barbies. By the third day, a Saturday, the pain began to subside enough that I could sit up and read, but I still felt I was being ripped in half when I tried to stand. I called a friend from church and asked if he would drive Doran and Tim to the evening service. I didn't realize I had fallen asleep until Doran gently shook me awake.

"Mom, Dad refuses to get ready for church," he said.

"What? What time is it?"

"It's 5:00. You said Mr. Hanson is coming over at 5:30. I need to get Dad ready, but he won't cooperate."

I was perplexed. "Your dad's the one who asked me to make the arrangements. Now he doesn't want to go?"

"He says church starts at seven, so he told me to leave him alone." Doran said, "He won't start getting ready until six."

"Seven? That's strange; it always starts at six. I think it has started at six since Christ himself walked the earth. Why does he think church starts at seven?" Doran shrugged his shoulders.

I smiled and shook my head. "Okay, here's what we're going to do. What's your dad doing right this minute?"

"He's in his room. He's leaning back in his wheelchair doing that 'centering' thing that he does."

Brittany, Suzanne, Doran, and Tim. (Photo by Jane McBee.)

"You know that clock he keeps on his nightstand? Can you get it for me without him knowing?" I asked my son, who began to see the sheer genius in my plan and smiled.

"Mom, I could play the trombone in there and he wouldn't know I was there." He walked down the hallway in mock stealth fashion, slipped into Tim's room and emerged seconds later with Tim's clock.

"Good," I said. I moved the clock forward one hour and handed it back to Doran, who stood over me, grinning.

"Now, it's six," Doran said cheerily as he snuck into the room to return the clock. Then, louder, I could hear him say, "Time to wake up, Dad!"

Chapter Five

Visibility

It was a scramble just to get out the door. I was teaching again, at a private high school, and Brittany was enrolled at the Lutheran school. But she was running a fever—99°, mild by medical standards but high for her—and her nose was runny, so I decided that she should stay home from school. Tim's CNA David called to say he was running late, and I told him that Brittany would be in the house when he got here and that my neighbor Pat would be coming over around 10:15. I asked David if he could remain in the house until Pat arrived and reminded him that I would be leaving his last two weeks' pay on the dining room table.

Doran had made eggs for breakfast. I started to call downstairs for him to come clean up his mess in the kitchen. Then I noticed that he had put a helping on a plate for me and another for Tim, so I filled the sink with soapy water and cleaned the mess myself. I took Tim's plate to his bedside and carried it back to the kitchen when he said he preferred to have his later. He asked for a half-cup of orange juice and 17 green grapes. I fed him the grapes and held the glass for him while he drank his juice through a straw. He reminded me that Curtis was coming by later to drive him to a meeting and asked what he should do with Brittany. I told him that Pat was coming over to watch her. Then I remembered that I needed to write a check to Pat, too.

In the kitchen I filled the cats' bowl with water and then I filled another bowl with cereal, poured some milk into a small pitcher and set up a tray for Brittany. She was sleeping when I took the tray to her room, so I set her breakfast on the bed stand. I picked up Lady, and, despite her meowing protest, I carried her out of the bedroom and closed the door behind me, setting the cat afoot in the hallway.

I carried a stack of graded student papers and my sack lunch out to the car and started the engine. I went back in the house, checked to make sure the keys to the van were hanging by the front door for Curtis, and called downstairs for Doran. He galloped up the stairs and yelled "Bye, Dad," before disappearing through the front door. I glanced up for a look out the bay window and saw him glide into the driver's seat of the station wagon, his head bobbing in rhythm to whatever was playing on the radio.

I grabbed my purse, took a last look around the room and stepped over the threshold. The phone rang. I thought about ignoring it, but it might be David…. The phone rang again. I returned to the kitchen, set my purse on the counter and looked at the caller ID. "Archangel Gabriel." I balked. No way, I told myself. The phone rang again. I turned and walked away.

WHEN WE RETURNED HOME that night Tim told me I had a message in the voicemail from Archangel Gabriel Monastery.

"Where's that?" I asked. I set my purse on the counter and reached for the phone.

"Beats me," Tim said absent mindedly.

The caller identified himself as a monk. "We have lit a candle for your family," he said, in a voice that was soft and melodic, like the voice of a person who is singing to himself. "For healing." He had a strange accent, not like any I had ever heard, and I strained to understand him. "Please call us if you have any specific requests." He left a long telephone number and rang off. I wrote the number on a piece of paper and hesitated before pushing the button that would erase his voice from my phone.

Suzanne and Brittany as Professor Dumbledore and Harry Potter.

I felt comforted just knowing that somewhere someone who had never even met us was taking the time to light a candle for us and say prayers on our behalf. It made me smile to think of the monk who had placed the telephone call, but I felt sorry, too, that when the call had come, I had refused to answer.

TIM'S HEALTH CONTINUED to deteriorate. He could no longer use his hands, have a natural bowel movement or live through a day without repeated doses of pain relievers. It took three hours for a nurse to help Tim with his morning routine and over an hour for me to get him into bed at night with Doran's help. He was spending more of each day — and, often, all day — in bed, so we cleared our furniture out of the living room and made space there for Tim's bed, his hoist, the hospital table, a dresser and a television. Two large wooden screens served to protect his privacy when his CNA came over in the morning or when we got him ready for bed at night.

Although Tim had retired from the university, he had a contract to revise his book and worked with a few colleagues on some consulting projects, so the university had installed a computer with voice-activated software in our living room for Tim's use. Doran and I figured out how to rig up a hydration system using Tim's old Camelbak bags, so Tim could get water to drink on demand. My mother had attached a bell to Tim's bed that he could ring simply by knocking it, and the bell would make a noise loud enough to carry throughout the entire house.

We had a lightweight French provincial sectional couch we would move near the bay window when we wanted to sit with Tim in the living room. When it was time for a family meal, we could move the couch out of the way and roll our dining room table, which was on wheels, close to the bed so Tim could join us for supper.

Toward the middle of autumn Tim's parents told us they would be travelling to Colorado to stay for the winter and help care for their son. We had a spare bedroom now that Tim's suite was in the living room, so I scoured second-hand stores and yard sales for furnishings that would be appealing to the in-laws.

I was having trouble paying for Tim's nursing care, so I also planned a yard sale of my own. If Tim had been in an institution, the nursing care would have been paid by Medicaid, but private, at-home care was not covered. We were mid-way through the month of October; the CNA would be working fourteen more days between now and the end of the month, for three to four hours a day, and I did not have the money to pay him. So I placed an ad for the upcoming weekend edition of the local newspaper and commenced a mission to clear the household of unneeded or unwanted clutter.

Brittany and Doran got into the spirit. Doran contributed plastic bags full of clothing he had outgrown and boxes filled with Goosebumps books, Matchbox cars and knick-knacks. Brittany wanted to get rid of her stuffed animals and old coloring books. She also wanted to have her own "booth" where she could sell sodas and ice water. She had plans for her profits: she was going to buy a Harry Potter costume for Halloween.

I had a lot to sell, starting with the furnishings I had recently removed from the living room and clothing I could no longer button or zip. There were boxes, too, of miscellany from the Anitra house: trinkets and tools that had had their niche in the old place but had never even been unpacked at the new. As the yard sale neared, I found the motivation to sit in the garage and sort through the boxes that had sat there, untouched, for two and a half years.

The simplest way to accomplish the task, I thought, was to make dollar boxes: a one dollar box, a two dollar box and so on, and to put each item in the box where it was most likely to sell. I had a stack of blank price tags and a marker handy for unusual items—things that would sell for more or things that needed some explanation. A large table sat ready to hold the things that were too fragile or too bulky for my dollar-box system. I was fortunate to have a warm sunny afternoon, and I opened the overhead door to the garage, sat on a stool in a patch of sunlight and went to work.

The garage cooled considerably after the sun shifted position. I looked at my watch and realized it was almost time to fix dinner. I had only a few boxes left to look through, however, so I pressed on. I reached for an unlabeled bankers' box, which turned out to be quite heavy. I carried it to the table, set it down and lifted the lid. Neatly labeled file folders revealed the names, in alphabetical order, of the shards of my career as a writer. "Adams, John. Bentham, Jeremy. Biographies, published. Biographies, finished but unpublished. Buber, Martin. Children's books, ideas. Children's books, finished. Famous economists, contract. Famous economists, first drafts. Famous economists, finished. Friendship, biblical view. Friendship, Greek lit." I reached for the two remaining boxes, which were also unlabeled bankers' boxes, and I set them on the table and looked inside. My photography collection, labeled again, in alphabetical order and sorted into sections distinguishing published and unpublished images.

I sat on the stool for a few moments and looked at my labels. Not so long ago I had been happily productive with my writing, and I had felt inspired to try so many new things with my photography. The file boxes contained the seeds for countless projects I had yet to harvest. As I looked through the labels, though, the ideas seemed only vaguely familiar, like the musings of a person I used to know. Would I ever write again? The question seemed ridiculous, a bit like wondering if a salmon filet would ever swim again. I had no time for ridiculous questions. Without a shred of regret I tipped the contents of the boxes, one by one, into the large mouth of a Hefty trash can. Then I stood and surveyed the scene in the garage.

It looks as ready as it can be, I thought, as I pressed the button to close the overhead door. I switched off the garage light and stepped over the threshold to the kitchen. Without looking back, I pulled the door closed behind me.

TIM HAD A BLADDER infection, a problem that occurred frequently now that he was using a catheter, or as his doctor called it, "a germ highway." As infections went, this one was mild; I was able to get Tim up, in his wheelchair and into Dr. Goldin's office for a routine examination rather than having to call an ambulance to take him to the ER. As expected, Dr. Goldin prescribed an antibiotic. As he was writing out the prescription I told him that I had serious concerns about being able to continue to take care of Tim at home.

"Well, as you know, assisted living is not an option," Dr. Goldin said, and I nodded. In the State of Colorado, anyway, assisted living was limited to people who could handle their own bladder and bowel health, and this requirement excluded Tim.

"Have you given any more thought to a nursing home?" he asked, looking at Tim.

"No," Tim and I said in tandem. I had made several "field trips" to nursing homes in Colorado Springs, trips Tim did not know about. Of the numerous facilities in the city, only three accepted Medicaid, the insurance we would have to use since the university's health insurance carrier did not cover long-term nursing. I couldn't see Tim thriving in any of the homes I had visited.

Dr. Goldin paused and leafed through Tim's chart. "Hmmm. It's been two years since we have tried any new treatments for the MS itself," he said. That was true. We had tried the ABCs (Avonex, Betaseron, Copaxone), the drugs that had seemed so promising several years ago, and we had tried several other treatments to no avail. For two years we had done nothing but treat uncomfortable conditions that accompanied the disease, such as infections and bowel obstructions, not the disease itself. "There is one thing I can do," the doctor said, closing the chart. "I can make the determination that you are 'terminal'—there's really no set of criteria defining that diagnosis, other than I say that I think you have six months or less to live. Now, I don't really think that to be the case, but I can make that diagnosis."

"Why would we do that?" I asked.

"It would qualify Tim for hospice care, which is covered by your insurance. What would happen is you—Tim—would receive home hospice nursing care, most likely three days a week—and some other care as well. The downside is Tim would have to agree not to take measures for prolongment-of-life, that is, he would have to stop treatment for the MS, which, as I have said, it appears we have already done."

I chose my words carefully when I spoke with Tim's parents after the children had gone to bed that night. "So, they are coming back around to a diagnosis of 'terminal,'" his mother said drily.

"What do you mean?" I asked.

"They told Tim his disease was 'terminal' when they first diagnosed him," she said. "They told him then not to expect to live past the age of 50."

THERE WAS A FLURRY OF activity the first week hospice got involved with our family. The organization did, in fact, provide a CNA five mornings a week. David cheerfully agreed to both a reduction in his hours and a schedule that involved working on Saturday and Sunday mornings, days hospice would not provide care. A registered nurse came to the house twice the first week, as did a chaplain and a volunteer visitor. Tim used his computer system to make a schedule for the weekly visits each person would make, working around his weekly civic club meetings, the Tuesday evening beer parties he hosted at home and our worship schedule. From henceforth, hospice would provide all pharmaceutical and other medical supplies, which we would keep in a locked cabinet,

Brittany, wasting away but still active, skateboarding in the garage at the Flintridge house.

and administer according to a typed schedule, also provided by hospice. We put a pen between Tim's fingers and he marked an X on the hospice contract, signifying that he understood all of the instructions he had been given and affirming that he was not seeking treatment to prolong his life.

NOW 15 YEARS OLD AND weighing 79 pounds, Brittany continued to have the "dark pain" headaches that had caused such frightening trouble in the past. She developed purplish-grey smudges under her eyes from a chronic lack of sleep. She frequently was constipated. And she had begun vomiting daily. She would eat, heartily, and vomit immediately. She had difficulty concentrating. She was irritable at school. One of her classmates had told her that the dry skin on her hands made her look like a monster, and he teased her about her repeated trips to the bathroom to throw up, she said. She begged every morning to be allowed to stay home. I wondered if it was anxiety about Tim that made her dread leaving the house, but I also wondered what would happen to her general outlook if she didn't leave the house. Finally, with the middle of the school year approaching, I decided I would forfeit my teaching position and teach Brittany at home.

"So, you want to quit," Tim said when I told him what I wanted to do.

"If I stay home, Brittany will be able to learn, better, and your parents will feel like they can go back home."

"How do we make it financially?"

I shook my head. "I don't know, Tim. I've always managed to get the bills paid. Always."

"What has happened to you?" he scolded. "You used to have ambition. Now you're just…tired…all the time."

I stared at the cats that were snoozing peacefully on a table in the bay window.

"Every day you complain about being tired," Tim said, and he turned his face toward the television.

DORAN ASKED PERMISSION to spend New Year's Eve with some of his friends from church. I had become quite close to Marie, one of the young women he wanted to see, and I was confident that Doran would be celebrating with responsible people in a safe setting. It made me nervous to have him out on the roads on New Year's Eve, but Marie had already agreed to be driver and chaperone for the younger revelers, so I agreed that Doran could go. He was in his junior year in high school and hadn't once asked to go out in the evenings. He made sure Tim was comfortable in his bed before calling Marie and asking for a pick-up.

Brittany, Tim and I had made a pact to stay awake. There had been some snowfall but the skies cleared as the evening drew on, and we were anticipating the fireworks display that would begin when the clock struck twelve. At 11:45 I called Brittany to the bathroom to brush her teeth. She later wrote the rest of the story:

> I was watching a movie called the Next Karate Kid movie. I rented it at Hollywood Videos movie store. We were trying to stay up till midnight on New Year's Eve. My mom told me to come to the bathroom to brush my teeth, and I paused my movie. Me and my mom were brushing our teeth.

> We heard a very loud sound and we ran out to see what it was. We had a car accident in our driveway! A teenager driving a white car—his friends' car—drove across our yard very fast and crashed.

> We saw our van and Doran's blue car smashed to the grounds in the driveway and both cars were stacked together and our garage got smashed too, a dent in the door.

> My mom ran outside to help the kid! She brought him in the house! And she put a blanket around him!

> My mom called 911 and the police came and the ambulance to ask that kid what happened. I was so angry and scared a little bit. When Doran got home he was very upset when he saw his car smashed to the grounds.

New Year's Day fell on a Friday, and it was three days before an insurance adjustor could come to the house to evaluate the accident scene. The white car, driven by a 19-year old who had been high on methamphetamines when he crossed our yard at roughly 90 mph, had been towed away by the police shortly after the accident. Doran's blue car, knocked ninety degrees off-kilter and ten feet west of the concrete driveway, lay where it fell, on the grass, its nose shoved ignobly into a shrub, the grass around it littered by bits of shattered glass and fragments of blue and white steel. The van lay sideways in the driveway, the front passenger side smashed beyond recognition. All weekend Tim watched as the neighborhood walkers would stop, stare and then continue walking, as if they had witnessed a scene that defied understanding.

DOING SCHOOL AT HOME, Brittany and I were able to adjust for her ups and downs, concentrating on more bookish tasks when she felt well and other activities when she felt puny. When Tim's visitors came to the house, Brittany and I usually left, to get books at the library, shop for groceries, play in the park or ride our bikes. She became very interested in writing and made booklets and posters about many different topics, preferring social studies and geography. She avoided math and showed no aptitude whatsoever for counting money or other so-called "life skills" involving numbers.

When she was at the house she frequently donned her 'Visibility Cloak, as she called it, the floor-length cape that had been part of her Harry Potter costume at Halloween. She especially loved wearing the cloak when she entered her own bedroom, her make-believe Hogwart's School. She had me write in her notebook:

I watched movies in my room and wrote scripts for my class. My pretend class was in my room because I wanted to be a teacher like my teacher and like my mom, a writer. Here's how I wrote scripts: I watched the movie with the words and I paused the movies at the spots where I wanted to write about it. Then I wrote it down.

I wrote scripts for myself from the Lion King. Sometimes I wrote The Three Musketeers. I also wrote one for each person in my pretend class. One at a time because I only had two hands.

I would sing in my room with the music up high. Because my brother Doran used his CDs up loud, so did I.

I made cookies with some friends. They were heart-shaped cookies. I made a diorama of Alaska; I wanted to learn about it because I wanted to know what Alaska looked like and because I had studied about St. Herman and St. Peter the Aleut who were from Alaska. There were a lot of things about St. Herman that I learned. St. Herman crossed the ocean on a boat from Russia to Kodiak, Alaska. He wanted to teach people about Christ. St. Herman loved to make cookies for little children.

I studied about St. Patrick. The shamrock is used to teach the Father and the Son and the Holy Spirit. St. Patrick taught us that. St. Patrick lived in Ireland and it's green there. I studied Ireland in home school. There are peat bogs there. I watched a movie about St. Patrick.

I learned about the myrrh-bearing women. My saint, Mary Magdalene, was one of them. She went to the tomb to find Jesus and the angel told Mary Magdalene that Jesus was not there any more, because he rose from the dead. The only one person Jesus appeared to that day was Mary Magdalene, and she went to tell all the others. I learned this from my mom.

I studied about George Washington. I learned how to draw maps. I learned about gases. I saw the gas bubbles in my soda when I stuck my straw in it. All the gas bubbles clung to my straw. That was kind of funny. My mom taught me how to measure things with a ruler and a tape measure.

I did some writing in home school and other things. I did presentations to my grandparents and to my mom and dad. I got smarter in home school from reading and learning about everything. It was wonderful to be in home school.

NEAR THE MIDDLE OF January Tim went into a coma. For the better part of a day he had stared dreamily at the ceiling, and then toward nightfall he closed his eyes. His parents and I took turns sitting up during the night, watching for any changes. Tim slept peacefully. The next morning, we were unable to wake him. The RN came over, examined him, and told us we should prepare for the end. Our priest came to the house and gave Tim last rites. The family kept by his bedside. We took turns reading the psalms and keeping the vigil candles lit. I held Brittany as she cried herself to sleep.

The next morning, I took a load of laundry downstairs and stopped by Doran's bedroom to talk with him. As I neared the top of the stairs I could see Brittany in her 'Visibility Cloak sitting on a stool near Tim's bedside. My neighbor Pat sat next to her. They were holding a tissue near Tim's nostrils. "See, Brittany," Pat said. "See how the tissue flutters? That's because your daddy is breathing, see?" Brittany nodded. "If your daddy is breathing, that means he is alive."

Brittany looked up in relief. "It scares me when Daddy sleeps like this. Makes me think he's dead."

Later that day, Tim opened his eyes and spoke, resuming with his dad a conversation he had left off three days earlier.

OUR NORMAL ROUTINE was restored: Doran returned to school, Brittany and I resumed our studies, Tim's beer group reassembled, we all went to church, the regular hospice CNAs returned per their usual schedule. Tim's favorite CNA, Val, was emotional when she returned on her day. She had grown very close to Tim and had felt cut off, it seemed, by her inability to see him during his critical time.

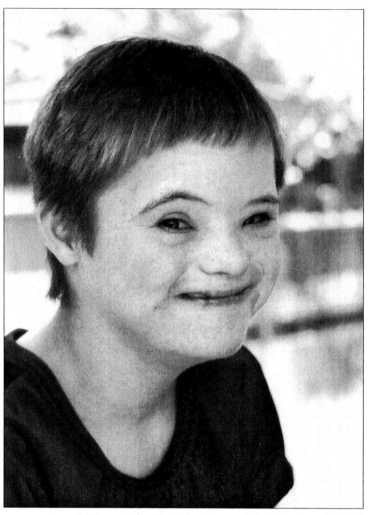

Brittany at the Flintridge House. (Photo by Jane McBee.)

Val usually came early, shortly before Doran left for school and about an hour before Brittany normally woke up; the schedule allowed me some personal time that I normally used for a brisk walk with my friend Pam. I was waiting for Pam to knock on the door one morning, idly working on a picture puzzle I had started at the dining room table, when Doran walked upstairs, his backpack in one hand and the keys to our Jeep Cherokee in the other. He sat down and helped me with the puzzle; Tim and Val chatted like old friends behind the wooden privacy screens.

Val said something about Tim's undershirts, and Tim responded, "After seventeen years of marriage I still haven't trained her to fold my laundry properly." Val giggled.

Doran looked up in disgust, picked up his keys, and walked out of the house without saying good-bye.

ALTHOUGH I ENJOYED MY walks with Pam, I lucked into a low cost membership at a fitness center in a downtown hotel and I began to use the fitness center more frequently. I had slipped off the edge of a handicap ramp and had broken my foot early in the autumn. Though the break had healed, my foot still got sore and cramped up after a long walk. And I still had problems with pain in my lower back. So I favored workouts at the club where I could take aqua-walks followed by a soak in the hot tub.

One morning I checked in at the fitness center early, signed the visitor log, got a towel and a key from the attendant and went into the locker room to change into my swimsuit. I walked in the pool for a little over a quarter of an hour before being joined in the water by another patron. He was an elderly gentleman—in his mid 70s, I was guessing. He had a clean shaven face and a head full of thick silver-white hair. The silver hair was thick on his chest as well, save for a long vertical strip that looked like freshly mowed grass right down the center. In the middle of the strip was the zipper-like raised red scar that signaled a recent heart surgery. I asked him about his recovery, and we talked and talked and talked. Twenty minutes later, we sat in the hot tub and talked some more.

His name was Otis; he was a retired physician. He told me about his upbringing in the Midwest, about his family, their farm and, finally, about his military service. He had flown planes during the Second World War, a bomber pilot assigned to missions over Nazi Europe. He told me how his conscience had struggled with his task, with the fact that innocent people died from the bombs he had carried, with his personal role in horrific consequences that were contrary to everything he had ever been taught or had come to believe about himself and his world.

Upon receiving word that his mother was in the final stages of her struggle with cancer he was given leave to return home for two weeks. He told me how during his precious time with her he broke down, sobbing like a child in pity for himself and disgust with the war. He told her that he could not return to military service, that he would accept the consequences for desertion, that he could not bring himself to harm another person. "I expected her to understand and to bless me," he said, "my mother was a religious person. But instead she told me I had to return. That it was my duty to my country, my responsibility to my fellow soldiers and, most of all, my privilege to help destroy the evil specter of Nazi Germany.

"But she told me I must do one thing. She told me that when I returned I must dedicate myself to the healing of men," Otis said, smiling at the recollection. "And that is what I did. I went back to Europe, and I broke the bodies of many more people. After the war I went to medical school and studied orthopedics. I worked as an orthopedic surgeon until I retired."

I left Otis to his memories and walked to the dressing room. As I closed the seal of the Ziploc bag containing my wet swimsuit, I imagined Otis as a younger man, kneeling by his mother's side. I pictured her, physically weakened by disease and yet so strong in her understanding of her son. I left the locker room and stopped at the reception desk, handed my towel and key to the attendant and picked up the pen to sign out. There were no names on the sheet except my own, and I mentioned this idly to the young man tending the gate.

"There's been no one in there but yourself," he said.

"Well, there's Otis, the older fellow…"

"I've been here all morning," the attendant said firmly. "No one but you has been in the facility today."

TIM SLIPPED INTO ANOTHER coma. As was the pattern before, he had spent hours gazing at the ceiling. We watched him smile sweetly at the images he saw there, and we tilted our heads to look, but no one else could see what he saw. We offered him drinks of water and tea but he was unresponsive. That night, I went downstairs to say good night to Doran, tucked Brittany into my bed, and sat on the couch, reading the Psalms out loud while Tim slept. The next morning I woke early when Brittany pulled my hands, which had been crossed, off my chest. "Don't sleep that way," she said crossly. "Makes you look like you're dead." I jumped to my feet and headed toward the bed.

"'SOkay," Brittany said. "Daddy's breathing." She showed me the tissue she held in her hands. "I checked."

"Thank you, Baby," I said, and I gently nudged Tim. No response. Fifteen minutes later I nudged him again. Again, no response. I called hospice and talked to the on-duty RN, who told me she would cancel the CNA visit and have Tim's nurse stop by later that morning.

Over the following days and nights, the children and I took turns sitting with Tim, Doran alternating times with Brittany and I, who kept watch together. We read the Psalms, sang songs and lit candles. As it had happened the previous time, Tim woke the third day, alert and conversational, with no inkling whatsoever of the passage of time.

Months later, after Tim cycled through a third coma, his RN told us it was time to move him to the hospice facility. CNAs now spent an average of about five hours a day in our home; Tim's care demanded more time than the agency could provide in a home setting, and none of the eligible nursing homes could take him. With the hospice chaplain on hand to support her, the RN gently but firmly told us that there really was no other option.

The next day an ambulance arrived at the house to transport Tim to hospice. I don't know what day it was, what week or even what month. It is one of those chasms in my memory that yields nothing but eerie silence when I call into it. I don't remember if Tim's parents were there or if they had gone. I don't remember if Doran was home when the ambulance came. I don't know if it was winter or fall. I only know that the exterior wall of the house felt warm when I sat on our deck and leaned against it, pulling my knees to my chest and holding them tight with my arms. And I remember the warm pressure of Brittany's hand on my shoulder and the sound of her voice in my ears: "We have to let him go, Mommy. We have to."

Chapter Six

Switching Gears

Brittany began to have a recurring dream. "We were walking in the fields, our whole family," she told me. By "the fields" she meant a twenty-acre patch of former pasture once a part of a ranch, now held in trust by a local family. The fields bordered a craggy, juniper-filled public park, known as Palmer Park, a popular destination for hikers, mountain bikers and dog walkers. Lapping along the park's northeast boundary, "the fields" were a sea of tall grass waving gently between the rocky cliffs of the park and busy Union Boulevard, with its clamor of traffic, concrete and noise.

When we first moved to the Anitra Circle house, walks along a footpath cutting through the fields were a regular part of our family's routine. It was a long walk, two miles from start to finish, so we would take a small lunch box that the children had filled with juice boxes, Goldfish crackers and any other goodies we might need for an informal picnic along our way. As Doran grew and mastered his bicycle, he would take the path on wheels, always offering to carry the lunch box in his backpack.

One spring we were returning to Colorado Springs from a road trip to Southern California, where we had visited Tim's relatives. We were sharing laughs from the trip as I steered our Suburban onto the Austin Bluffs

Parkway exit off of I-25. As we reached the crest of a steep hill, we could see that "the fields" were gone, replaced by a long row of regularly-spaced bulbous swaths. If you had viewed the scene from a small airplane the patterns cut in the earth may have appeared mystical and beautiful, but from our vantage point on the hill there was no mystery or beauty in the design: it was a portent of cul-de-sacs, houses, lawns and driveways. The fields had been dissected into parcels soon to be marketed under the name "St. Andrew's Estates."

When Brittany began dreaming, ten years later, of "the fields," she was dreaming of an earlier time, a time before earthmovers ravaged the fields and before disease ravaged her dad, for the rest of the dream went as follows: "We were walking in the fields, our whole family, and you didn't have to carry me, because Daddy was walking, too, and he could carry me, the whole entire way, without dropping me, even once."

THE DAY AFTER TIM moved to Hospice, the medical supply company sent two men to our house. They deftly disassembled the hospital bed and loaded it, the bed table and the hoist onto a large van, courteously asked me to sign a document and drove away. Doran put the dresser in the guest room and asked if he could have the TV, which he then carried downstairs. The wooden screens he put in the garage. He asked if I needed anything else before he grabbed his backpack and headed off in his Jeep to go to play practice. Brittany was next door, jumping on the trampoline in the neighbor's backyard. Doran had left the door ajar, and I could hear the girls giggle and scream.

I stood in the living room, feeling small and exposed in the open space. Feeling a chill, I buttoned my sweater and folded my arms tightly. I noticed one of Tim's soiled undershirts sitting pell-mell on the floor, and I picked it up and carried it to the laundry basket. I returned to the living room and looked around. Some of the candles on the fireplace mantle had burned down to little stubs, so I replaced them. I picked up the Bible, open to the Book of Psalms, and I closed it and set it down again. Next to the Bible lay the notebook we had used to track Tim's meds; I closed it, too, and put it in a "catch-all" drawer in the kitchen. I stopped at the dining room table and tried to fit together a few pieces of the jigsaw puzzle, but the effort exhausted me, so I moved a section of the couch into the stream of sunlight shining through the bay window, and I sat down. Hector jumped on my lap, his purr box vibrating loudly.

I was vaguely aware of the screen door slamming and Brittany entering the room. "Don't sleep like that," she said as she grabbed my hands and moved them off my chest. "It scares me."

I sat up and patted a sunny spot on the couch. Brittany sank into it and snuggled alongside me, but she was too excited to sit still for long. "Me and Hadley had so much fun," she said. "And it was so funny. Hadley's dog, he got under the trampoline and he barked at us. And he went to the side of the trampoline and he tried to jump on. It was sooooo funny!

"And now I'm sooooo hungry!" she said, "when's dinner?"

"Well, it's just you and me tonight. Doran's having dinner with some friends. We'll go see Daddy for a while and help him with his dinner, but after that we're on our own, so, how does Michelle's Restaurant sound?"

Brittany jumped off the couch. "Yaaaaay," she yelled, and she spun around the room with her arms extended, filling the vacant space with her joy.

BRITTANY BREATHLESSLY told Tim about Hadley, the trampoline, the barking dog and our upcoming "dinner out" at Michelle's Restaurant. "Can I go watch the TV now?" she asked, and when he nodded, she kissed him on the forehead and walked down the corridor in the direction of the Hospice waiting room.

After she left, Tim filled me in with his news. His friends from the university's computer sciences department had come by earlier and set up his computer system, even hooking the voice-activated software to a telephone unit. By this time tomorrow, Tim predicted, the system would be wired through the Hospice phone lines, enabling him to make phone calls, via a headset and microphone, directly through the computer using voice commands. He had started making a spreadsheet in his Excel program with times of day on one grid and days of the week on another. Already, the grid for next week was filling fast, the names of Tim's friends and hospice volunteers neatly arranged in rows and columns on the spreadsheet. "I already have you in for Saturday dinners before Vespers and for Sunday breakfasts and lunches for church. I need you to come in at breakfast times for the next few days, but lunches are covered and all dinners except Monday," he said. "Can you come in Monday at dinner?" he asked.

"Of course," I said.

Tim faced the computer screen. "Go to C:2," he said and he paused. "Suzanna. Go to D:2 ... Suzanna. Go to E:2 ... Suzanna. Go to F:2 ... Suzanna. Go to B:4 ... Suzanna." My name now occupied eight cells on his spreadsheet. I did not ask whose names occupied the other cells, but he offered some information. "I've got beer group here on Tuesday, Sertoma on Tuesday lunch—if I can't go to the meeting, one of the Sertomans will just feed me here—Russ is here on Thursday afternoons and he can stay through dinner, Matt is here on Wednesday...." He went through the list. "Most people can come every week, and I'll get someone on those breakfasts and Monday dinners.

He looked at me. "You'll just have to come in when someone cancels."

"Wow." It was the only thing I could think of to say. I started cutting up the Salisbury steak on his tray. "Salt and pepper?" I asked. He nodded.

"And could you get the grapes?" he asked. "I asked the staff to prepare some cups with grapes and have them ready in the refrigerator. They're down in the break room. When we're finished, can you remember to bring me some grapes?"

"Sure," I said, and I smiled. He asked if there was any news from home. I didn't have the heart to tell him that the van had picked up his bed, so I told him simply that Doran was at a play practice and would be having dinner with friends. We chatted while he finished his meal, about Doran, the play, people from church, the university's search for a new chancellor, our nephew Brian's decision to study for the ministry. When we finished I walked down the hall to the waiting room and tapped Brittany on the shoulder. "It's time to say goodbye to Daddy."

"Yaay, Michelle's!" she said as she leapt to her feet and scampered down the hall. I walked into the break room and opened the refrigerator. On the top shelf were 10 plastic cups in two neat rows, each filled two-thirds full with green grapes. I carried one back to the room and Tim smiled, "I asked them to put 17 grapes in each cup," he told Brittany as she took the cup from my hand and lifted out a grape to feed him. "Do you want to count them and make sure they got it right?" he asked her.

She looked at him as a bartender might size up a patron before agreeing to refill his drink. "No," she said finally, "that would be boring."

I SHOULD HAVE KNOWN I was setting a precedent. When I took Brittany to Hospice the next day, she chatted cheerfully with Tim, complied with his request to walk down to the break room to get the cup of grapes, patiently read out loud a story she had been learning in home school, and instantly cooperated when I told her it was time to put on her shoes to leave. But the skies darkened as we left the building and she began talking about Michelle's Restaurant. When I told her we were going home for dinner she planted her feet firmly on the sidewalk outside Hospice's huge double doors, crossed her arms defiantly and refused to walk to the van. "That's not fair," she said hoarsely.

"We can't go out to eat every day, Brittany. You know that."

"You said we go see Daddy, then we go out," she said, glaring at me through narrowing eyes. "You lied!"

"I said we would go out yesterday. I didn't say we would go out every time."

"Then I'm not coming here. I don't like this place." She thrust her hands in the pocket of her sweatshirt and stomped across the parking lot to the car. I pressed the remote, unlocking the passenger side door. She climbed in and slammed the door behind her. I hummed the Jeopardy song silently to myself—two times through—before I opened the driver side door and got in. Brittany stared out the windshield, arms crossed, an angry pout on her face.

"This is where Daddy lives now, Brittany. This is where we come to see him."

"I don't want to see him," she said, her eyes still staring straight ahead of her. "Get me out of here."

I knew there would be no way to reason with her until later—much later—and that she was not in the mood for a hug. "Buckle your seat belt, and we'll go," I said. She started to resist, and then complied, scoffing and rolling her eyes while she latched the belt around her.

WITH TIM NOW AT HOSPICE, Brittany and I began to explore activities to complement her home-school curriculum. We started working cooperatively with some other home-school families and furnished a small library/classroom at our church where we could have joint study times. We participated in a science and history fair where local homeschooled children could come together to show exhibits, do presentations and win awards for their academic contributions. We took field trips to museums, wildlife centers and swimming pools.

One day we got word that the local Special Olympics organization would be offering bicycling, and Brittany instantly embraced the idea of participating. We called Tom Gomez, the coach, and learned that practices would take place twice a week. I thought Brittany would burst from excitement as we loaded her bicycle in the van and headed off to her first Special Olympics practice.

Brittany with Tom Gomez, Colorado Springs Special Olympics cycling coach.

Practices took place at Memorial Park, located just blocks away from Hospice. In my innocence I had hoped that Brittany's bicycling practices might serve as a bridge to visits with Tim. With the exception of her first visit there, the one followed by dinner out at Michelle's, getting her to visit cheerfully had been like spinning straw into gold. A wizard may have been able to do it, or a demon perhaps, but I was neither wizard nor demon; the more I tried to encourage Brittany to go, the more obstinate she became. Cycling practice and visiting Tim were activities that could naturally dovetail off of one another, I thought. To my astonished delight, I had spun a golden plan!

More or less.

Two weeks into the season I had to acknowledge the flaw in my design. Going from practice to Hospice was a poor strategy; by the time Brittany finished practice she was exhausted and a stop anywhere other than her own home was beyond her mental and physical limitations. Visiting Tim before practice worked better. Having the assurance that we had a fixed time we were leaving Hospice and knowing that cycling practice immediately followed "Hospice time," as Brittany called it, gave her the encouragement she needed. However, Tim got frustrated—as did I—with Brittany's incessant clock watching: "What time is it now?" "5:30." "What time is it now?" "5:32." "What time is it now?" "5:35." "Is it time to go yet?" After the second pre-cycling visit, Tim asked me to leave Hospice "off the cycling track," and I agreed. Brittany would be much happier, we all would be much happier, if her visits to her dad were disentangled from her Special Olympics participation.

She loved Special Olympics bicycling. With every revolution around the track she seemed to grow in strength and confidence, and she discovered a new way of looking at herself. She looked in the mirror and saw an athlete looking back at her. Years later I helped her write in her journal:

> I did biking since I was only 15 years old. I had to go around and around on a hard dirt track. I had a few team members with me, the same team as me.
>
> We were the Power Pedalers!
>
> Sometimes the others were riding their bikes faster than me, because sometimes I got exhausted riding too fast on my bike. Sometimes I rode faster. In practices we went twice a week, so we can get better at riding so we could do the tournament competition. So we can try to do our best.

I got a first place ribbon when they called my name. I wore a jersey, a bright orange team uniform on the back it said our team name. I also wore bicycling gloves, black shorts and a helmet.

I loved being in biking with my coach Tom Gomez. He was a good coach. I don't know if you might want to meet him some day.

When her coach announced the upcoming Southeast Area Summer Classic and explained to Brittany and the other athletes that cyclists, tennis players, bocce players and entire softball teams would travel to Colorado Springs for competition from other cities in Southern Colorado, Brittany was mesmerized. She asked me to repeat the information—over and over again—and called Tom Gomez on the telephone to see if "it was really true." When she finally assured herself that, yes, the competition would actually take place, she gathered paper and markers, asked me for some "ventilopes," and positioned herself at the dining room table where she wrote and colored invitations to her "first-ever" sports competition. It was a full day's effort, an effort I obliged by setting aside home-school lessons and encouraged by working alongside her. When she completed the invitations, she set one aside for Tim and one for a family at church. Then she donned the bright orange Power Pedalers team jersey, distributed by her coach at the previous practice, strapped on her helmet and stuffed the remaining invitations in a plastic grocery bag. I opened the garage door so we could get our bikes. I was putting on my helmet when she said, "'SOkay, Mom, I can do it myself. I know where everybody lives." She mounted her bike and took off.

A postcard-perfect Colorado day greeted the uniformed Special Olympics athletes as one by one they arrived in mini-vans, SUVs and pickups, and unloaded their bicycles, helmets, softball gloves, tennis rackets, water bottles and other gear. Under a bright green tent volunteers from a local bike shop examined the athletes' bicycles, airing up tires as necessary, adjusting brakes and tightening the clamps holding seats in place. Under another tent volunteers distributed cold water and hot coffee. Another group of volunteers, clad in bright orange vests, gathered around a coordinator and received clipboards, timers and credentials to identify them as tournament officials.

I had stopped at Hospice to pick up Tim and had backed the van into a handicap parking place near the finish line of the bike track. I opened the hatch on the back and draped a large towel over it, making a tented seat for myself and two friends from the neighborhood. Tim sat in his wheelchair on the grass, shaded by the van's veiled hatch; next to him, three other neighborhood friends sat on the ground, a blanket between them and the grass.

After forming huge circles where they stretched out and listened to announcements, the athletes herded into groups behind large placards announcing the names of their hometowns. In the middle of the crowd behind the Colorado Springs placard I could see Brittany nervously clutching her coach's hand. Music blared over a loud speaker as the athletes processed onto the tracks. The music stopped and everyone stood at attention as the colors were presented and the pledge of allegiance recited over the loudspeakers. An announcer welcomed the athletes and handed the microphone to an athlete who said, with the other competitors repeating in unison, the Special Olympics athletes' oath: "Let me win, but if I cannot win, let me be brave in the attempt."

It was standard form for athletes to compete in three events, and the Summer Classic was no exception. By the time Brittany was called to get on deck for her third bike race, however, she was ready to call it a day. She had found us, made herself comfortable on the blanket and removed her shoes. "No," she told Coach Tom, when, clipboard in hand, he found her on her blanket oasis. "I'm not going."

"Last event, Brittany, let's go," he said. Our neighbors clapped, "Yeah, let's go, Brittany." She smiled but hesitated.

"I'm so tired," she collapsed into the blanket.

"Last event, Brittany," I said. "I'll go to Subway; have a meatball sandwich waiting for you."

"I'm outta here," she said, grabbing Tom's extended hand and her shoes in one fell swoop. "Extra cheese," she called to me as Tom led her away.

"Save my parking spot?" I begged my neighbors, as I closed the hatch and dug in my pockets for my keys. I closed my eyes and briefly said a prayer, "Please get me back in time."

Brittany was on her fifth trip around the track by the time I returned with the sandwich, and she was lagging behind the others. When she saw me she picked up steam and by the end of the tenth revolution she narrowly led the pack. She finished the fifteenth and final round, dismounted, reclaimed her spot on the blanket and had the meatball sandwich unwrapped before her nearest competitor could cross the finish line. "This is like a heaven," she said. "I gonna inhale it," she added and, indeed, she ate the sandwich so quickly I was afraid she would be sick. Compared to the sandwich, her first place ribbon paled in comparison, at least it did then in the heat of the moment. As she recalls the event, she remembers the ribbon and the first-place finish; not the meatball sandwich that got her there.

IN FACT THE SANDWICH did make her sick. Not right away, but later. When we took Tim back to Hospice, Brittany said she felt weak and hot and asked to stay in the van, while I got him settled in his room inside. I made her promise she wouldn't leave the van or unlock it for anybody. I put the windows down slightly and removed the key from the ignition, gave Brittany my bottle of water and kissed her. "I'll be out as soon as I can," I said, and I was, but it wasn't soon enough.

"I threw upped," she said, "my sandwich, all of it." She pointed to a plastic grocery bag she had used.

"Ah, Honey, I'm so sorry," I said as I reached for the bag.

"Wait," she said. I opened the bag and she leaned forward. She vomited again. "Okay," she said as she sank back in the seat. "I feel so weak."

"I'm going to throw this bag away over there," I said, pointing to the trash bin. I left her door open while I turned and walked away from the van. When I returned, I latched the seat belt around her and reached behind the seat for the Subway bag. I put it on her lap. "Here. Just in case."

She used the bag three times before we made it across town, but she didn't have the volume she had had before and she seemed defeated with the effort. "Do you want me to pull over and stop?" I asked.

"No." She was adamant. "Home."

"Okay, Baby," I said, grateful to be turning onto Flintridge Drive and on the last quarter mile of our journey. I pulled into the driveway, cut the engine and got out of the car. I walked around to the passenger side and opened Brittany's door.

"Come here," I said. She looped her arms around my neck and her legs around my waist. I hoisted her out of the van, and carried her bony little body into the house. I set her on the couch with the plastic bucket we used on occasions such as this. "I'm going to get you some water," I said. "Drink it when you can, and when you feel like you can, get your teeth brushed, okay?" She nodded, but my words were lost in the nausea that propelled her forward. Her shoulders heaved as she held her face over the bucket and groaned.

By Sunday morning Brittany felt like herself again; nonetheless early Monday morning I asked Doran to stay home with her while I drove to the pediatrician's office. I took a seat in the waiting room where I told the receptionist I would stay until I was able to speak with Brittany's physician. When Dr. Hoover took me back to his office I unleashed my words in a hailstorm of emotion, opening with the patter of "Why can't we solve this?" picking up a deafening drum with "She shouldn't have to live this way," and finally exhausting myself in the pitiful, whimpering cry: "It just isn't fair!"

Two weeks later Dr. Hoover called me at home. "I want you to call this number in Denver," he said. "They just opened a pediatric gastroenterology practice. I just met one of their guys, Dr. Yazdi. I think they can help us."

BRITTANY AND HER FRIEND Rebekah had spread blankets and pillows on the floor, making a big bed for the sleep-over. They had decided on a movie and were tugging on their pajamas when the phone rang. It was Hospice. "We have been trying to wake Tim to get him washed and medicated for bed, but he's unresponsive," the nurse said.

"Heart rate and blood pressure?" I asked.

"Low but stable," she said. "Temperature normal. Lungs sound clear." Of course they do, I thought, there's nothing wrong with his lungs.

"How long has he been this way?"

"He was awake at dinner, but didn't eat. He just kind of stared at the ceiling," she said. I was walking with the phone to check in on the girls. They were lying on their stomachs, propped up on their elbows, eyes glued to the screen of Brittany's movie player. Brittany had the remote in one hand, ready to hit "Play" when the previews got boring.

"Who's on the phone, Mom?" she asked, turning her head to look at me when she sensed my presence in the door.

"Gramma," I said, my hand cupped over the speaker.

"Oh, tell her Hi," she said and returned her attention to the movie. I walked back to the kitchen.

"I've got a guest here, one of my daughter's friends," I told the nurse. "I'll come over in the morning. Please call me if anything changes."

"Yes, ma'am," said the nurse.

I slept with the phone on the bed next to me and called Hospice first thing in the morning. There was no change in Tim's condition, so I called Rebekah's mother and told her that Tim was in a coma again. She told me she would pick up Rebekah at 10 and offered to pick up Brittany as well. I went into Brittany's room and nudged the girls awake. "You're going to go play at Rebekah's for a while now. Let's get some breakfast."

Brittany rubbed her eyes. "I thought…"

"You've been invited to Rebekah's house."

The girls looked at each other and said "Suh-weet," mimicking a scene from the movie previews they had watched.

From Hospice I called Doran, who was working at my brother's lumber mill and staying at my mother's house on the western slope of Colorado. "Should I come home, Mom?" he asked. I told him that I didn't have any reason to think this episode was any different from the last few, but that I would call him if things changed.

"Just stay near a phone, will you, Hon?" I asked him.

"No problem. I wasn't going to go farther than Gramma's kitchen today, huh, Gramma?" he teased. "Love you, Mom."

The next evening I called Doran from the Hospice waiting room. "Everything's back to normal," I said. "Your dad picked right up where he had left off. He's perfectly okay except that he thinks it's Friday."

Doran laughed, "Like you said, Mom, everything's back to normal."

I told Doran I loved him and hung up the phone. I walked to the break room to get a cup of grapes and started down the hallway to Tim's room. The charge nurse intercepted me. "Can we talk a moment?" she asked and nodded toward the small room marked with a placard that said "consultations." I stepped inside. "Have a seat," she said.

Is this it? I asked myself.

Is this the part where they tell me they know that Tim isn't really terminal, that he doesn't belong in Hospice, that he's been here for a year and that they're sending him home? As I took a seat I thought about the cells on Tim's spreadsheet. Would we be able to fill those cells with the names of volunteers once we took him home, or would it be just me and the kids…

"I understand Tim has had events like the one just experienced before," the nurse began.

"This is the fourth time he's gone into a coma," I said.

"And are the events alike?" she said. I nodded. "How so?"

"Well," I began, "Each one seems to come out of the blue. Each time he tells us he saw angels on the ceiling. Each time it lasts about three days. During that time, he seems to be on the edge, between this world and the next, low blood pressure, very shallow breathing, completely unresponsive. And each time he awakes and resumes whatever conversation he had been having before he slipped away."

"Yes, I can see this in his chart," she said. "I find it very puzzling." I suddenly realized the nurse was an ally, not someone looking for an alternative placement for Tim. "Is it your understanding that these comas are typical of MS?" she asked.

"No, not at all," I said. "I mean, maybe if Tim had huge patches of brain damage, I could see how this would happen, but his damage is confined to a very small area. As I understand it, the damage in his brain is all concentrated in the area at the top of the spine, and that's why he's paralyzed. There's never been any evidence of damage anywhere else in his brain."

She nodded. "When did these comas begin?"

I struggled out loud to place the first one. "Let me ask you this," she said. "Did they begin before or after Hospice began providing care?"

I thought about it a moment. "After." She nodded her head knowingly.

"Okay, let's switch gears. What can you tell me about Tim's alcohol use?"

"What?" I asked, but she did not repeat herself. "Well, he likes to drink, not a lot at one time, but frequently. A glass of wine at dinner, an evening martini with his dad, beer night with friends from church, a glass of beer at civic club meetings, an occasional Scotch with that guy here, the one whose room is down the hall ..."

"And how does he drink?" she asked.

"How?" It suddenly dawned on me what she meant. "Through a straw. Someone has to hold the glass for him; he drinks through a straw."

"Mrs. Tregarthen..."

I interrupted her, "Suzanna."

"Suzanna, the chart indicates that when Hospice began doing home care for Tim, we shifted him off of Morphine and replaced it with another pain reliever..."

"Methadone," I said. "I remember. Morphine wasn't cutting the pain in his back and legs."

"Suzanna, serious side effects can occur with methadone, especially if the patient uses alcohol while taking the drug. This should have been explained to you when the prescription was begun."

"I don't remember..." My eyes drifted away from her face, over her shoulder, and back to a memory of the first day Hospice nurses came to the Flintridge house. "I remember the log book, I remember Tim signed the contract. We put a pen in his hand and he signed an X. I remember the crinkly paper bags with the medicines in them; I don't remember anyone telling us Tim should stop drinking."

"Methadone and alcohol should never be mixed," she called me back to the consultation room, to her shoulder, her face. "Never, ever."

"Are you telling me these comas are drug reactions? That they aren't real?" I asked.

"Oh, they're real," she said. "What I'm telling you is that they may have been unnecessary."

BRITTANY PRESSED THE elevator button for the second floor. "Is it a boy doctor? Is he going to make me pee in a cup? Do I have to get undressed?" The questions continued as I signed the patient register and guided Brittany to a seat in the waiting room. "Is he going to be like that other guy, 'Dr. Hamburger'? Eewww, why did he want to see my poop? I hate barium. Do I have to swallow barium? I don't want any IVs. How do you say his name again—Dr. John Yazdi?"

"Brittany?" a young nurse called from an open doorway. Brittany looked up. She clenched my hand.

"I'm scared," she said in a hoarse whisper.

The nurse looked at Brittany and smiled, "It's your turn now," she said perkily.

Brittany gulped dramatically. "Get this over with," she said. She stood up and skulked toward the nurse, clutching my hand in hers and avoiding eye contact with everyone else in the room.

Within moments Dr. Yazdi entered the patient room. He sat on the foot of the examination table, smiled, and greeted Brittany. Tall and olive-skinned, with short salt-and-pepper hair and a broad, pleasant smile, he engaged his new patient in a conversation about Disney movies, which he discussed knowledgeably. She chuckled at his accent and said, "It's Finding Neeee-mo; not Finding Nai-mo."

"Naaaaiiii-mo," he repeated.

"Neeeeeeeeeeee-mo," she said, giggling.

"Now tell me, young lady, what's troubling that belly of yours?" She described her symptoms, telling him how it feels like she's got nails in her stomach and how she just can't help it sometimes, she just has to throw up. She pointed with her finger to the spots where it hurts the most. "How are you sleeping?" She told him that she props her pillows up and wakes up a lot during the night. "Does it ever hurt in your head?" he asked, and she nodded and told him about the dark pain, and how sometimes it makes her want to die.

"And it makes me so sad," she said, "especially when other kids look at my hands and call me a monster." He held her open palms tenderly in his own hand and brushed his thumb across her dry, cracked skin.

"Now that looks like it hurts," he said and she nodded. "And lotion probably doesn't help." She frowned and shook her head. He lowered her hands to her lap and smiled. "Care if I look at your chart, here?" She smiled.

"You've had the swallowing study," he said, smiling when Brittany dramatically made a gagging gesture. "And Dr. Hambert did a thorough exam."

"Gross!" Brittany said. "He looks at peoples' poop, their butts, actually," she added in a whisper.

"Yes, that is gross," Dr. Yazdi said. He looked at me, "You've been to cardiology…"

"Yes," I said. "Numerous times. They say everything looks good. The last time I took her in there, the cardiologist said Brittany probably just has 'little girl stomach.'" Dr. Yazdi raised a thick eyebrow. "I know," I said. "I just wanted to punch his face."

"Mom!"

"Sorry."

"Well, Miss Brittany," Dr. Yazdi said, "I have a pretty good idea what's going on with you." Brittany looked at me, and then at the doctor. "Do you remember you had to do some blood tests for me?"

"Uh. Yes!" she said, rolling her eyes. "I couldn't have nothing to eat for the longest time."

"Well, I'm afraid I have to do one more test, and this time, Brittany, I'll have to see you at hospital." Brittany started to protest, but Dr. Yazdi interrupted her. "I think I already know what's making you feel so sick, my dear, but we must do this test to know for sure. You'll come in to see me and leave on the very same day. I promise." He patted her arm and turned to me.

"It is fortunate that you are coming to me now," he said. "I just attended a very good conference and learned a great deal about children with Down Syndrome. I strongly suspect that Brittany has a condition known as Celiac Disease, which is an intolerance to gluten, found primarily in wheat. The incidence of Celiac Disease among the population with Down Syndrome is significantly higher than it is in the general population. Her blood work points to this diagnosis, as do her symptoms, and I am virtually certain that Celiac Disease is what we're dealing with here—along with, perhaps, GERD, or gastroesophageal reflux disease.

"We need to do a procedure down at your Memorial Hospital to take a biopsy to be sure. We'll also insert a monitor we can use to help us diagnose the reflux problem. If Celiac Disease is the problem, the good news is that we can help our young lady here to feel much better simply by changing her diet."

"Should I start changing her diet now?" I asked.

"No, not yet. It could throw off the test results. We'll get this thing scheduled right away." He looked at Brittany and winked. "I promise."

I guided Brittany to the elevator and watched her push the PL2 with her small index finger. She held my hand as we stepped into the parking garage and skipped to the spot where we had left our van. She asked for the remote and I handed it to her. Headlights flashed and the door locks clunked when she squeezed the remote with her thumb. She jumped up into the passenger seat, latched the belt around her and pulled the door closed in what appeared to be a single movement. I plodded around to the other side of the van, opened my door and climbed in. "Can I turn the key?" Brittany asked and she reached over.

"Mom! What's the matter, Mommy?" I heard her deep voice and felt her hand on my shoulder. "Why are you crying?" I shook my head but I couldn't find my voice to answer. Brittany reached behind her seat for the tissue box. "Here, Mommy," she said.

I took a tissue and blew my nose. "You know what?" I said, after drying my face with another tissue. "I think we're going to solve this problem. You're going to get better."

A smile wiped the concern off her face. "I know it. I can *feel* it."

Chapter Seven

Eat My Dust!

Brittany developed the annoying habit of calling everybody "Steve." She would carry on a normal conversation with someone and then suddenly call the person "Steve" and burst into laughter. When she met someone new she would ask the person his or her name and then cock her head at an angle, smile and say, "Hi, Steve." With previous acquaintances she would wave, smile that peculiar smile, say, "Hi, Steve," and then snort and giggle.

I asked her to stop, and then I told her. I yelled at her. I threatened to ground her for the rest of her life. Still, the dog, the cats, the grandparents, the priest, everyone became (dorky smile) "Steve." One day I noticed Doran stifle a laugh when Brittany used the name at church. "What's this about?" I asked him, exasperated.

"Nothing, Mom. It's just something from a movie I watched with Sis." My son made a move to leave my company, but I reached out and grabbed his forearm.

"What movie?"

"Just a movie. 'Multiplicity,'" he said, looking sheepish. "It's nothing, Mom."

I didn't have the time to watch this movie and I darned sure didn't believe it was "nothing." Whatever the meaning behind the irritating behavior, I wanted it to stop. So I sat down with Brittany and I took out a sheet of paper. It was time to start planning for her birthday party, and she always wanted me to write her "cake order" on paper before I started baking. "I want half chocolate and half white," she said, not suspecting that she was being set up. "And I want it to say, 'Happy Birthday and Congratulations, Brittany.'"

I drew a rectangle and squeezed the words inside. "Happy Birthday and Congratulations ..." I wrote. And then I wrote, "...Steve."

She glared at the paper and then at me. "All right," she said. "I'll stop."

WE MOVED TO A THREE-bedroom condominium, located within walking distance of our church on Colorado Springs' west side. The condominium development, one of the older ones in town, encompassed little more than three acres. Twenty-one homes, crowded tightly into groups of three, lined a single arrow-straight street. A concrete pad set off with a privacy fence served as the "back yard" for each condo; a narrow strip of grass between each building constituted the development's "public greenway."

Unit B was the second building on the right once you turned onto Plumtree Drive; our home was sandwiched in the middle of the unit. A steep staircase greeted you when you stepped into our entry way, as it did, surely, in every unit in the development. Upstairs were two spacious bedrooms, each with its own bathroom and walk-in closet. I had the bedroom overlooking the city and the vast plains to the east; Brittany's room looked out over the parking lot and offered a beautiful view of the mountains to the west.

With binoculars I helped her locate the Eagle Mountain house, which you could see from her bedroom window if the sun was right.

Doran had a room in the finished basement, off the so-called TV room that we had already turned into a home office. He, too, had his own bathroom. On the main floor a fourth bathroom was tucked into a cranny just off the kitchen, sharing a wall on one side with a nook for the refrigerator and on the other side with a coat closet. The main level of the condominium was deep and narrow, just wide enough for a couch on one side and a bookshelf on the other, but not for a coffee table between them. We shoved our dining room table against the wall to make room for a person to pass from the dining area to the kitchen if someone else happened to be seated in a chair at the table. So long as it was just the three of us eating there this didn't create a problem, and we seldom invited guests to dine with us. In fact, Doran was a first-semester university student and he worked at an Italian restaurant, so he rarely ate at home; Brittany and I often forsook the dining room table altogether and ate at the breakfast bar that delineated the kitchen's share of the long, narrow space.

Brittany was learning how to be home alone. I had taught her how to react if people called the house when I was gone, what to do if someone knocked on the door. She knew how to call 9-1-1 and where to go if the fire alarm activated. Even so, I rarely left the condo without Brittany except to go to the church, and if she was staying home I always drove, in case she needed me home in a hurry. The home-school library we had started at the church had blossomed into a private school/home-school cooperative. On occasion I would go there to work on bulletin boards or lesson plans while Brittany stayed at home. She had memorized the phone number at the church school, but I had also shown her where it was written, in case she was panicking or flustered when she needed to reach me.

BRITTANY WAS SCARED but optimistic when we checked her into the outpatient surgery department for the upper GI endoscopy ordered by Dr. Yazdi. At her request we had stopped at our church so that we could attend morning matins, and Brittany could receive a blessing from our priest before entering the hospital for her procedure. She later wrote:

My mother and I went to the church school and dropped by and did the beginning prayer of our church day. I couldn't stay that long, because my mom had to take me to Memorial Hospital. I couldn't have anything to eat that day, because my doctor John Yazdi had to take pictures of my stomach: the insides.

I checked in and got ready, and the nurses put the IV in, so they could be ready for the doctors to take me in. When they got ready to put the mask on I really wanted to turn my head and I did, because I didn't want the tube thing in my throat. I saw Dr. Yazdi and the other doctors, the surgeons and the nurses. I wished that my mom could stay in there. They said, "It's time to start."

My mom was waiting in the recovery room.

I remember I could feel the tube come out of my mouth. It was hard and stiff, and I was so tired. I wanted to go back to sleep, but they took me to recovery room. I was still sort of asleep, later on I woke up and I saw my mom. I could taste something weird, like I smelled like hospital.

I told my mom that I tasted like hospital in my mouth, I could feel the stuff, and she gave me some cough drops and I felt better, but I was so weak.

Dr. Yazdi released Brittany later that afternoon, sending her home with a battery-operated device that had a button on the top. He asked her to push the button every time she felt a sick feeling in her stomach, no matter what time of day. He had taken biopsies from three places along the upper gastro-intestinal tract and had inserted a Bravo capsule, a tiny monitor that would collect and transmit chemical data each time Brittany pushed the button on her power pack. When we got home I carried her into the condo and laid her on the couch. I set the power pack next to her. From the kitchen I watched her sleep while I waited for the kettle to warm my water for tea.

Three days later Dr. Yazdi phoned me at home and told me that his initial impression had been correct: Brittany had Celiac disease and GERD. He would write a prescription immediately for Preva-cid to help her manage the GERD and would schedule an appointment for us to meet with him and a nurse/nutritionist at his Denver office. In the meantime, he suggested I do my best to eliminate from Brittany's diet anything containing wheat, rye, barley and oats. He then asked if he could speak with Brittany. She took the phone tentatively.

"Fine," she said after he had time to ask how she was feeling. Her face as she listened to him speaking was expressionless as a stone. "Uh-huh," she mumbled occasionally. "Uh-huh." Then she grinned and said, "It's Neeeeee-mo, not Nai-mo…Geez!"

BRITTANY AND I gradually reached a truce where visiting Tim was concerned. I insisted that she visit him regularly but did not think it was necessary that she visit, as I had, every day. At the Flintridge house we had the support of neighbors whose houses were open to Brittany when I went to Hospice. But condominium life did not lend itself to the development of such relationships, and even though Brittany was learning to stay home alone, she was not ready to be on her own when I was on the other side of town with no specific time of return. We continued to pick Tim up for church every Saturday evening and Sunday morning, and together, Brittany and I came up with a plan for the rest of the week: I would go to Hospice two other times during the week and she would go with me, and as much as I had resisted offering bribes, part of the arrangement was that she could buy a soda pop from the machine on the first floor of the facility after every visit to her dad.

When Tim went into a coma we would shift into crisis mode. The nurses would call us at home, and I would notify Tim parents, my family, our priest. If Doran was at work or school I waited until he got home, and then tell him. He would increase the frequency of his visits, and Brittany and I would visit every day.

As Tim's regular visitors came to the facility we would allow them to take over, reading the Psalms or saying prayers. We would go somewhere for a meal, for a walk around the park or for our "tea." Then we would return to Hospice, where we held vigil until it was time for us to go home and go to bed.

The nurses at the facility had talked with Tim about eliminating Methadone as a tool in his pain management, but he had refused. Morphine had lost its effectiveness and opium made him unable to think and, therefore write, coherently. The other drugs, extra-strength Ibuprofen and Tylenol, were constipating. So, he continued to use Methadone, and continued his Tuesday night beer nights, and continued to have, from time to time, episodes that brought him dangerously close to death.

Brittany felt the sting of grief as Tim wove in and out of these episodes. Whenever the phone rang unexpectedly, she stopped whatever she was doing and found shelter on the stairs, where she would sit and wait until my telephone conversation had ended. Then, she would peek over the stair rail and gauge the climate of the room before resuming the activities she had begun before the interruption.

Many years later she reflected on these experiences when she wrote:

> I have sorrow when my mother tells me bad news. It feels like, after they're done talking on the phone, it feels like there's going to be bad news. My heart fills with sorrow and I'm very beyond nervous.

I BEGAN TO COMPREHEND—fully—that Brittany had been suffering from malnutrition. She had always had a good diet, but a person with untreated Celiac disease has damaged intestines that cannot properly absorb nutrients from the food they eat. Most of Brittany's symptoms—insomnia, dry skin, cracked lips, inability to gain weight, headaches, irritability, inability to recover from sickness or injury, and frequent vomiting—were the consequence of lesions in her digestive system, lesions that had been present most likely since birth but were only now revealed, thanks to the "horrible" procedure Brittany had endured at Memorial Hospital.

By the time Dr. Yazdi confirmed his diagnosis of Celiac disease, combined with GERD, I had completed my own crash course on the diseases, having read everything I could find on the symptoms and treatment. Certain things began to make sense: that as an infant, Brittany could not tolerate formula or cereals of any kinds; that she had always experienced discomfort when eating; her chronic problems with constipation; her painstakingly slow dental development; the fact that, even on the Down Syndrome growth charts, Brittany's height and weight never exceeded the five percent mark.

"It isn't fair," Brittany howled, when she found out that a gluten-free diet meant no more Ramen noodles. "Tell Dr. John Yazdi that it's not fair. If I can't eat Ramen, everybody can't eat Ramen right in front of me!" she said.

"I know it isn't fair, but you want to get better, and getting better means no more wheat," I said.

"Tell Doran he can't have Ramen," she said.

"Doran doesn't have Celiac disease, honey," I told her. "And even though other people can still eat wheat, we mustn't let you eat it. We want you to feel better," I said. "You know how I can't eat shrimp?" I added. "I would love to eat shrimp but I can't."

"It makes you sick," she said.

"Yes, it does. But other people can eat shrimp. You can eat shrimp..."

"But I hate shrimps," she whined.

"I know. I tell you what, for the first six months, I will go on the diet with you. Does that help? I'll go gluten-free, too. We can do it, don't you think, the two of us?"

She nodded but refused to look me in the eye.

The first several months were extremely difficult. The nurse/nutritionist had given me a comprehensive product catalog that listed all the foods and commonly-used household products that contained gluten. Still, it took almost three hours to accomplish the weekly grocery shopping, because I had to read the labels on everything. It seemed like gluten was an ingredient in almost every item in the supermarket—all the canned soups, nearly every brand of packaged ice cream, in numerous over-the-counter medications, in many types of candy.

The convenience foods that Brittany was learning how to prepare for herself were terrible culprits, as were snack foods I would have bought for her to eat on picnics, road trips or sleepovers. I learned I had to plan ahead for birthday parties, potluck suppers and baseball games, packing extra food for Brittany to eat at such events. My list of acceptable restaurants shrank as I began to scrutinize the menus and ask questions about brands used in food preparation.

I figured out how to bake breads, cakes and cookies that used flour made from grains other than flour. As the months went by, Brittany and I both became more aware of what she could and could not have, and menu planning, shopping, and eating out became easier.

Feeling like we were getting enough to eat was another matter. Pasta, bread, crackers, and other products containing wheat provide the bulk of many meals, and the absence of these ingredients made our helpings seem meager. We used potatoes for bulk when we were eating at home. I discovered I could use potatoes to thicken soups and many other foods, resulting in a meal that would help Brittany feel like she was full after eating. It took a long time for us both to learn, however, how to dine at a restaurant and feel like we had had enough to eat. There was nothing sorrier, we agreed, than the sight of a bunless hamburger on a plate!

Many years later, when we were sitting on our front porch with a notebook and a pen, Brittany asked me to write down her "thoughts and feelings about Celiac disease." She dictated:

> I wish I could have Ramen! And spaghetti and meatballs and meatball sandwiches! I can't because these things have wheat in them and I can't have wheat.
>
> This is upsetting and not fair at all! I see everybody eating wheat and I want some. Like at restaurants and at home and in town and picnics—everywhere people are eating wheat right in front of me. That is obnoxious. I wish everybody would stop eating wheat in front of me.
>
> My mom makes bread and birthday cake with the kind of flour I can have, so I sometimes have food I want. I wish I could just buy this food for myself at restaurants and stuff. When I order a hamburger at a restaurant my mom makes me to order the food by myself. I have to look at the waiter and say, 'No bun.' Because the wheat in the bread will make me sick. If there is a birthday cake at somebody else's party, I just eat the frosting, that's all.
>
> I will always have Celiac disease. I will never grow out of it. Never, ever, ever, ever. That sucks! Gosh darn it!

Despite her complaints about the diet, convincing Brittany to avoid foods with gluten, even Ramen, turned out to be relatively easy. Very quickly she learned that staying on the diet meant she would feel good, and that cheating on the diet had terrible consequences. If she "snooked" a cookie or crackers—or if I fouled up and accidentally allowed her to eat something that had gluten in it—she would vomit almost immediately.

We learned through trial and error that soy had the same effect. The horrible and physically draining results of going off-diet helped Brittany develop the self-motivation to stick to her gluten-free diet. Likewise, her medicine, which helped her control GERD, had such dramatic positive effects on how she felt that I never, not once, had to remind her to take her daily Prevacid capsule.

BRITTANY DEVELOPED A fascination with maps. Even though she could read the mileage signs, she wanted me to tell her, over and over, the names of the places we would pass whenever we took long drives in the van. When I finally bought her a laminated map of the State of Colorado you would think I had given her the world. She toted it around, from the van to the house, from the dining room table to her bedroom, from the condo to the school, from the school to the Hospice waiting room. She carried with it a notebook of lined paper and a pen, which she used to transcribe the names of towns, rivers and mountain ranges she read on the map. After several months of transcribing names and tracing routes with her index finger on the map's laminated surface, she started drawing her own maps—maps of her bedroom, maps of the neighborhood, and maps of an idealized town, the place where, she said, she would someday like to live.

One day I asked her to tell me more about the fantasy town she had drawn. The long rectangle was a school, she said, and the dotted line around it was a fence to keep out dogs. The square with the cross on the top was a church. She pointed to parallel lines with hash marks down their centers: these were the roads where only bikes were allowed, not cars. The shapes that looked like squares with one side missing and a U hanging off the top bar—these were swing sets, and Brittany's town had quite a number of them.

"Does your town have a grocery store?" I asked her.

"Oh, yeah," she took the paper from my hand. "I'll put it... here." She drew a rectangle next to one of the swingsets. "But there's no hospitals," she said when she handed the paper back to me. "The peoples in the town don't need a stupid hospital!"

"Brittany," I said one day when she was busy drawing one of her maps. She looked up. "Let's make a map of your life."

She gazed at me quizzically, as if she hadn't heard accurately. "What do you mean?" she asked.

"A map that shows your life, the things you want from your life, and how to get to the things you want," I said.

She smiled. "You're weird," she said and she returned her attention to her work. The next day she brought me a notebook and a pen. "I want a map of my life," she said. "Show me."

"Okay," I said. "But first we make a list of things we call 'goals.' Goals are like towns on your map. We make a list of goals you want in your life."

"Okay..." she said tentatively. "Like I want not to have Celiac disease!"

"We'll start with that." I wrote it on the notebook paper.

"I want to be a singer, like Elvis. I want to go to California. I want to win medals in Special Olympics." The words tumbled out like sugar spilling from a tear in the bag, and I wrote while she talked. "I want to go to Florida. I want to not be a woman. It's gross. I hate getting breasts. I don't want to have my period. Gross! I don't want to be a woman! Ick!" She paused. "That's all," she said. "Now what?"

Brittany doing a presentation in homeschool.

"You're finished?" I asked and she nodded. "Okay, now we make 'towns' using positive talk." She rolled her eyes indicating that she understood my meaning and disapproved. "First we make a circle showing where we are right now." I ripped out the paper with the list of goals and handed Brittany the notebook. "Go ahead and make a circle like it's a town and write the word 'me' in it."

"Okay, I'll put it...here," she said. She made a small circle in the center of the page and wrote M-E inside of it. "That's me," she said triumphantly.

"Okay, now make another circle and call it 'Athlete.'" I said. "Because when I see your goals I see that you really want to be an athlete."

"Where I put it?" she asked.

I shrugged. "It's your map."

She considered the paper seriously. "I put it way up here." She made a circle in the upper right corner of the page. "How you spell 'athlete'?" I gave her the spelling, two letters at a time, which she wrote in her small, neat script.

"Good. Okay, now, here's where the positive talk comes in," I said. "I know you want to not have Celiac disease, but you understand that you can't change that, right?" She frowned but nodded. "So, let's use positive talk. Can we say, 'I, Brittany, want to be healthy and strong?' Does that work? Can we say it like that?"

She flexed a biceps muscle and said, "Yeah! Healthy and strong!" Then she made another circle on her paper, anticipating that she needed a bigger circle than she had made before, and she said, "Spell 'healthy'." And then, "Spell 'strong'."

"You know that one," I said. "How does it start?"

"S-T."

"Uh-huh."

"R."

"Uh-huh."

"O-N-G."

"Good."

In similar fashion Brittany drew a circle for "Singer" and a circle for "Travel." With five circles now on the page we talked about her other goal: that of not becoming a woman. We talked about the difference between a goal and wish and about wishes that are realistic and wishes that are not. "You can't change that you will be a woman, honey," I said finally, "because that is what God intended for you to be. But look," I took her pencil and used the tip of it to point out places on her page, "Look, you can choose to be a woman who is strong and healthy. You can choose to be a woman who is an athlete, a woman who is a singer and a woman who travels. You can be that kind of woman."

"How?"

"Well, how do you get from one town to another?" I asked her.

"You go on a road."

"That's right. Well, let's put some roads on the map." I handed her the pen. "You're right here, right," I asked, pointing to the circle that said ME. "Let's draw a road from here to 'Athlete,' and then we'll talk about some of the towns you'll pass along the way."

When we were finished, Brittany's map had roads winding their way from the center "ME" to the other destinations on her map. Along the road to the town of Athlete she had made signs for "Winter-Special Olympics Skiing," "Summer-Special Olympics Bicycling," and "Hospice-Take Bike Ride around Memorial Park." Along the road to the town of "Healthy and Strong," she had written, "Take Medicine," "Stay on Diet," "Brush teeth every day" and "Eat More Meat." Along the road to Travel, she wrote "Go to California," and having agreed that she would like to accompany me on a trip I would be taking later in the year to Alaska, she had made a sign saying "Alaska" along that route. In our discussions about being a singer, Brittany had told me that Elizabeth, a friend at church, was giving voice lessons, and I had agreed that we could talk to Elizabeth about lessons for Brittany. So, along the road to the town of Singer, Brittany had made a large sign with the words "Lessons!" and, another, equally emphatic, "Studio!"

Brittany held the map at arm's length and nodded her head approvingly. "I need to make it again," she said, as I knew she would, "color it and makes shapes and stuff," she added. "But first," she laid the map on the table, "I need to get busy on my studio!"

She ran upstairs, and I went to the kitchen to put on the kettle for tea. I picked up Lady and stroked her soft fur while the kettle warmed. When the whistle signaled that the water was ready, I set Lady afoot, poured the water over a tea bag that had been waiting in my mug and spooned in some sugar. I watched the shadows darkening over the eastern plains and stirred my tea. It occurred to me that it had been many years since I had set goals for myself. "Write my books" was the first goal to come to mind as I idly sipped my tea, but my own words about realistic versus unrealistic goals echoed back to me. "Stick to writing corporate reports and grants," I told myself out loud, "that's where the money is."

I headed up the stairs to check on Brittany. A handwritten sign hung on the door to her room, which was closed. "Girl Working," the sign read. "Stay out." And in smaller script she had written the word "please."

I GUIDED OUR BICYCLES, one at a time, from the back patio through the condo and into the van. Brittany went downstairs to get our helmets and water bottles and her bicycling gloves. She was making good on her objective, written as a sign on the way to "Athlete" on her map: she would go for a bike ride around the lake at Memorial Park when we visited Tim at Hospice. After discussing the matter we decided we would take the ride first and then drive to the facility. "I be too exhausted," she reasoned, to ride after visiting her dad. We unloaded the bikes at the park, strapped on our helmets and started pedaling. "Eat my dust, Mom," she told me as she picked up speed.

"That was fun," she said as I caught up after the long loop, and we loaded the bikes into the van. She climbed into the passenger seat. "Whew. I'm hot. Can I get my soda now?" she asked.

"Nope. After we visit Dad."

"Pleeeeeeeeeeeease!"

"Nope. You have water."

"Pleeeeeeeeeeeeeeeeeeeeeeeeeeease!" She dragged out the *e*'s all the way to Hospice. "Pleeeeeeeeeeeeeeeeeease!" she wailed again as we passed the Coke machine and boarded the elevator. "Gosh dang it," she muttered, and she pushed the button for the third floor.

We stepped into the third floor elevator lobby and nearly ran into Val, the homecare CNA who had been so intimate with Tim before he moved to Hospice. "What's she doing here?" Brittany asked as Val waved and stepped on the elevator. Hospice's home-care offices were located on a different floor of the building and the homecare staff rarely came to the third floor.

"I don't know, Hon," I said. "Probably visiting your dad."

Brittany skipped down the hall ahead of me. As I watched her I wondered if Tim and Val were having an affair, and if Tim had had an affair with the nurse in California, and I surprised myself with the silent wish that he had.

When I reached Tim's room Brittany was telling her dad about the "studio" she had organized inside her walk-in closet. The items that had been in the closet—her clothes, blankets, shoes, stuffed animals and books—these items were heaped in a mound on the top bunk of her bed. The rods and shelves of the closet had been stripped and the floor cleared except for a lap table she had moved into the center of the closet. On the lap table was her CD boom box and a cassette tape player/recorder with an attached microphone. Her closet bookshelf held a folder containing sheet music Elizabeth had given her, a small electronic keyboard she had received for Christmas one year, and her CDs and cassette tapes stacked in piles. She used the studio, she told Tim, to play music and practice her singing, which she did by playing a CD in the boom box, pressing the record button on the cassette player and singing into the microphone. Sometimes, she said, she would add her own electronic piano accompaniment to the mix.

"Can I go watch TV now?" she asked, after she had described the whole get-up. He nodded and she turned to leave him room.

"Brittany," he called, and she turned to face him. "Will you go get my grapes?"

"So how's the sound in that place?" Tim asked after Brittany brought the grapes and headed down to the waiting lounge. "When she's singing in this 'studio,' I mean," he added.

"Amazingly good," I said. "When she closes the door of her room, I don't hear a thing. I don't think the neighbors do either; I know I never hear electronic noise from their places."

"Didn't you tell me the previous owner had a daughter who turned that closet into a studio?" he asked, and I nodded. "How old was she, 10?"

"Yes, I think that's right. Around 10 anyway," I said.

"Hmmm."

After a long pause Tim spoke again. "I am thinking about leaving here and moving into the condo with you," he said. "I know there's nothing we can do about the inside stairs, but we could set my room up on the main floor where you've told me the dining room and living room are. I have a friend who thinks he can make a hoist to get me up the concrete stairs in the front...."

Tim waited for me to say something, but I sat in silence.

"I know you're concerned about the cost of home nursing," he added, filling in the void created by my own silence. "But I've thought about that, too. You can go back to work full time, maybe at the college, some place where you can earn more than from writing or teaching, that will help us afford to have someone come over in the mornings. Doran is there to help at night."

He paused again, waiting for a response. I said nothing.

"And Brittany is smart," he continued. "She can be trained to take care of almost everything I will need during the day."

"You want Brittany to be your CNA?" The intensity of my voice startled him.

"Well, why not? She can be trained," he said hotly.

"Maybe she can and maybe she can't; that's not really the point, Tim. We can't require her to devote her life to taking care of us, that shouldn't be the focus of her life. She's got plans..."

"What, for singing? She can sing and take care of me. God knows we've taken care of her!"

I instinctively raised my hands to my ears as Tim continued speaking. Suddenly I knew what I had to do.

DEEP INSIDE, I MUST HAVE known it all along, but like a person who is disoriented in the woods, I had been slow to recognize my predicament, stumbling to find my way along a ridge when I should have been building a shelter.

I was lost, or, at least, I was not on the path that I had chosen when I was young and idealistic and recently married to a charming, attentive husband. The plan had been simple enough: we would walk through life as one, live and work together, celebrate wedding anniversaries, watch our children grow, feed our grandchildren pancakes in the very house where we had raised their parents. By the time Doran and Brittany were in elementary school, I could see that we had changed course. Tim's interest in me waned as my professional interests expanded beyond his chosen field, his support for my work weakened, his attention strayed. He couldn't keep his eyes off other women. And why not? I was no longer Tim's young protégé, or his clever business partner: I had become an air-headed, humanities scholar and fretful mother, an embarrassment to him and a bore at economics department cocktail parties.

As the years passed, my position in the marriage shifted even more. I was the manager who maintained a house and paid bills, the administrator who monitored meds and nursing schedules, the overweight, anonymous person who pushed the wheelchair, and finally just another name on a spreadsheet, a substitute name put in a cell when the first choice cancelled. I was aware of these changes as they took place, knew I was playing cards I'd been dealt, not the cards I wanted. Nothing to complain about; it happens to people all the time, I told myself. Just keep your head bent to the wind and your feet moving forward. You'll get there.

It wasn't some rigid rule of my church that kept me moving, or any expectation on the part of my family, or even a sense of duty. It was a combination of pity and shame and love. My heart ached for Tim as I watched what his disease did to him. I prayed faithfully for his healing, worked tirelessly for his comfort, wept deeply in the sharing of his sorrow. Everyone who knew Tim felt profound sympathy for him, a brilliant scholar and young father wasted by a horrible disease. If I hadn't been married to him I would have cried for him no less.

But I was married to him. As a wife, a partner and a person, I wasn't getting the affirmation or the love I needed, and that had more to do with personalities and habits—Tim's and mine—than it did with the fact that Tim had MS. But I couldn't leave him, criticize him or even feel angry at him, because he was sick. He was a man, to be sure, and my husband, but he was also an MS patient. I was ashamed to need the things I needed, to feel the way I felt. My desires seemed so trivial compared to the suffering he experienced. Yes, I was lost, but I was too embarrassed to admit it.

It was love that finally put me in survival mode. So long as Tim remained in institutional care, love meant believing that my continued bond to Tim was healthy, that it reflected important values regarding family and faith. But Tim wanted to come back home, now, just as the children were taking steps to define themselves, to explore possibilities, to chart their own courses in the world—and just as I finally had reestablished myself as a writer. He wanted to take us all back to a time when Doran felt guilty for wanting to spend evenings with friends, when Brittany fearfully checked to see if her dad was breathing, when giggles behind the privacy screen reminded me how little I meant to my own husband. Suddenly I saw love from a different vantage point. It was time for me to face reality, to take cover, and to make plans.

Chapter Eight

Anywhere but Here

Brittany stuffed her backpack with her portable player and headphones, CDs, crayons, extra batteries, spiral notebooks and coloring sheets, and she set the backpack in the hallway near the top of the stairs. I stood by my bed, folding laundry. I put half of the folded clothes into our suitcases, which lay open on the bed, and the other half back into the laundry basket, to put away later. I asked Brittany to pick out two church outfits, and I looked through my own closet for two skirts that would be dressy enough for church but casual enough to match the clunky shoes I was wearing, the only shoes that didn't pinch my feet, which were swollen and sore from the bunion surgery I had had four weeks earlier.

I was drawing my bath when Brittany came back with two dresses. She stood in the bathroom doorway and held them up. "These OK?" she asked and she put them in her suitcase when I nodded. "Can I come in when you have your bath?" I told her she could come in as soon as she had her pajamas on and had brushed her teeth, and she turned on her heel to head back to her room. When she returned to my bathroom she rolled up her sleeves, got a washcloth off the towel bar and filled it with bath soap. "I wash your back," she said, and I leaned forward in the tub.

"Alaska will be cold?" she asked as she rubbed the cloth gently across my shoulders.

"I don't think so," I told her. "It wasn't cold when I went last year. But sometimes it rains a lot. That's why we're taking rain jackets."

"Who are all the peoples who are going?" she asked. I rattled off the names of the ten people travelling on the mission trip from Colorado Springs, as I had numerous times before, and then I reminded her that other people were going from other towns in Colorado and that we wouldn't know them until we met them in the Denver airport. Brittany asked where we would stay and I reminded her that we would be at a college, staying in dormitory rooms normally occupied by the students who had returned to their villages for the summer.

She poured more soap into the washcloth and said, "Tell me, again, Mommy, what was my first word."

I smiled. Brittany's love for travel was legend among all the members of our family; her willingness to pick up and go at any moment, the thrill she experienced from room service and motel swimming pools, her ability to make friends in any place at any time. "Your first word was 'hotel,'" I told her, and she giggled.

"Is that true?" she asked.

"It's the truth if ever I told it," I said.

"Oh," she said. "I just can't wait until tomorrow."

WE WERE GOING TO Kodiak Island for two weeks, a trip we had been planning through our church since the previous summer. We would be part of a mission team, sent to Alaska to complete badly-needed repairs on a seminary building, two small chapels, and a house that served as a rectory for a seminary priest. I had had surgery on both of my feet and had just graduated from my walking casts, so I was in no shape to climb ladders or haul construction material. I would be participating as a camp cook, and Brittany would be my assistant. Tim agreed to postpone his plans to move home until our return. I didn't tell him I had no intention of moving him into the condo; I needed the time in Alaska to work up the nerve.

Before Brittany and I left for Alaska I made several attempts to convince Tim that our whole family should relocate to California, where his parents, siblings and cousins could help us care for him at home, but he refused to consider the idea. His life, his friends, his work—everything important to him was in Colorado, he said; he had no interest in starting over somewhere else.

As I made preparations for the trip, my priest and I had long discussions about Tim's future and mine. He agreed that I needed support I was not receiving in my relationship and, to my surprise, gave me his blessing to end my marriage with Tim. He recognized the intensity of the physical care Tim needed and felt that Tim should remain in institutional care. He hoped, as did I, that my two week retreat would help get me the distance I needed to assess my situation, the clarity to plan my next move.

IT TOOK NEARLY 36 hours to get from Colorado Springs to Kodiak, including an overnight we spent in our sleeping bags on the floor of the fellowship hall at the Orthodox Cathedral in Anchorage. By the time we finally arrived on the island, Brittany and I both felt a close kinship with all of the other participants on the trip, including those we had just met, a small group from a tiny church on Colorado's western slope. As we were shuttled from the Kodiak airport to the seminary where we would be staying, we learned that our team would be divided in two: one group would stay in Kodiak; the other would travel by boat to Spruce Island where they would make repairs to a chapel built over the burial site of St. Herman, the Russian missionary who had introduced Christianity to the native Alaskan people more than two hundred years ago.

We now needed two cooking teams, one for Kodiak and one for Spruce Island. There were four women designated for the work; since the Spruce Island mission team was smaller and would be

Suzanne and Brittany on a fishing charter, watching as Kodiak disappears from view.

operating in more primitive conditions, we decided that team could get by with one member. I, Brittany and Joan would remain on Kodiak. The three of us would assist the Spruce Island cook by packing coolers with food, which we would send to Spruce Island whenever a boat went over.

The Spruce Island team needed to be ready to leave within an hour, we were told when we reached the seminary, to take advantage of the availability of a vessel large enough to transport them. The boat captain delivering the news offered to take us to the grocery store for provisions, and we four cooks piled into the back of his pickup truck and got to work.

It turned out to be the only time a vehicle was available to support the work of the kitchen crew. We had 15 construction workers to feed and a remote crew to support, however, so we figured out a system. We requisitioned the three largest wheeled suitcases in our party and after breakfast each day, Brittany, Joan and I rolled the suitcases down a hill and across town to a corner grocery store located directly across from the local boat harbor. It was only a half-mile walk (shorter if you jaywalked), but the bags were heavy on the return trip, and my feet were still healing, so we made slow progress getting back to the seminary each day.

After our fourth "bag lady trip," Bo, the construction crew supervisor, noticed us hobbling back to the seminary kitchen. As we headed down the hill the next morning, he deputized a member of the group to oversee specific tasks in his absence, set his tool belt aside and walked with us, so he could drag the heavy bags back himself. The next day, he added two more suitcases to our convoy, tossed his tool belt aside, and convinced a seminarian to join us. We hauled back enough food to tide us over the next three days.

By then, the island inhabitants had discovered us, and we were showered with gifts of cod, halibut, salmon, seal meat, salmonberry jam and fresh muffins. Each day, several people stopped by the seminary and left us baskets of food or cups of piping hot coffee. Often, they stayed and visited, and we made it a routine to set extra plates at the long dining table. After suppers we shared stories about our elders, about ourselves and about our lives in the church. We sang each other songs, put on skits and went for walks. We sat on the lawn in front of the seminary in the long bright hours of evening and smiled at the simple faith of the locals, who would make the sign of the cross reverently as they went past the onion-domed church in their cars or on their bicycles.

"This island has a deep mystery," I said to Bo one night as he chatted with me and Brittany on the steps in front of the kitchen. I was knitting a sweater for friend's baby, and he was sipping coffee. "Someday I would like to come here to stay," I said.

Bo nodded. "I've been wanting to live here for years," he said.

Bo came from one of the other Colorado churches, a small parish on the western slope of the state. We hadn't met one another until all the mission teams had melded into one at the Denver airport. Since that day, he had become my confidant. He had been marvelous with Brittany, had given her piggy-back rides, teased her, convinced her to finish her chores, listened as I told him about the challenges she faced in her life, her dreams for the future. He understood the delicate situation I was facing back home and he offered a fresh perspective on my struggles. And he always seemed to be there when I needed help; no matter what my task or what I might need, it seemed Bo was there to lend a hand, even as he directed the crews in the difficult construction projects outside.

As we sat on the steps and I laughed and kept making errors in my knitting, I realized Bo had done something else: he had reached into that dark place where my soul had retreated, and he had found me.

WHEN WE RETURNED FROM Alaska, I left Brittany at home with Doran and I went to see Tim alone. I asked him once more to relocate to California and I explained why I thought it was important. "You don't seem to be able to comprehend..." he started to say, but I cut him off.

"Tim, I am going to file for divorce." But instead of telling him how deeply I resented the fact that he wouldn't let us move closer to his family, how I couldn't forgive him for continuing to use Methadone, how sick I was of making sure each cup had exactly seventeen grapes, how small his womanizing had made me feel, how appalled I was that he would adopt two children having been told he would not be around to raise them, how angry I was that he would now seek to exploit them, instead of telling him the truth and exposing the depth of my own misery, I said the one thing that would hurt him the most: "There's someone else," I said, and I could see immediately the severing impact of my words.

I HARNESSED THE MOMENTUM of Brittany's wanderlust and watched her energetically pack her things, once again, into moving boxes. She was sad about losing her studio, but excited about the idea of moving to a new town and enrolling in public high school. I had drawn a map of the western Colorado town of Rifle, with dotted lines for major streets and squares labeled Park, High School, Safeway, Aunt Peggy's House, Aunt Tina's House and, on the rightmost corner of the page, Uncle George's House. She drew a star over Grandma and Aunt Bonnie's House and colored it yellow to show that that's where we would be staying temporarily.

I picked up a small moving van on a Saturday morning, and all that day and the next Brittany and I packed and taped boxes, wrapped wall hangings, and dismantled furniture. Doran and two of his friends loaded the household items we would need in the immediate future into the van. I had offered the condo to Doran, suggesting that he find roommates from the university, but he had already set his heart on an apartment closer to the campus. He wanted to keep some of the furniture, however, so we went through the place and put sticky notes on the items that he could keep.

Our plan was to drive over the mountain passes late Monday evening, after cleaning the place and visiting with my friend and former employer, Timothy Fuller, who wanted to come over to say goodbye. We had cordoned the cats in an upstairs bathroom and had the cat carrier waiting for service by the front door. A real estate agent had already taken measurements and been given a key; he would let himself in next week and take photographs. I put the kettle on for tea and was leaning against the sink when Doran came upstairs wearing his white waiter's shirt and black pants. "Well, Mom, it's time for me to go to work." He stood tall and faced me, "Drive safe," he said, and then he took two long steps into the kitchen and hugged me. "Call me when you get there?"

I nodded, fighting tears.

"Sissy!" Doran called. Brittany slid down the carpeted stairs on her bottom. "Be good," Doran said, hugging his sister.

"We'll see you again in just a few weeks," I managed to say, and Doran smiled.

"I hate you call me 'Sissy'!" Brittany said, pretending to be angry.

I stood in the kitchen and Brittany in the entry way. We watched Doran climb into his Jeep and drive away. Brittany scampered back upstairs as I stood there, staring at the empty parking spot. If only Doran would go with us, I mused, but he had his own studies to consider, his own path to forge. Even though, he said, he could understand why I was leaving, he felt that he should stay at the university and here, in the city, close to Tim. "God," I said out loud, "please don't let that boy feel abandoned by me, and please, God, don't let him be ruined by his dad."

The loud "whooOOOO" of the tea kettle brought me back to my task. My friend Timothy would be here any minute; I put two bags of tea in the pot, filled it with boiling water and put it on the center of my tea tray, along with two mugs, some cookies on a plate, the sugar bowl and some spoons. I carried the tray out to the front step, sat on the concrete and rested my chin on my hand. Not much of a view, I said to myself, but at least the sun feels warm upon my face.

"I'M HAVING A DIFFICULT time understanding why you are leaving; you can be divorced and stay right here," Timothy said. He was finishing his second cup of tea, and, having shared with me the most recent developments at the college and the hilarious exploits of some of our mutual friends on the faculty, Timothy finally came to the point of our conversation. "You could come back to work at the college...."

"It wouldn't be the same, Timothy, with someone else in charge," I said, happy that he would suggest returning to the college, but knowing that he didn't have the power to hire me at will, the way he did when he was the dean of the college. "Besides, I'm just not strong enough."

"You are one of the strongest people I have ever known," he said.

I scoffed. "Let's say Hospice tells Tim he can't be there anymore, which is a strong possibility," I said. "Let's say that happens, if I continue to live in this town, even if I am divorced, I would still take care of him; you know I would. It would be the same thing, all over again."

"But now there are facilities here where he can go, four or five of them built in the last few years," Timothy said.

"I know, I've told Tim about them. He won't even consider them. He would insist on moving here, with us, and I wouldn't be able to say no."

After reflecting on my words, Timothy nodded. "Yes, I can see." He stirred some sugar into another cup of tea and took a sip. "But your friends…"

I smiled and looked away. "My friends-base has shrunk to almost nothing," I said. "The past five, six years have been concentrated on taking care of things at home. I haven't really maintained contact with anyone outside the church," I said, facing Timothy, "the exception being you, of course."

He smiled. "I'm very glad for that."

"Me, too," I said. "But my friends at the church… I can count on those friendships being over," I said. He looked at me quizzically. "You don't leave a sick man. You just don't do it. Especially…the way I just did."

He looked into his tea. "You mean by saying 'there's someone else.'"

I nodded. "Yeah. That was stupid." Even my mother, I thought, who had encouraged me to separate from Tim years ago, had told me my actions were "terribly blunt" and "not very smart." And my priest, who had been so supportive, had turned away from me in disgust. I set down my teacup and stared down at my empty hands.

"Well, you said that because you wanted it to be over, and I think you were right, it's probably the only thing Tim would respond to. It buys you some time," he said as he drained his cup.

I smiled. God, I was going to miss this man, this friendship. We had covered so much ground together as colleagues and then, gradually, as close friends. We had read the same books, attended the same conferences, worked jointly on the same research projects and even suffered many of the same personal sorrows in our ten-year relationship. I would see him rarely now, and the thought saddened me, but I felt encouraged, too, by the knowledge that at least one soul in Colorado Springs understood and appreciated me.

Timothy put his cup next to mine on the tray. "So what about this man, Bo? Do you think you will see him?"

"I have no idea. I mean, I hope so," I said. "But…"

"I hope so, too," my friend said, fixing me in his gaze. "You have so much love to give, and it's been a very long time since you've had a partner in your life to give it to." He stood. "Now, where's that Brittany? It's time I give her a proper good-bye."

AFTER TIMOTHY LEFT, I WASHED the tea tray, the pot and the cups and set them on the drainer to dry. I dried my hands and hung the dish towel over the oven handle; then I grabbed the cat carrier and headed upstairs. "Time to go," I said, as I tapped on the door to Brittany's room. She was sitting on the carpet outside her bathroom door, which was closed to keep in the cats, and she was poking her finger under the door. She giggled when a white furry paw reached back. "Let's get the cats and go," I said.

"Highway hounds!" she yelled. "Yes!"

"Yes, that's us, the 'Highway Hounds.' Do you have everything ready?"

"Yes, everything. Here's my map," she reached down and pulled the laminated State of Colorado map out of her backpack. "Right here, front pocket." She slipped the map back into the pocket and pulled the pack over her right shoulder. She laughed while I shoved the scolding cats into the carrier. I closed the latch and stood up.

"Here we go," Brittany said skipping ahead of me. She slid down the stairs on her bottom, her pack bouncing on her back behind her. I carried the meowing, hissing load down the stairs and grabbed my coat and purse and keys, which were hanging by the front door. I closed the door of the condo, locked it with the key and squeezed the cat carrier onto the front seat of the moving van. As I turned the key in the ignition Brittany grinned and howled.

"Not yet, Highway Hound. You have to wait until we hit the highway!" I said. Three minutes later, as I steered the van off of Fillmore and onto Interstate 25, Brittany howled again, and this time, I howled with her.

WE ARRIVED LATE AND I slept poorly on a small bed at my mother's house. The next morning I woke to the smell of coffee and the sound of my mother padding softly around the house. She and I shared a cup and chatted, but she had been drinking coffee for over an hour and outpaced me in the art of conversation. I took a shower to help quicken my brain and I got dressed. I peeked in on Brittany and saw that she was still sleeping soundly, so I got a tall glass of ice water, sat at the table and stared absent-mindedly at the Colorado River, which was framed for my view by my mother's dining room window. Now what? I wondered.

I had lived in my own home—in the same city—for 23 years. I had grown comfortable in a church, taken care of a family, made friends, found a niche in a community. Now I was starting over, and I had no idea what to do first. The print in the local newspaper was unfamiliar; I didn't know my way around the local supermarket. I needed a cafe where I felt comfortable having a cup of coffee alone. I needed a new dry cleaner, a dentist, a school, a physician, a contact for Special Olympics, an organic grocer, a mechanic, a church, a house and most of all, a job: it was overwhelming.

Money was an issue, a huge issue. My retirement accounts were nearly tapped out, my life insurance payments past due. Tim had income in the form of disability payments and royalties from his textbooks; I had income from freelance writing, but it would be hard to maintain my Colorado Springs clients from a distance. Computer technology had changed a lot since I last worked in an office; I knew nothing about the Internet and my database management skills were outdated. I didn't have the chutzpah, either, that I once had. Confidence, it seemed, was one of the casualties of taking care of things and people so long at home.

I tapped my thumb anxiously on my mother's table, and then got up, slipped on my shoes and my sunglasses, and asked my mother if she minded me taking a walk. I needed the movement of my feet upon the sidewalk, the warmth of the sun on my face, the taste of sweetened tea on my return—the familiar, routine experiences to help me anchor my soul. My mother, giddy with excitement to have her oldest daughter home, slipped on her sweater and chirped, "Don't leave without me."

I hadn't been at my mother's house long before Bo tracked me down there. He had been worried about us, he said, but confident I would make my break with Colorado Springs and Tim. He apologized for taking so long to call. "I have a proposition for you, though," he said. He was going antelope hunting near the Wyoming border. Would Brittany and I like to tag along, eat camp food, take in the smell of sagebrush, lie awake at night and stare up at the stars? It sounded like the opportunity to sink my feet into the soil from which I had sprung, I said, and it was. He picked us up the following day and returned us to my mother's house three days later. As we pulled into her driveway, I told Bo how much I appreciated his company, the trip, that beautiful place and I said I didn't think I deserved so much happiness. "It's not about what we deserve," he said. "It's about making the most out of the gifts we receive."

BY BRITTANY'S SEVENTEENTH birthday, we had found a small bungalow on a large corner lot, not in Rifle, but in the small town of Cedaredge, which was about an hour away. Built in the early twentieth century, when most of the residents of the town were farmers, the house was solid and quaint, with cypress wood floors, small cozy rooms and the ornamental concrete frame so common among the old Sears "kit homes," of which this house was a model.

It needed work; that was certain. I had removed the carpet, soiled from years of indoor pet care, the very day I got the key to the place, and I had already ordered window coverings to replace the tatters left by the previous occupant. The kitchen was a disaster, no other word captures the condition of the appliances, the countertops, the floor, but it was situation I could live with and improve as time went by.

While I frosted a birthday cake in my make-do kitchen, Brittany and Bo worked cheerfully in the living room, dipping rollers in a five gallon drum of neutral beige paint and putting a fresh face on the walls of our new home. Other than my tea kettle, the utensils I needed for baking Brittany's cake, our painting supplies, and two beds made from air mattresses, we had no furniture or household goods yet in the house. So when the cake was finished, I tapped the lid onto the paint bucket with a hammer to make a small table, and Brittany and I sat next to it, cross-legged on the floor, while Bo carried the cake, lit with a single candle, from the kitchen. He also carried two gifts he had bought for Brittany, a dark blue Colorado T-shirt with wildlife images on it and a book of Native American stories. I must have had gifts for her, too, but Brittany's delight over Bo's presents outshines any recollection of my gifts, whatever they might have been. Over the next few years she would wear the T-shirt so often that there were times I threatened to use the scissors to remove it from her body just so I could get the thing into the laundry.

BRITTANY ASKED ME TO write one day in her notebook:

I been moving away so much from one place to another, and I miss the places where I was living at. Like one thing is my home where I was born in Colorado Springs, where I used to live.

My dad Tim doesn't look at mom, I noticed. My dad was always flirting with someone else. In my heart, my mom thinks, "Hey, snap!" (She snaps her fingers.) My dad is looking through her like she's a window.

My mom told me that my dad doesn't want to move with her to California, because he wants to live in Colorado Springs because that's his home and his friends are there with him.

Then my mom grabbed me instead of leaving me with my dad, when the time came to move.

My mom and dad's wedding was at Crystal Park, they got married there in 1985. I have a photo of them. Every time I look at it it hurts my heart so much because they were a good couple then, but now they're not. Divorce is so full of sorrow, when you're seeing the divorce. It kind of broke my heart, me and my brother Doran, and it was very sad for me and Doran.

Then my mom finally decided to move to Cedaredge, Colorado, because she wants to not live in cities. She doesn't want to be a city girl anymore. That broke my heart, because I love cities a lot and I miss it so much. I had been there a long time, since I was born in 1987.

BRITTANY AND I DROVE to Colorado Springs one weekend a month, so she could visit her dad and she and I could spend time with Doran. It was a 550-mile drive round trip over mountain passes, through rocky canyons and across windswept plains dense with sagebrush and antelope. It was a gorgeous drive, wasted, mostly, on Brittany who was more interested in towns than in scenery, but breathtakingly beautiful to me. We usually left our house early Saturday morning, stopped along the way for lunch and met Doran in mid afternoon at a Colorado Springs tea house that had become a family favorite. There we would sip our drinks and chat, ending with an agreement to meet somewhere for dinner, and then I would take Brittany to Hospice, where Tim had asked me to bring her, always, no earlier than 4:00; no later than 4:30 p.m..

At Hospice Brittany would help Tim with his Saturday evening meal and then accompany him to church for the evening service. I would pick her up at church at 7:15, and then she and I would meet Doran for dinner. The next morning, I would drop Brittany off at the church, where she would meet Tim, and then I would return and pick her up at 1:00 p.m. Then, she and I would stop at a gas station for fuel and snacks and hit the road, howling as we started the long, beautiful drive back to our new home.

As the months went by, the trips to Colorado Springs became difficult for both of us. Places change over time, and people too, in small ways that one may fail to notice when one sees them every day. But when your visits are infrequent the small changes seem magnified, until one day the places and people bear little resemblance to those you once knew. Brittany was devastated by the closure—by the IRS—of Michelle's, her favorite restaurant, and the announcement that Redeemer Lutheran School would close its doors forever. Equally shattering was the sight of a huge "For Sale" sign plastered on the abandoned building that once housed Penrose Community Hospital, where Brittany was born, and massive changes to the layout of Memorial Park, where she had competed in her Special Olympics bike races.

Her friends, too, had changed; outgrown the images Brittany had fixed in her mind of them. We had an hour of free time one sunny afternoon, and Brittany asked me to drive to the Anitra neighborhood to visit her old neighborhood friends. As we rounded the turn near our old house we saw one of the boys, Brad, grown now and driving a car in the opposite direction, a sight that shocked us both. "Never mind," Brittany muttered from the back seat, "don't stop." I drove slowly past the old house, and caught myself staring at two unfamiliar children playing in the sandbox Tim and I had built for Doran and Brittany. I glanced in the rearview mirror and saw that Brittany had noticed the children too. I stopped at the T at the end of the street and turned left toward town. As we drove away I could hear Brittany muffling sobs in the back seat and taste the salt of my own remorse.

Chapter Nine

Right Turn

Brittany gazed wide-eyed at the building as we pulled into the "visitor parking" spot outside the public high school. "This is the school," she said as her eyes took in the monstrous brick building, the boys in green football jerseys, the clusters of teens leaning against the wall outside the entrance, the bleachers lining the football field, the rows of vehicles in the parking lot. "I'm scared," she said, staring out the windshield. I wanted to say, "Me, too," but instead I got out of the car, walked around to her side and opened the door. "C'mon, let's go," I said, holding out my hand.

I gave the pig-tailed cheerleader at the front desk my name and told her that Brittany and I had an appointment with Mrs. Bichon in Special Ed. The girl pointed around to her left. "Down the hall, second door on the right," she said. We passed a row of lockers and started to tap on the door, when a young girl, wearing denim jeans and a checkered shirt, stopped us. "I'm Stacy," she said to Brittany. "You are new here."

Brittany shrugged. "I guess so," she said quietly.

"These are our lockers," Stacy said, gesturing along the wall we had just passed.

"You mean...you mean, I get a locker!" Brittany stared at Stacy open-mouthed.

Stacy smiled. "Mrs. Bichon is in there," she said, pointing to the door in front of us. "You just go in." Then she turned and walked away.

We opened the door and stepped into a large classroom, divided into two sections, one that resembled a home economics classroom, with countertops and stoves, and the other, on the side we had entered, that looked like a typical classroom with rows of wooden desks facing a dry-erase board at the front. A lanky, olive-skinned boy doodled on a sheet of paper at one of the desks, and a petite woman wearing wool slacks and a sweater stood over in the kitchen area. Otherwise, the huge room was empty.

The woman looked up. "I'm Suzanna," I said. "We have an appointment...."

"And you must be Brittany," she said, approaching us with her hand extended in greeting to my daughter. "I am Mrs. Bichon."

Brittany reached her hand out tentatively. Then she looked at Mrs. Bichon and smiled. "I'm just the same tall as you!" she said, giggling. "That's cool."

THE HIGH SCHOOL WAS one of several in the Delta County School District, which had an open enrollment policy allowing all students in the district to choose whichever school they wanted to attend—and a transportation system that provided busing to each student's school of choice. Delta High School had the most comprehensive Special Education program in the district, so most parents of special needs teenagers chose placement in that school, and I was no exception.

For Brittany, this meant boarding a bus in Cedaredge at 6:45 in the morning and returning home at 4:30 in the afternoon—a long day for her. I worried about her stamina, but I would be working and could not home-school her during the day, so I put her on the bus each morning and prayed her health would hold out.

She had grown much stronger and more resilient on the gluten-free diet and she enjoyed going to school, so most mornings she was up, dressed and ready for action by the time I warmed up the car. One morning she emerged from her bedroom in her bicycle helmet. "I can ride to the bus barn, Mom," she said. I stared at her over my coffee cup, which I held suspended in front of me. "It's just right there," she said, and she pointed to a square on a map she had drawn of our new neighborhood.

"You don't have a lock for your bike," I said.

She buckled the strap of her helmet. "Matt says it's okay I leave my bike in the office at the bus barn. I already checked." She had her hands on her hips and spoke definitively.

"Okay, as long as you let me take you when the sky gets dark or when there's snow," I said, and she mumbled assent as she headed for the backdoor. "Brittany!" I called after her. She stopped. "Breakfast?" I said. She pointed to her back pack, indicating she had packed a protein drink and a fruit snack, which she would eat at school before the bell rang for first period. She turned for the door, and I called out to her again: "Coat!" She lifted her jacket off the hook, slid it over one arm and left.

I watched from the kitchen window as she rode across the gravel drive, the jacket tied around her waist, a wide grin on her face. I finished my coffee, slipped on my sweater and grabbed the keys to the car. I backed slowly out of the driveway and turned right at the stop sign, hooking another right at the street Brittany should have taken to get to the bus barn. I turned left onto Birch Street and pulled over when I saw her on her bike ahead of me. She turned right through the open gate of the huge lot used for the district's school buses and disappeared from my view. Satisfied, I turned the car around and returned to the house to enjoy another cup of coffee before heading off for work.

I had found several new clients for my freelance work, including a farm and ranch magazine, an outdoor magazine and several newspapers that ran my feature stories. I had applied for a position as a reporter at a regional weekly newspaper but couldn't get my foot in the door for an interview. A library in another county was looking for a librarian for their children's section, and I applied even though I didn't have the credentials. I never heard from them either. A resume with a six-year gap in employment proved to be a hard sell. I applied for every job in every office, school and store that advertised and settled, finally, on a job I got through a temporary employment agency. I would work three days a week in Paonia, a town located 30 miles away, typing classifieds and designing display ads for a weekly shopper. It paid eight dollars an hour and was the only thing I could find that got me home in time for Brittany's return from Delta.

I was waiting for her one day on the front porch, sipping my tea and writing in my journal. She rounded the turn onto our street and dismounted at the head of the driveway. She pushed her bike to the edge of the porch and then let it fall on the ground. Then she loosened the strap of her helmet, threw the helmet to the ground and sank with a heavy sigh onto the chair next to mine. "I want you to write this," she said. "I want to say something." She dictated:

> I hate that Kent calls me a shorty. I am short, but I hate being short. I say to Kent: I am not a midget anymore. I don't want to be the shorty in the school. The youngest in the school should be the shortest; not me.
>
> I hate having Celiac disease in my body. It's not fair I can't have wheat. I want wheat like Ramen and noodles and spaghetti and meatballs. Why do I have Celiac disease?
>
> I wish I had no cracks in my tongue and no missing teeth. I want braces on my teeth. I can't have them until my teeth come in but they can't because of my disease.
>
> I wish I had no brown hair. I wish I was back to my blondeness. I'm letting my hair grow down to my shoulders.
>
> My eyebrows are not white. My eyes are a good color.
>
> I hate breasts because every day my mother asks me to put on a bra or an undershirt. I don't want to. I hate them.

I don't want a period. I want my mother to have them; not me. I have them because I'm turning into a grown-up woman. It hurts. It's painful. Awful. Traumatic. Hideous.

I don't like to take a shower, because I don't want to get cold. If I wear my clothes I am warm. If I take them off to go in the shower I'm cold. I want to take a shower but not every day.

My body is so flexible. I can put my feet back of my neck and I can make my legs and arms into pretzels. I like to do this because it tightens my leg muscles. That feels good. It makes me stronger.

Brittany interrupted me several times as I wrote and asked me to read passages back to her. She made some edits, choosing new words in some places, striking whole ideas in others. When she was done, she asked me to read the entire piece. She nodded satisfaction, and then she got off the chair, picked up her helmet and her bike and headed off toward the garage. As I watched her walk away, I realized that my daughter had become a bona fide teenager. Even more illuminating was my other realization—that she had become, also, a writer.

AT SCHOOL BRITTANY spent about half the week in the large classroom with the other Special Education students and the other half taking electives, "mainstreamed" with two or three other Special Education students into a regular education class. Her first semester she had choir, which was a thrill for her. It was a huge class, however; the instructor had little time to offer help to individual students, and there was no teacher aide. Brittany complained that her two peers in the class, Dawn and Amber, "always screw around and get us all in trouble," and that "the other peoples in the class tease my singing, because my voice is different." She despaired over the volume of material she had to learn, but she practiced every day in her bedroom to master it.

I was working on display ads one day when an ad request for an upcoming Winter Concert at Delta High School landed on my desk. I drafted the ad, printed it on the office printer and took the rough draft home to show Brittany. "Mr. Smith, the director of this concert, isn't he your choir teacher?" I asked her, showing her the teacher's name printed on my ad.

She squinted to see the name. "Yep, that's him," she said.

I made a short hand note in the margin to increase the size of the type on my ad. "So, are you singing in this concert?" I asked.

"Oh, yes!!! I'm so nervous!" she said, hugging herself in a mock shiver. "I been practicing and practicing!"

"The songs you're singing downstairs, are these the songs you're performing in the concert?" I asked. She nodded, and I asked her to get the copies of the songs for me. She disappeared into her room and emerged several minutes later with a battered folder. I leafed through well-worn sheets of lined paper with lyrics written in her small neat script. "Where are the copies from the music books?" I asked her.

"We not allowed to bring them home. I write the words and bring them home," she said, pointing to her folder. "Except one: Beebles Mebley, I don't have that one. We listen to the tape and sing. No words for that one."

I put my hand on her shoulder. "Tomorrow at school I want you to ask Mr. Smith for copies of the song sheets for each one of your songs—and a copy of the tape for 'Beebles,' okay? The song sheets and the tape, can you remember that?"

"I think so, but I'm scared."

The first call I made from work the next morning was a personal call to the high school. I asked for Mr. Smith, expecting to leave a message, but he was available to take my call immediately. "It's very important to Brittany to learn the selections you're teaching in class," I said. "She is supposed to ask you, but in case she forgets, I would appreciate it if you would give her copies of all the sheet music you're using for her class and a copy of the tape they're using in class for the 'Beebles,' she calls it."

"Beatles Medley?" he asked.

"That makes more sense!" I said. "And one other thing, could you allow Brittany to stand apart from Dawn and Amber? Dawn's behavior especially is distracting for her and frustrating, because she really wants to pay attention and learn in choir. Brittany said she's afraid to ask because she doesn't want the girls to get angry with her."

"Sure, I can help out. I am getting ready to group them for the performance anyway, and Brittany will be in the front row," Mr. Smith said, and he added, "I had no idea my class was so important to Brittany."

Despite the teacher's assurances, the sheet music for the Winter Concert never made it home, and the Beatles Medley tape was never duplicated. When I asked Brittany about it she would tell me the teacher "promised" he would make the copies but always said he ran out of time. Using Brittany's hand-written sheets and my own recollection of Beatles lyrics, she continued to practice at home, but we had an ongoing argument about whether the medley contained the words, "Hey, Jude," as I said it did, or the words, "Hey, Dude," as Brittany insisted.

The night before the concert Brittany hung her gown in my car and furiously searched her room for her dress shoes. She was too nervous to eat dinner she said, but I convinced her to eat a little, and when dinner was over I excused her to resume her hunt for her shoes. A half hour later, she carried her shoes to the dining room table, and then she went into the bathroom to throw up. "Ugh," she said, sinking into a chair at the table. "I'm so nervous."

"Why? You know all the songs." She did, but all of the students—even those with intellectual disabilities—would be expected to sing without using song sheets as prompts, and that was asking a lot, I thought. They might as well require the students with poor vision to go without eyeglasses. "You'll do great!" I said. "Now remember, don't get on the bus after school tomorrow. I'll pick you up at school."

"I remember," she said, and she put her face down on the table.

She was waiting in the Special Ed classroom when I drove to the high school. In a much more cheerful mood, she hugged Mrs. Bichon goodbye, grabbed her backpack, and scuttled to the car. "Is Grandma coming? And Aunt Bonnie?"

"Yes," I said, "We're meeting them right now at The Stockyards for an early, early dinner."

"Yay, The Stockyards," she cheered. "What about Daddy?"

She meant Bo. For several weeks she had been calling him "Daddy" or "Dad," an arrangement that, it seemed, suited him as well. When Bo's children, eleven-year-old Jason and eight-year-old Keeley were with us, she would call him by his name—or at least she would try to remember to call him by name—but most of the time Bo was Dad, a kinship felt and expressed in Brittany's speech and actions towards him. Tonight, I assured her, he would be joining us for the concert, after he got off of work and had some time to freshen up and drive to Delta.

We had all finished our meals and were having our second or third cups of coffee by the time Bo made it The Stockyards. He ordered a meal, and my mother and sister shared a piece of pie, while I helped Brittany change into her gown in the bathroom. It was her favorite gown, made of dark purple satin embroidered with silver thread, ankle long with spaghetti straps and a flattering neck line. She had worn the gown at a graduation party for Doran and at her cousin's wedding, and she loved how it made her look "grown up." Tonight, the dress was a little snug, the zipper on the back resisting closure. "I guess your diet is helping you gain some weight," I said, shaking my head at the irony. "Stand up straight," I said, and the zipper gave in. Brittany looked at her reflection in the mirror and smiled. "Radiant," I said.

"Okay," she said. She took a deep breath, slipped her feet into her shoes and turned on her heel. "Let's go."

As it turned out, it made no difference that Brittany continued to say "Hey, Dude" when she sang the Beatles Medley; at the winter concert she didn't belt out the lyrics like she had at home. In fact, she did not sing at all. As she stared out at the audience from her front-row position, she stood mute, wearing a surprised, semi-terrified look on her face while the other students sang. She refused to communicate or even make eye contact with me during the long drive home. "I was way beyond nervous," was all she would say when she finally talked about the concert the following day.

BRITTANY HAD A LONG face when I picked her up at the bus barn. It was mid-January, and we were having our fourth snowstorm in as many days, typical weather for Colorado. Everyone, it seemed, was suffering from cabin fever. Brittany sat in icy silence while I made the short drive home, and I thought about her teachers, and felt sorry for them, remembering when I was a teacher and those long weeks when snow storms kept the children indoors. Little problems always magnified under the weight of gloomy, cold skies.

When we reached the house, Brittany hung her jacket on the hook by the door and headed to her room with her pack. I lifted the lid on the pot I had left on the stove, gave my soup a stir and sat down at the table to read the newspaper. The door to Brittany's room made a familiar creak, and I heard the sound of her footsteps on the stairs. She sat heavily on a chair at the table and handed me a sheet of lined paper and a pen. "Write this," she said.

"Wait just a minute," I said, and I reached onto the bookshelf behind me. "I got a special notebook—a green spiral notebook—for when you want me to write something," I said. A smile cracked the ice on her discouragement. "Go for it," I told her.

> I wish Dave and Kent and Dawn and Laura would stop saying cuss words and lies at school and stop telling me what to do. I wish Dave would not sit by Kent. He should sit by me, because he picks fights with Kent. I wish Dave would never talk to Dawn and Kent again. I want Dave to talk to me and Charles again.

I want Dawn to stop telling lies and stories. She always tells me that Dave's not smart and talks weird because he has Down Syndrome. That makes me feel upset and disappointed. Laura tells lies and stories about Amber and Dave. They are going to jail. Laura said Dave broke her arm. She blamed him to her mom, and her mom works for President Bush! She was going to put Dave in jail. Laura fell and broke her own arm.

And Laura in geography class fifth period, Amber was crying because she was afraid she was going to jail because Laura said: I'm happy you're going to jail.

I wish Kent would stop calling me names like "Charles-lover" and "midget"—about my body. I hate being teased, and so I called Kent "Fatty," because that's what Laura told me. Now I wish Chris would stop calling me "Duncan-lover" and "Charles-lover."

I told on Chris about teasing—my teachers—and he got in trouble and he had to run around the tables and then write sentences with a timer.

I hang out with my friends; we hang out outside together unless it's bad weather.

Brittany nodded her satisfaction with her essay and walked back down the stairs to her room. I closed the notebook and went to the kitchen to stir the soup. I replaced the lid on the pot and turned to look out the kitchen window. The snow, visible only in the light of the street lamps and the headlights of passing cars, had a mesmerizing effect. I focused on the large, fluffy flakes and thought about friendship, how difficult it would be for Brittany to have real, authentic friends.

Her peer group was limited, no larger really than the group of kids in her classroom at Delta High. And each one of those kids experienced profound delays in analytical reasoning, communication skills, the ability to interpret verbal and non-verbal clues, the ability to experience empathy, the ability to appropriately express feelings, the whole range of what we call "people skills," those characteristics that enable human beings to engage fully in relationships with other people. What are the odds, I wondered, in that one classroom that another student could balance Brittany's particular mix of interpersonal skills with his or her own mix and share with Brittany that wonderful feeling of having a true friend? I had placed great hope that Brittany would develop a friendship with Laura, who lived near us and who also had a parent with MS, but Brittany's journal entry dashed that hope. Imagine, Laura telling the other students that her mother works for the president of the United States! Imagine, the other students believing her! Brittany believed her! Sheez!

I pulled myself away from the window, got some plates and bowls out of the cupboard and started setting the table. Wait a minute, I thought. I opened the cover to the green notebook and reread Brittany's essay. "Charles-lover?"

"Duncan-lover" I could understand; many years ago Brittany had had a crush on my friend's son Duncan. But who was Charles? Charles. Charles. The olive-skinned boy who sat doodling at the desk Brittany's first day at Delta High! "Brittany!" I called down the stairs.

By the time she answered I had thought better of it. Better to let her express her thoughts without being questioned. "What?" she hollered.

"Come help set the table," I said, and I put the napkins, glasses, spoons and forks on the counter where she could easily find them. I pointed to the stack of dishes when she entered the kitchen. "Bo will be here; that's why there are three," I said, anticipating the question she was forming in her mind.

TIM'S MOTHER CALLED ME from Colorado Springs to tell me that Tim had slipped into a coma. I asked her if she thought I should bring Brittany over right away, and she said she thought it wouldn't be necessary. Two days later she called to tell me that Tim had recovered and that Hospice would be eliminating Methadone from his pain management regime. She also told me that Tim would be moving into a skilled nursing facility, one of the newest "bridge" facilities on the west side of Colorado Springs. She would call again later, she said, to let me know when the move would be taking place and how to reach Tim once he had left Hospice.

I continued to drive Brittany to Colorado Springs once a month to see Tim. The nursing facility was gorgeous, home to many of El Paso County's retired judges, doctors and generals. Beautifully draped windows lined every hallway, and comfortable overstuffed chairs and couches welcomed visitors. A full slate of concerts, lectures and performances kept the residents entertained, and there were many recreational programs, even a weight room and an Olympic-size swimming pool, for residents and visitors. But it was still a nursing home, with nursing home smells and sounds, and Brittany dreaded the weekends she visited her dad. By the time I picked her up on Sunday, she was ready "to hit the road," and she would chat cheerfully about the people she saw at church or about the movie she watched in Tim's room, but she refused to talk about her dad except to say that he was doing "Okay."

After the first few trips to Colorado Springs a disturbing trend developed, not with Brittany, but with me. Without fail I would develop a urinary tract infection after visiting the Springs. On the drive home I would begin to feel a prickly sensation in my bladder and would drive the last one hundred miles or so feeling feverish and weak. I'd wake in my bed on Monday morning with a full-fledged infection, which I would try to ignore. By Wednesday I would drag myself into my physician's office and leave a sample in a cup. The pattern became so predictable that my physician would call in the prescription before my sample even reached the lab, and I came to expect the medical expense I would incur each time I travelled east.

I wracked my brain to try to figure out what was going on. Bo teased that it was the "filth of the city" causing the problem. The only explanation I could suggest was that somehow stress was causing the infections, and it was stressful to visit Tim. But the few minutes I spent with him each time I dropped Brittany off or picked her up—were those encounters really that stressful? As the months went by and the pattern repeated itself, Bo grew impatient with searching for an explanation. Whatever was happening, he said, it was unhealthy for me, so he cleared his schedule so that he could join us each time we went. With Bo sharing the chore of driving and providing companionship, Brittany and I both began looking forward, if not to the destination, at least to the trip, and Doran and Bo got the chance to become acquainted with one another.

OUR TRIPS TO COLORADO Springs interfered with the schedule for Special Olympics skiing, so Brittany sat out her first season in Delta Area Special Olympics. But the words "Delta Globetrotters" in 48-point type on a light blue flyer signaled the advent of the Special Olympics basketball season, of which Brittany was determined to be a part. She pulled the crinkled flyer out of her pack when I picked her up at the bus barn and shoved it in my hands. "Look! Basketball! I wanna go!"

It was the only note I had seen come home from school since Brittany enrolled. "Wow," I said. "Let's see, practices twice a week in Delta, there's a phone number for the coach, Judy...."

"I call her," Brittany said, "when we get home!"

It was a unified sport, the coach explained to me, when Brittany finally let me have the phone. That meant that intellectually disabled people of all ages played alongside volunteers. The "partners," as they were called, would help move the ball up and down the court, protect smaller players from accidental encounters with larger players and assist the athletes in scoring points. As much as possible, she explained, the partners don't score, rather they help move the ball and pass it to the Special Olympics athletes who would attempt to score.

"Brittany weighs only about 100 pounds," I said, "and that's soaking wet."

"That's okay," Judy said. "Trust me, there are all sizes, shapes and ages on the team. Everyone gets to play and everyone plays safe."

It sounded wonderful, the only problem was that practices started at 6 and Brittany usually got home at 4:30. "You'll have to come in the house, change clothes and eat, and then leave again—back to Delta," I told her. "Two times a week."

"I don't care. I wanna play." She was whining.

"Then back to the house, into the shower and straight to bed. Twice a week."

"I hate showers," she said. "I won't shower."

"If you want to play, you shower," I said firmly.

"So, I can play?"

I SAT IN THE BLEACHERS at the Delta Middle School gym, knitting and chatting with other parents while Brittany and thirty other athletes and partners stretched, ran laps and divided into groups for skills drills.

The real estate industry had begun to slow, and housing starts were on the way down. Having endured the previous recession in Colorado, Bo anticipated that the worst was yet to come, so he retreated from the construction industry and took a job doing store security for a new Wal-Mart store. The security job often involved working nights. If Bo had an evening open, however, he joined me in the bleachers at the gym.

We enjoyed watching the athletes play. Judy, the coach, had been absolutely correct: there were athletes of all ages, shapes and sizes, but Brittany was by far the smallest in the group. And the most timid. It surprised me: all her life she had been a thrill seeker in sports, riding as fast as she could on her bike, skiing at top speed without poles, diving into the deepest water she could find and swimming like a shark. And when she was on the basketball court, she could shoot the ball as well as ever, sinking free throw after free throw to the astonishment of all the other members of the team. But team play was another story. When the skills drills were done and the players divided into teams for scrimmages, Brittany became a mouse. She would cling to the edges of the court, hang back when the other players ran down court, and scurry when they ran in her direction.

I couldn't really blame her. Some of the players were huge, and play often got rough. The partners did a fabulous job blocking the more disabled players from harm, and the more advanced athletes did the same, but Special Olympics basketball was still a great deal more robust than I had imagined it would be. As time went on and the coaches became more aware of Brittany's limitations, it was determined that Brittany would participate in the "Individual Skills" part of the competition and not team play. In Individual Skills, she would be scored by how well she performed the drills—dribbling, shooting, free throws—and would compete against other players who performed the same drills. She would be spared the frightening prospect of playing on the court with nine other players running at full charge. Still, the coach said, she should remain at practices while the teams scrimmaged so she could support the team and become more familiar with the sport. The arrangement suited Brittany: she could stretch out, and do the warm ups and drills with the team, and then play the part of social butterfly while the teams pressed each other back and forth on the court.

And she was quite the butterfly. Bo and I watched in amusement as Brittany became acquainted with every parent, every sibling, every volunteer that sat in the bleachers every practice. By the second month of practice she had memorized everyone's birthday and knew everyone's middle name, data that had become very important to her. Occasionally, the coach would ask Brittany to focus her attention on the sport, and occasionally Brittany would comply when asked, but most evenings Brittany simply circulated in the crowd, meeting people and making small talk.

"Give her five minutes," Bo said after watching her one evening, "and she knows everyone in the room."

Chapter Ten

A Long, Long Road

Bo came out of the bedroom looking perplexed. His security shift started at 7:30 this morning, and he could not find the set of handcuffs he had put on the bedside table when he had undressed last night. His glasses were there, his belt, his wallet, his keys and his ballpoint pen. But no handcuffs.

"What'd she do with them?" he said as he sat at the table, irritated.

"Why would she have them?" I asked, also irritated. It was silly to think that Brittany would have gone in our room and taken something, especially handcuffs. "We've been up all morning," I said. "We watched her leave for the bus; she was never in our room."

"I know," he said, skeptical. "I'll look again." I offered to help. We moved the bed, the table, the small rug. We opened the drawer of the bedside table and looked through the books stacked in the opening underneath. No handcuffs.

"You're sure you set them here?" I asked. But I knew the routine. Every night after work Bo set the handcuffs on the bedside table; the other items he put there, every night, before going to sleep. But last night he didn't get home from work until 11:30, and then he went straight to bed.

Maybe he did something different with the cuffs. Maybe he left them at work, or in the truck.

"That girl!" he said, exasperated, and I stiffened, feeling defensive. But I was sorry, too, for Bo, who now was running late for work. My new husband could be said to be a lot of things—stubborn, maybe, opinionated, but never would anyone call him late, for work, especially. It was a simple matter of respect, he believed, to show up on time. "I guess I'll just have to go without them," he said, tying the lace on his boot. Great, I thought, let's hope today's the day Bo doesn't have to tangle with crack-heads and gang-bangers stealing CDs.

The phone rang and I grabbed it. "This is Delta County Sheriff dispatch," a static-scratched voice said. "Is this Suzanne?" Bo was getting up, but I reached for his forearm and I lowered myself into a chair. "Don't worry, this is not an emergency," the woman said, and I felt my shoulders slacken with relief. She started to laugh. "Your daughter has...well, she has handcuffed herself to the school bus."

SHE DID IT ON A DARE, she told Bo when we met the bus, the cuffed passenger and the curt bus driver at the Cedaredge Bus Barn an hour later. "The other kids on the bus told me my dad didn't have handcuffs, and I said, 'Yes, he does, I will show them.' And when I showed them they said 'Those aren't real,' and I said, 'Uh-huuuuh,' and they said, 'Oh, yeah, show us, we dare you,' and so I did." She slid one cuff around her wrist, and the other around the leg supporting the bench seat, the driver explained to Bo, and when she tried to wriggle out of the cuffs at the high school...

"...they just got tighter," Bo said, and Brittany nodded, tears now welling up in her eyes. "Crying isn't going to help you," Bo said, and the bus driver concurred.

"The sheriff tried using his keys on them," the driver said.

Bo nodded. "Law enforcement's universal keys don't work on these." Bo released Brittany's hand from the cuff, looked at her squarely and told her to get in his truck. "I'll take you to school," he said gruffly.

"I want Mom," she said, looking to me for sympathy.

"Mom's not going to Delta. I'm going to Delta. Get in."

I watched them pull out of the parking lot, keeping my eyes fixed on them until they turned left onto Main Street and the truck disappeared from view. "You are in for a long, long ride," I said out loud, and I realized immediately I wasn't sure to whom I was referring. I pictured Bo herding Brittany into the cab of his truck, tender even though he was angry. I pictured Brittany getting into the cab and choosing, as she had, not to put distance between her and her new step-dad by sitting near the window, but sitting where she did, right next to him on the bench seat of the truck. I thought about myself standing there, watching my husband and daughter leave together. It dawned on me that finally Brittany and I had found a companion, for me a husband, for her a father, for both of us a steady and faithful friend to share our life adventure. No matter where the road would take us, I realized, Bo would be there— to help us get ready to go, to take a turn with the driving, to enjoy a cup of tea at a roadside cafe and to join us as we laughed over mishaps and wrong turns taken. Yeah, it will be a long ride for all of us, I thought, and I had to admit I was really looking forward to the trip.

BO AND I HAD MARRIED in early spring, in a quiet, unannounced courthouse ceremony we managed to squeeze in between his work schedule, my work schedule, our trips to Colorado Springs, Special Olympics practices and the calendar limitations imposed by Bo's visitation schedule with his children.

Jason and Keeley stayed with us every other weekend and would stay for longer periods during school vacations. We had modified the floor plan of the bungalow to accommodate each of the three children in rooms of their own, while still finding a little nook for my home office and space on the walls for Bo's hunting trophies. By now, our little house seemed filled to bursting with toys, computers, books and files, hunting equipment, baseball and paintball paraphernalia, bicycle helmets and the usual household necessities. Soon the house would get even cozier.

A month after Bo and I married I got a call from Doran, "Come and get me, Ma," he said. "I'm ready to get out of here." Bo gave me the keys to his truck and I drove, hell-bent for leather, across the southern Colorado mountains to retrieve my son, whose pale voice had revealed the anguish he had tried so carefully not to express in words.

It had been a difficult semester for Doran; he had done the kinds of things typical of college sophomores, but unlike most young men his age, he had already learned the value of time and the value of money, and he felt that he had been squandering both. He had fallen behind in all of his classes except theatre, in which he excelled. He had developed great talent as an actor, having earned respect in his thoughtful portrayal of characters, his ability to quickly memorize long scripts, and his understanding of the nuances of great dramatic performance. His friends in the theatre crowd undermined his personal values, however, and he had struggled to maintain their friendship while measuring himself according to his own conscience.

He was having difficulties with Tim as well. The staff at the nursing home did not respond to Tim's needs as readily as the staff at Hospice had, Doran felt. It upset him that Tim often had to wait until after lunch before he would be bathed and dressed for the day. The head nurse had classified Tim as a "two-person assist," meaning the process of hoisting him for a bath or for transfer to his wheelchair required two staff members. The nursing staff typically dressed their "one-person assists" first thing in the morning, and then devoted the time necessary for the others later and as time dictated. Doran complained to the head nurse that Tim needed attention earlier in the morning, at the very least getting assistance with changing his position so that he would be less susceptible to bed sores. The staff finally compromised by lifting Tim out of the bed each morning and transferring him to his wheelchair, getting

Brittany and Keeley (on the far right) clowning around with some of Keeley's friends at the Cedaredge house.

him set up with his computer, and coming back after lunch to bathe and dress him.

Even as Doran was negotiating on Tim's behalf, Tim was on the phone with me, complaining first about Doran's grades, and then, strangely, accusing Doran of stealing money from him. One day Tim told me that Doran had taken some cash out of his bedside table. Several weeks later, he called to say that Doran had stolen $5,000 from his personal checking account. "The man who helps me with my accounting, my financial adviser, traced the cancelled check," Tim said gravely. "And Doran's signature is on it."

"Well, what does Doran say about it?" I asked Tim. "Was the check for tuition? Do you remember you promised him you would help him with tuition?"

"Doran denies knowing anything at all about it. Flat out denies it," Tim said. "This is very serious. I am thinking of pressing charges against him."

I was floored. How could such a thing happen? What had happened? I refused to believe Tim's story, but the thought of a cancelled check with Doran's signature and the police knocking on Doran's apartment door scared me to death. I tried to reach Doran, but no one ever answered the phone in his apartment. I thought about driving to Colorado Springs that night.

The next day, Tim called again. One of his colleagues, the instructor of a course in which Doran was enrolled, had mentioned to Tim that Doran was failing the class. "I don't know what he's doing, but apparently he isn't turning in homework," Tim said.

"Did you find out any more about the check?" I asked.

"What check?"

"The check for $5,000 that you called me about yesterday, the one you said Doran signed," I said, exasperated.

"Oh, that was a check for $8,000. I forgot that when he was here my father transferred that money from one of my accounts to another," Tim said. Tim's father is also named Doran.

"So it was your dad's signature on the check, not Doran's?"

"Huh? Yes. I talked to Doran about it. I apologized to him. Everything's okay," Tim said. "He accepted my apology."

The final straw, Doran said, from the top of Monarch Pass, where we had pulled over to give the truck's overheating engine an opportunity to cool, was the sale of Doran's classic Jeep. Doran had bought the old Wrangler using money I paid him in exchange for his Jeep Cherokee, and he had invested nothing but time and money in the off-road vehicle since the day of the purchase. When he was in hock to the mechanic for several hundred dollars and fed up with the whole idea of Jeep ownership, Doran had convinced his dad to pay the mechanic bill—Doran would sell the Jeep and pay him back.

Doran already had a buyer in mind but would be out of town when the buyer was available to see the Jeep, so he left the Jeep and the keys with his dad, with instructions not to sell the Jeep for any less than $5,000, the "classic car" value. Tim's financial adviser looked up the "Blue Book" value of the Jeep and found that it was only $1,500, enough to pay the outstanding mechanic's bill and money Doran had previously borrowed from Tim. When the buyer came to Tim's room, Tim offered her the Jeep for $1,500, which she promptly gave him in cash, and Tim's financial adviser deposited the cash in Tim's account. When the dust settled, Doran was left with no vehicle, no cash to buy a replacement and an outstanding mechanic's bill, which, somehow, the financial adviser neglected to pay.

"You went to Dwayne, right?" I asked my son as the cool evening air flowed through the cab of the truck. "For the repairs—Dwayne was the mechanic?"

"Oh, yeah." Doran smiled. "Of course! Are there any other mechanics in Colorado Springs?"

"Well, let me talk to him, honey. Don't you worry about the bill. The rest—we'll sort it out, like we've always done." I got out of the cab and slammed the hood closed. "I'm so glad you're coming to live us, Doran," I said as I climbed back in, and Doran turned the key in the ignition. "And Bo is absolutely thrilled."

Doran smiled. "I'm so glad Bo came with you when you brought Sis to visit Dad. I really like him, Mom."

"Me, too," I said, watching Doran as he pulled cautiously onto the highway. In my mind I could picture Bo at home, rearranging furniture to make room for my son and the truck load of stuff he was bringing with him.

IT WAS OUR WEEKEND to have Jason and Keeley over, and I took them and Brittany to a paint-it-yourself pottery store. Jason picked out a dragon, which he was painting with dark colors, gold glitter, and drops of red for blood. Keeley was putting the final touches on a unicorn figurine and Brittany had drawn two figures on a dinner plate, a man in a tuxedo and top hat and a woman in a bridal gown. I thought she would label the figures "Bo and Mom," but I watched as she painted "Charles and Brittany" instead. She held up the plate and asked the rest of us how we liked it. Jason shrugged. Keeley stared at it and then said it was nice. "Cute," I said, nodding and holding my questions at bay.

I picked up the shiny, fired pieces of pottery the following week and put Jason and Keeley's wrapped pieces on their bedside tables. Brittany was sitting on the front porch, playing with Barbies. I unwrapped her plate and took it outside for her to see. Her face beamed her satisfaction. I stood watching her. Finally, she looked up at me. "What?" she said.

"Perhaps it's time you write something about Charles."

She handed me the plate, jumped to her feet and dashed inside, returning seconds later with the green notebook and a pen.

Yesterday Charles sat by me in class when we were playing Uno with Amber, Naomi and Kent. I told Charles to come sit by me, and he did. Kent came over to Charles and whispered in Charles' ear: Do you want to marry Brittany? And Charles said, yeah.

This means we're in love, totally in love. Charles is excited about getting married, but he wants to go on a date first.

I'm going to fix Charles' memory. He can't remember peoples' names. Well, he remembers my name. Every morning Mrs. Bichon says: Charles, who's this girl sitting in the desk next to Jose? And Charles says: Um...um...Brittany.

I want Charles to ask his Grandma to help him buy an engagement ring and a wedding ring. (Squeals of laughter.) Okay, that's embarrassing, isn't it?

When people get married they go on a honeymoon. My honeymoon will be three days at California. A honeymoon is that you spend time alone for a while with who you got married to.

Married people move in together. You stay in the house, watch movies together, go to work, drop off your kids, eat, give your children chores.

We should have a son and a daughter to live with us. We need to get to know each other and tell my family that we got married. You tell all your best friends.

We are going to live in California.

It feels nervous to be in love, and excited and joyful and compassion and freedom.

I finished writing Brittany's words and straightened in my chair to read it back to her. But she picked up her dolls and, giggling, ran into the house and down the basement stairs to her room. Bo stepped out on the porch with two mugs of hot tea and asked me what I was doing.

"Just sitting here wondering," I said, reaching up for my tea, "what happened to my baby girl."

BASKETBALL SEASON ENDED, and practices for Special Olympics swimming began promptly thereafter. Even though it was her first year of competitive swimming, Brittany quickly became the strongest female member on the team, a natural consequence of the years Tim had spent instructing her and of her own fearlessness in the water. As summer neared, the swimming coach sent news home that the team would compete in a regional tournament in Craig, a ranching town located about 85 miles north of my mother's place in northwestern Colorado. Opening ceremonies would include a barbecue and carnival Friday evening; competition would take place all day Saturday and Sunday morning, and medals would be awarded Sunday after lunch. It sounded fabulous, and I was only too anxious to agree to the coach's request to be one of the chaperones for the trip. My meals and lodging would be provided, and I would be compensated for my fuel. I was delighted that the arrangement would provide the financial resources I needed to travel to Craig and watch Brittany compete.

I gassed up the Cherokee and stopped at the high school at 1:00 Friday afternoon, as the coach had previously arranged. I checked in at the office, gave the secretary the names of the three high school athletes in my carpool, and she used the loudspeaker to call the girls, including Brittany, to the office. "There was another girl, a junior high girl, who was going to meet us, but I don't see her. Has she checked in here?" I asked the secretary. She shook her head, so I walked out to the car with the girls and helped them find a place in the back to load their gear. They were giddy with excitement about leaving school and about the tournament. I waited for a break in the chatter and asked, "Anybody know where Heidi is?"

"Her mom 'posed to bring her," Brittany said.

"Okay, well, let's go inside and see if we can use a phone. Anybody know her number?" The girls shrugged as one and followed me back into the building.

The secretary handed me a phone book and I scanned the Delta listings but couldn't find the girl's last name. "It isn't here," I said to the secretary. "Does anybody in the office know Heidi Salinger's phone number?"

"What's the name, Salinger?" She asked, and I nodded. "I don't know their number but I can show you where they live," she said. She took out a piece of paper and drew a map to the place, which, it turned out, was only a few miles from the school. "That's great," I said. "Thanks. And if they should happen to show up here, would you ask them to wait for us? I'll come back if there's no one at the house." The secretary smiled and turned to the ringing phone. She waved vaguely as the girls and I turned to go.

Heidi's house was a tidy single-wide mobile home, white with dark blue trim, on a grassy lot on the north side of town. It seemed quiet as a tomb, but I knocked anyway, and I could hear a tentative shuffling sound inside. A tall, middle-aged woman opened the door and looked out, a confused expression on her face. I looked at her matted hair, the pajamas she was wearing. "I'm sorry if I woke you," I said. "I'm here to pick up Heidi. For the Special Olympics tournament in Craig?" The woman thought for a moment and then nodded. She beckoned for me to come in, turned slowly and padded tentatively down the hall, leaving me standing in the entry way. I stared after her, trying to recall where I had seen her. She looked so familiar.

When she returned with her daughter in tow I remembered: of course, the woman was one of the athletes on the Special Olympics Basketball team! "I couldn't drive to the school today," she said as she handed Heidi a grocery bag filled, presumably, with the things Heidi needed for the trip. "I'm sick."

"Oh, no problem," I said, and I ran through the weekend's events with her to make sure she understood that I would not be bringing Heidi back until Sunday afternoon. She nodded and bent forward to kiss her daughter on the forehead. "Have fun," she said. She smiled weakly and turned to walk toward the couch. I stepped out, and Heidi followed, pulling the door closed behind her.

"My mom is diabetic," Heidi said, when I opened the hatch so she could put her grocery bag in the back of the Cherokee.

"Well, is it okay to leave her, Heidi?" I asked. I did not feel confident leaving the poor woman alone in her little trailer. "Did she see a doctor?"

"It's okay," Heidi said, gesturing to a larger mobile home on the same grassy lot. "My gramma lives right there. She takes care of us."

"That's nice," I said. "You hop in right there," I said, pointing to the vacant spot on the back seat. "I'm just gonna go let your gramma know we're leaving."

WE ARRIVED AT THE Craig Holiday Inn about an hour later than everyone else from the Delta team, but of the four girls in my troupe only one seemed agitated by our late arrival. The coach greeted us in the lobby and I apologized, explaining what had happened. "Oh, don't worry about it," the coach said, "there's still plenty of time to check in, sit in the hot tub, swim in the pool and change before the barbecue."

"Pool?" said Brittany. "Awesome!" Hot tub, I thought... Awesome!

We got our key and the girls skipped down the hall ahead of me, anxious to join all the other athletes who had converged on the hotel and who now chatted in happy clusters around the pool. I made a beeline for the hot tub, as did Dawn and Amber, the two other girls in my charge. As I lowered myself into the blissfully hot water, Dawn nodded recognition to a young man already sitting in the tub. She climbed in next to him and within nanoseconds, the two had limbs and lips entwined, greeting one another after, apparently, a long separation. Amber sat on the edge of the hot tub, awkwardly gaping at the lovebirds. "Get a room," she finally said, as she left the hot tub and found Brittany, surrounded already by new friends and engaged in a happy, splashing game in the middle of the large pool. Dawn and her boyfriend exchanged giggles and nervous whispers as I held them in my gaze. Finally, Dawn looked up and saw me staring at her. "Let's go," she said, and she and her friend climbed out of the hot tub to cool off with their friends in the big pool.

The opening program for the athletes took place at the middle school, where one civic organization served a full barbecue meal in the cafeteria and another entertained the participants on the lawn with a carnival and street dance. Local merchants had provided a generous bounty of prizes and refreshments, while musicians performed on a stage under a cheerful yellow awning. I wasn't sure how closely to watch my four girls, who all seemed to want to go different directions; finally the coach assured me that Dawn and Amber had travelled to Craig before and did not need much assistance. I should stick with Brittany and Heidi, who were travelling for the first time, the coach said, and that suited me. The girls got their faces painted, tried their luck at various ball-toss games, danced and drank sodas which were available in abundance. At nine o'clock everyone boarded buses and headed back to the hotel, tired but happy, and we listened to volunteers' instructions for the following morning: what time we needed to be in the lobby, what we needed to take with us, who needed to be ready to compete and where.

Dawn held back as the other girls climbed off our bus, smooching her boyfriend who sat on the seat beside her. Finally, she and the boy de-boarded. I gestured with my head and firmly said, "Let's go!" She rolled her eyes but complied, first giving her boyfriend a peck and whispering something in his ear. Brittany and Amber changed into their pajamas the instant we got back to our room and settled into the bed near the window. Dawn secluded herself in the bathroom, and Heidi sat on the foot of the bed in front of the TV, absorbed in a Tom and Jerry cartoon. When fifteen minutes passed and Dawn hadn't emerged from the bathroom, I suggested to Heidi that she simply change into her pajamas there in the room. We would all look away, if that helped.

"That's okay," she said. "I'm sleeping in this." She gestured to the outfit she had on.

The other girls looked up and said, "Finally!" I looked behind me and saw Dawn coming out of the bathroom. Brittany and Amber grabbed their toothbrushes and scampered to the bathroom, chatting and giggling, while Heidi continued to sit, eyes glued on the TV.

"Do you want to brush your teeth, Heidi?" I asked when the others came out, but Heidi only smiled and shook her head.

"I'm on my period," Dawn suddenly announced. "I need you to go get me some pads," she said, looking at me.

"I think I have some," I said. I tossed my suitcase on the rollaway and riffled though it, finding a small plastic bag with about five sanitary napkins inside of it. "Here you go," I said, holding the bag out for Dawn.

"Not that kind," she said. "I have to use another kind. I need you to go to the store and get some."

"Hmmm." I stalled. She seemed to want me out of the room, but why? "Let's call the coach. Perhaps she can go get some." I picked up the phone. Dawn sighed.

"Oh, those'll do," she said, grabbing the bag off my bed and stomping to the bathroom. I watched the door close behind her and suddenly realized the motivation for her puzzling behavior: she wanted me to leave the room so that she could skip out and join her cowboy for a romp in the hay! This girl is only 15 years old, I told myself, and I wondered what I should do to protect her from her raging hormones. The only thing I could think of was to keep her in for the night, so I tugged my rollaway bed closer to the exit of the room, and I climbed into bed. Anyone wanting to leave would have to walk over me first. Dawn might join that boy for a tryst, I thought to myself, and it might even happen on this trip, but it isn't going to happen tonight!

The next day, when Heidi left the hotel room dressed in the same clothes she had worn since I picked her up, I figured out the problem. The grocery bag she had brought on the trip had her swimsuit and a towel and some stuffed animals, but nothing else—no change of clothes, no toiletries, no jacket, nothing. I loaned her a shirt from my own suitcase and got a toothbrush and toothpaste at the hotel front desk. I asked the clerk if there was anything in the lost and found that could be considered unclaimed and could be used for my young traveler, and she gave me a jacket, a hairbrush and a pair of sweats. During our afternoon break I asked the coach to keep an eye on my girls while I drove over to Kmart, where I picked up some underwear and socks, and I left these, along with a pack of gum and some glitter lip gloss, on Heidi's pillow.

Brittany swam like a champion in her events, and she won two gold medals and one silver. She got leg cramps after her third race and started to panic, but I rubbed her legs and got her warmed up, and she recovered, and then she and Heidi went in the locker room where they showered, got dressed and brushed their hair. By the time we loaded up the vehicles for the trip home the girls were exhausted. Even Dawn seemed anxious for a quiet, undisturbed drive. When we got home, Bo was waiting with mugs of hot tea, and Brittany was rested and ready for action. She showed Bo her medals and chattered about the trip, and then she joined me and Bo on the porch with the green notebook and a pen in hand.

SPECIAL OLYMPICS IS FUN

I like Special Olympics, because I want to be in Special Olympics forever and ever.

Special Olympics is fun because you can do your own sports like basketball and swimming and bike riding. Whatever you want. And you can win awards and gold medals if you win the race.

You have to go to practices all the time. If you don't go to the practices you don't get to go on the team. But I do go to the practices so I get to be on the team—on the Delta Globetrotters and the Delta Splash.

At practice we practice dribbling, swimming, bike riding, whatever the coach asks you to do. And stretches.

And when you go to the place where the tournament is you get to stay in a hotel and get dinners and stuff. Free dinners with no paying and you get to be with your friends.

I read it back to her and she made a few changes, and then she turned to go back into the house.

"Wait a sec," I said. She turned and looked at me. "Daddy thinks we should put all our writings together—yours and mine—in a book. What do you think?"

"Hmmm," she mumbled, and I could see the idea taking root. "That would be cool." She reached for the door and then paused. "Mom," she said, "would you call that chapter 'Special Olympics is Fun'?" I nodded, and she disappeared into the house.

Chapter Eleven

Crack the Egg

Our house was within walking distance of the city park, which was a favorite hang-out for every member of our family. Brittany and Keeley loved performing tricks on the swing sets and the monkey bars and seemed to find endless delight in tossing their Barbies into a creek that cut through the park and then running ahead and "rescuing" the dolls before they crashed into a grate at the mouth of a culvert.

Jason loved the creek, too, though he distanced himself from the Barbie games, preferring to roll up his pant legs, slip off his shoes and wade through the fast-moving water until his toes got white from the cold. A wide, meandering sidewalk with a moderate downhill grade provided a challenge for Doran, who worked on his skateboard skills when he wasn't working at the burger joint down the street. Bo and I found pleasure sitting close together on the park bench, holding hands and watching our suddenly large family at play.

From our front porch one day we heard the muffled, tinny sound of music and we knew from experience that a band must be playing at the park pavilion. Doran was at work, but the rest of us were home, looking for a way to pass a sunny Saturday afternoon, so we followed the sound — Brittany and Keeley on their scooters, Jason on his bike, and Bo and I on foot, toting collapsible camp chairs over our shoulders. When we reached the park, we could see Jason waiting for us near the fire hydrant at the corner; Keeley stood, her scooter in hand, not far from him. "Where's Brittany?" Bo asked, and Keeley waved vaguely in the direction of the crowd assembling on the grass in front of the pavilion.

The four of us strolled down the sidewalk, looking for a place to set our chairs and the picnic blanket Bo was carrying. We found a spot and spread out, Jason and Keeley on the blanket with their bike and scooter on the grass beside them. "There she is," I said, spotting Brittany's head in the crowd. I pointed, and the others saw her too.

She was working the crowd, the way she always did, stopping here and there, greeting the people she knew, introducing herself to the people she didn't know, laughing at jokes, making chit-chat. Jason stared at her and then shook his head. "I really suck at that," he said.

Without taking her eyes off Brittany, Keeley quietly said, "Me, too."

BRITTANY WAS EIGHTEEN years old and classified as a junior at Delta High School; Keeley, in third grade, would soon be nine years old; Jason, nearly 12, was in his last year in elementary school; Doran, 20, had completed three semesters in college, had experimented with living on his own and now was back home and working as many hours as his employer would have him. With no warning whatsoever and without taking a vote, Bo and I—the parents of these four children—had married and combined households, and our kids did their level best to adapt.

This was easier in some ways than others. Although she fussed when he called her "Sissy," and complained that he ate Ramen right in front of her face, Brittany was delighted to have her older brother home again. To Jason, Doran was the epitome of coolness: he did tricks on a skateboard, drank energy drinks, played paintball, had a tattoo and a pierced tongue. And, though Keeley was quiet and shy around him, Doran quickly won her over as well; she would fight to hide a smile when he teased her and stole food off her supper plate.

And Keeley enjoyed Brittany's company. When other people did not interfere, the girls played for hours with Barbies, coloring books or rough-housing on our trampoline. When Jason asserted his claim for his sister's attention, however, things got dicey. In fact, Jason and Brittany became fierce rivals: arguing not only over Keeley's attention, but Bo's attention, too, and any other thing that could possibly become a bone of contention. If Brittany called window seat, Jason wanted the same seat. If Jason wanted chicken for dinner, Brittany begged for burgers. If one said "white," the other, inevitably, demanded "black."

One Sunday afternoon, after Jason and Keeley had gone home and while Bo was waiting for the "WhooOOOO" of the tea kettle, I asked Brittany if she wanted to write about her experiences and feelings about the younger children. We were sitting on the front porch, and I had the green notebook already on my lap. Brittany looked at me. "I want to call it 'Brothers and Sisters,'" she said, and she dictated:

BROTHERS AND SISTERS

I want to talk about Jason first. I hate little brothers—12-year-old brothers. I wish Jason wouldn't be in my conversations. I hate to be told: Shut up. Every time I watch movies, he tells me to shut up or be quiet. And I hate being told what to do by stupid, little brothers.

Every time I get home from school I say: Hi, Jason, and he says: Whatever, or Shut up. Every time me and Keeley are on the computer he butts in. I tell him: Jason, this is my computer game, and I can tell Keeley what to do, not you. And I tell him: You may not come in my room and throw stuff and sneak up on me and Keeley.

On my birthday, Jason cannot be rude to my friends.

I didn't always hate Jason, but now he always tells me what to do. He says: Don't touch my things! And he is always acting stupid, like a clown, trying to get attention, because he's trying to be a teenager like me. I say: Oh no, only one in my family gets to be a teenager, and that's me—well, me and Doran.

Doran is more cooler because he's so hot and he's smart and he can spell things. He has a very cool hair color. He's a good actor in plays. He's so funny. He always drinks Mountain Dew a lot because that's his favorite drink. He likes Ramen noodles. Doran's an awesome teenager drama king. I like Doran a lot, except when he calls me Britt or Sissy.

I don't like Keeley that much, nine-year-old sisters. Because she is a smart aleck to me when her friends are here. Keeley says: Knock it off, Brittany; I've had it with you being in my room. This is when her friends are over. She's kind of okay when she's alone. She tells me what to do: Hey, Brittany, can you throw this away? I say: I'm not your servant.

I like Keeley a lot without Jason or her friends around. I like when we play Barbies downstairs in my room or watch movies together or eat or jump on the trampoline. We get along well.

If she asks me nicely I do things for her. If she doesn't ask me nicely I won't do it. She can boss her friends, not me.

Brittany made her customary edits as I read her words back to her, and then she held the front door open so Bo could come through with two mugs of tea. "I gonna go listen to my CDs," she said, and I could hear the floor creak under her retreating steps.

"Did she get some more writing done?" Bo asked. I handed him the green notebook and he sat down, took his reading glasses out of his shirt pocket and slipped them on to read. He chuckled as he came to certain parts which he repeated out loud, "only one person gets to be a teenager..."; "awesome teenager drama king..." and "I'm not your servant." He turned the book sideways, so he could read the notes I had made throughout the margins, and then he handed the notebook back to me and smiled. "This is important, what you two are doing here," he said.

He rested his hand on my knee and looked me in the eye. "I hope you'll keep this up."

I TRIED TO CONVINCE Bo to spend some time alone with Jason and Keeley when they had overnight visits with us, but he insisted on keeping everyone together. "We're a family now," he said. "Everyone best get used that idea. They'll come around, all of 'em; you'll see." They had come from such different worlds, though: Brittany had grown up in a big city and had benefited from many types of experiences with many kinds of people; Jason and Keeley had always lived on their mother's sheep ranch, relatively isolated from civilization. Having shared in the daily chores associated with life on a ranch, Jason and Keeley were no strangers to work; Brittany, on the other hand, hadn't worked a day in her life. She had always reaped the fruits of a life devoted to learning, the opportunity to discover herself and to develop talents in sports, the arts, reading and worship. Jason and Keeley, however, had not enjoyed such privileges and hadn't, when Bo and I got married, even had the experience of having friends over for a birthday party or belonging to a baseball team.

So we looked for activities Brittany, Jason and Keeley could enjoy together, starting with regular trips to the local library, where Jason and Keeley received their first-ever library cards, and outings to the Delta Recreation Center, where Brittany helped Keeley learn how to swim and Jason enjoyed watching the middle school girls play in their skimpy swimsuits. When we went camping or fishing, Jason and Keeley got to be the experts, teaching Brittany how to bait hooks, reel in fish and shoot an arrow from a bow. If Brittany had a Special Olympics practice when Jason and Keeley were visiting, Bo would bring the children to watch. As time passed, both developed a deep respect for Brittany's ability to make friends and for her tenacious athleticism—even though they were often mystified by her and had difficulty reconciling their knowledge that Brittany had reached the age of adulthood but still looked and acted like a child.

A POSITION FOR A PART-TIME news reporter opened at the *Delta County Independent.* It was the third time the position had opened since I moved to the area, and twice my applications for the job had gone unnoticed. But now I had been working for another publication and had established a foothold in the area, so my third application for a job at the DCI was a success: I got the job.

I was keeping an eye open for a full-time position, but jobs were scarce throughout the county—and getting scarcer. Bo quipped that the nation was probably heading for a recession, but we wouldn't notice it in Delta County when it finally happened: things were so tough already.

I had no medical insurance and my medical bills were mounting. I tried to keep a zero balance at the doctor's office, but the recurring visits for bladder infections stymied me. With the holidays approaching, I used my employee privileges to run free advertisements in the DCI, and I put three different sets of my jewelry up for sale for a hundred dollars a piece. When a mustachioed cowboy showed up at the house and handed me two fifty dollar bills for the pearl necklace and earring ensemble, I took the other $200 I had collected, put on my shoes and walked to the doctor's office with enough cash in my pocket to pay off my account and a feeling of utter relief radiating through my veins.

I was lucky, I told myself, that I didn't have any major medical problems—no diabetes, no heart disease, no broken bones—in fact I felt better in general than I had in years. I still had occasional back pain, but who didn't? It wasn't anything that couldn't be fixed by turning the shower to the hottest temperature possible and bending over so the water was directed toward the small of my back. And there was a small problem I sometimes had with bowel movements. Several times when I went to the bathroom there had been blood in my stool; when it happened it seemed to occur over a period of two weeks or so and then things would return to normal. When I thought about it, this did seem serious, but I didn't breathe a word of it to anyone—not my doctor, not Doran, not my mother, not even Bo. I was determined to find a full-time job with medical insurance, and I didn't want evidence of a preexisting condition limiting my coverage. So I kept the matter to myself, praying that in the end I would discover that it had been a minor problem all along.

EVEN THOUGH SPECIAL Olympics was not, strictly speaking, my "beat" at the newspaper, the editor gave me free rein to write articles about athletes and tournaments, and she even ran photographs I submitted of athletes at practices and other events sponsored by Delta Area Special Olympics. One day I was using my computer at home to review photos I had taken at a bowling practice and planned to use to draw attention to the upcoming Regional Bowling Tournament. Brittany had joined the bowling team and was at practice when I took the photos. She watched over my shoulder as I examined them, one at a time, on the computer screen.

"Which one do you think?" I asked her. "I want people to see the photo and say, 'Yes! I want to go watch this event!'"

She adjusted her glasses and moved her face closer to the screen. "'Scuse me," she said, taking the mouse from my hand.

She clicked through the photos. "That one," she said, enlarging for my view the photo of an athlete whose arms were raised in a gesture of victory.

"Yeah, that is a good one," I said. "Why don't you write the caption for it?"

She took her eyes off the screen and looked at me. "What's a caption?"

"See this photograph here," I said, pointing to the cover photo of this week's newspaper. She nodded. "The caption is right here. It's the words under the photo."

"What words I say?" she asked, warming to the idea.

I opened a word processing file on the computer, moved off my stool and gestured to her to sit down. "Well, you want to tell the name of who is in the photo and what he's doing. And then we want to tell people about the tournament, so they'll come and watch." She looked overwhelmed. "Let's start with who is in the photo?" I suggested.

"Klaus Davis."

"Right. I'll write 'Klaus Davis' on my paper; you type it, okay?" She looked at my writing on a paper and typed the letters, hunt-and-peck style, on the computer. "Good," I said. "Now, what's Klaus doing?"

"Klaus happy he got a strike," Brittany said.

Brittany practicing her archery skills at her grandmother's house in Rifle, Colorado.

"Yes, he is happy; that is how he is feeling. What is he doing?" I asked.

"He celebrating." Brittany looked on as I wrote "celebrates a strike" on my paper, and she typed the words into the computer.

When she finished, I asked "Where? Where did Klaus get the strike?"

Brittany smiled. "At Special Olympics bowling practice, silly!" She started typing before I could finish handwriting the words "at Special Olympics bowling practice in Delta" on my paper.

"Now what?" she asked as she finished.

"Well, how does anyone know that's a sentence? What do you need?" I asked.

"A capital at the beginning and a period at the end," she said in a monotone. I nodded.

In the same staccato fashion, we got through the rest of the caption, which told readers about the tournament that would draw athletes from across western Colorado to compete in Grand Junction at the end of the month. When my editor printed the photo, she ran it with this byline: Caption by Brittany Tregarthen; photo by Suzanne Bobo. Brittany saw the caption and gave a disinterested shrug, but she hovered over my shoulder as I evaluated photographs of the tournament itself, pointed to the photo she thought was best, said "'Scuse me," and positioned herself on my stool to draft the caption.

The next week she asked me to help her type an article. She had been invited to write an article for the monthly church newsletter. The article was due "tomorrow," she said, "so let's get crackin'!"

IT WAS TIME FOR MY one-year IEP conference at Brittany's high school, and I stopped at the school office to let the staff know I had arrived. Three young girls kidded and teased each other while I stood at the counter waiting to be acknowledged. Finally, I pushed the button on the bell to draw their attention my way. One girl looked up, gave another girl a friendly shove and then asked,

"Can I help you?" as if it was an afterthought. I told her why I was there, and she turned and walked into a back room, presumably to find an adult who knew where my conference would be taking place. I glanced at the clock to make sure I was on time. 12:50—a little early, I told myself. I may have to wait.

I leaned with my back to the counter and looked out over the atrium that did dual duty as the school lunch room. On the left, near the food service window I noticed three burly boys in letter jackets sitting with their chairs cocked back and laughing at something under their table. I tilted my head to look, and was surprised to see Nancy, one of the girls from Brittany's Special Ed class, on her hands and knees under the table. She had her face near the ground and was looking for something. What...? I realized she was picking up small pieces of trash. As she reached back to put some in her pocket, the boys wadded up small bits of foil from their candy wrappers and tossed them under the table. As Nancy meticulously picked up each piece, another fell, and the boys roared with laughter at their game.

I took a step toward the table and was startled by a light touch on my arm. "We're ready," a Special Ed aide said, completely unaware, it seemed, of Nancy's plight.

"Just a second," I said, motioning to the table.

"Ah," she said, and she walked to the table and crouched down. "Come on out, Nancy," she said, motioning to the girl. "You shouldn't be under there; you should be in class."

I WAS STILL UPSET ABOUT it when Bo got home and we sat together with our tea on the front porch. "Pricks!" he said. "Who were they?" I didn't know; I wish I did. If it had been Bo walking into the school he would have known them, and he would have put a stop to their humiliating little game. If only Bo had been there. Or, if Nancy's brother, a junior at the high school, if he had been there, he would have stepped in and stopped their play. I felt ashamed that I hadn't noticed what was happening sooner and that I hadn't stepped in immediately. But what would I have done? Knocked the boys off their chairs? Given them a tongue lashing? Grabbed Nancy by the hand and pulled her out from under the table? Or would I have reacted like the aide had, with words that made it sound like Nancy was at fault? You shouldn't be under there, you should be class.

"I asked Mrs. Bichon about it," I said. "She told me Nancy has a school job—it's a program that teaches kids work skills while they're still in high school—and Nancy's job is to help the custodian. That's why she was picking trash up off the floor."

"Typical." Bo said. "The Special Ed kids work in the background, for the custodian…"

"The popular kids work in the school office," I finished his sentence. "There's no reason the Special Ed kids can't work in the office, too. Stacy, for example, she would do well there."

"Stacy?" he asked.

"Stacy. The one who greeted me and Brittany the first day, that wonderful ambassador who made Brittany feel so welcome," I said. "She's articulate, she's friendly, she's helpful…"

Bo fell silent and sipped his tea. We heard the floor boards creak and knew that Brittany must have emerged from her room. Bo leaned back in his chair, opened the front door and held it ajar. "Hey, Brittany," he called into the house.

"What?" she hollered. She must be in the kitchen, I thought.

"Come out here," he said, and he leaned forward, letting the door close.

"Does Stacy have a job at the school?" he asked our daughter when she appeared on the porch. Brittany nodded. "What does she do for her job?" Bo asked.

"She help the janitor."

He leaned forward and tenderly held her shoulder in his large hand. "Don't you ever, ever, get on your hands and knees in front of anyone at that school or anywhere else, you hear me?"

BO AND I SAT ON THE front porch sipping tea and fantasizing about returning to Alaska. We had started subscribing to the *Kodiak Daily Mirror* and looking online at the Job Service announcements for the island. Housing prices seemed comparable to those in our county, but jobs were more plentiful and better paying. Bo wanted the chance to explore Alaska—to hunt mountain goats, black-tail deer and Kodiak brown bears—before he got too old. We missed the opportunity to attend worship services, felt isolated spiritually in an area where the nearest Orthodox church we could attend was more than 75 miles away. The Roman Catholic priest in Cedaredge had welcomed us warmly to services at the Catholic mission, but we couldn't have communion there, and we were missing our life in our own church. "I just don't think the children are in an emotional place, yet, where we can move," I said to Bo. "Especially Jason and Keeley, they need more time." Bo looked at the kids and nodded. "Someday, though..." I said.

Jason, Keeley and Brittany were jumping on the trampoline, and Jason was the odd man out. He wanted to do front flips; the girls insisted on crack-the-egg, and donkey kick and other games that left him, inevitably, out of the loop. Doran was working his shift at the hamburger stand; none of Jason's friends were home; and as Jason's mood soured, his hostility toward Brittany swelled. We got on him, Bo and I both, when he came into the house later and referred to Brittany as "It."

By Sunday afternoon, it seemed, the two had ironed out their differences. We sat around the table for an early supper, held hands and recited the Lord's Prayer. We had learned from experience not to seat Jason near Brittany, because he would refuse to hold hands with her and an argument always ensued. We had also convinced Brittany to give up her seat next to Bo when Jason and Keeley visited. It was a hard-won effort; she had howled at the injustice of it. But I finally helped her to understand that their time with Bo was very limited; she, on the other hand, could sit by him almost every day. With the supper-table-seating politics behind us and the prayer done, Brittany engaged Jason in a discussion about grandfathers. She had received a letter from her Grandpa Doran and she wanted to know about Jason's kin.

"I don't have a grandfather," Jason said.

"No grandfather!" Brittany said, stunned.

"No. My mom's dad died when she was very young, and my dad's dad died when I was two years old," Jason said.

As he spoke to her he looked at his food and his fork, but he looked up sharply when she said, "Oh, you poor thing! Well, you can borrow my Grandpa Doran. I don't mind."

Jason's eyes narrowed with anger. He glared at her and then at me. "Why?" he said. "Why do you get all pissy when I call her 'It,' but she can call me a 'thing,' and she doesn't get in trouble at all?"

The following weekend flew by with no episodes, tears or anger—as far as Bo and I could tell. As Sunday afternoon waned, Jason, Keeley and Brittany got on their bikes and instead of riding to the park as they usually did, they went down the dead-end road in front of our house. "They won't be long," Bo said as we sat together on the porch and watched them go.

Indeed, within minutes Keeley came back, huffing from the uphill climb. She tossed her bike to the ground and ran to Bo. "Brittany got hurt!" she said, pointing. Bo and I jumped to our feet and ran down the road, while Keeley mounted her bike and sped ahead.

At the end of the road there was a steep hillside, dense with trees and shrubs planted there to prevent motor traffic from accidentally descending. Instead of turning around where the gravel road ended, Brittany had gone over the hill on her bike; she had been frightened, Keeley said, by a deer that had darted across the road. We could see Jason on foot halfway down the hill, reaching a hand out to help Brittany climb back up the hill. From the looks of things, she and the bike must have tipped and slid some fifteen feet, under low limbs and through dense shrubbery. I grabbed Brittany's hand as she neared the crest; Bo and Jason went down the hill to retrieve her bike. She had a scratch on her upper arm, and it was bleeding a little, but otherwise she seemed okay, and when Jason brought her bike to her, she mounted it and rode ahead for home.

The four of us stood there, watching Brittany pedal away. "Geez," Jason finally said. "She didn't even cry!" He mounted his bike. "I would have been bawling," he said, as he, too, turned to ride for the house.

"Me, too," said Keeley, but she didn't mount her bike. Instead, she pushed it, striding alongside Bo and me as we joined hands and walked toward home.

Chapter Twelve

Bus Ticket

Seeing Nancy on her hands and knees at the feet of the football play-
ers was not the only shock I experienced at Brittany's IEP conference.
The other was seeing the stuff that Brittany did at school. Each school day
Brittany attended three regular education classes, but with the exception
of choir, she had never brought home any work from these classes. When
I asked her about her homework, she always said she finished it at school,
during the half day she spent in the Special Ed classroom. The explanation
seemed plausible, but I still wanted to see what she was learning, so I had
asked the woman who scheduled the IEP to have some of Brittany's class
work available for me to see.

Brittany and I joined Mrs. Bichon and four other women in a small
meeting room and we all pulled a seat up to a round conference table. In
the middle of the table was a three-inch stack of papers. About half-way
through the meeting, I was invited to look through the stack. I looked at
the top few papers, which all looked like they had been photocopied from
a first-grade pre-reading workbook. "Color the picture whose name starts
with the d sound." "Circle the picture that doesn't belong with the rest."
"Circle the pictures whose names begin with the same sound." Each page

had Brittany's name on the upper right corner, sometimes in her hand-writing, sometimes in Mrs. Bichon's.

I looked at Brittany. "So, this is, like, your busy work?" I asked, and she nodded. "Oh. Where's your geography work?" She pointed to the stack. "Your social studies, too?" I asked and she nodded. "Art?" She pointed to the stack. I riffled through the rest of the sheets, all of which were some variation of the first few, each one looking like the sort of thing she had mastered during her first year at the Lutheran grammar school.

"So, that is what she does all day?" Bo asked when I joined him later on our porch and told him about the stack of papers. "What's the point of that? What is she supposed to be learning from that?"

I shook my head. "I don't know. Maybe at this age, it's all about just learning how to be with the group, how to go with the flow. Keep quiet. Look busy," I said, but it didn't sound convincing not even to myself. "I know I shouldn't project my feelings onto her, but I believe that she can keep learning, and I hate to think that this is all there is for her now," I said. Bo stared at his teacup but said nothing. "It wouldn't be enough for me," I said.

"Nor me," my husband said quietly.

IT TURNED OUT NOT TO BE enough for Brittany. A few weeks later, with the Christmas holiday approaching, Brittany told me that she did not want to return to Delta High School after the break. "They are not teaching me what I want to know," she said, with all the confidence in the world that I would hear her. And I did, oh, how her words went straight to my heart! And though I could only wonder how I would find time, I expected to hear—was delighted to hear—the words that followed: "I want you to teach me, Mom. You teach me?" she begged.

"I can try, but I guess I need to know what it is you want to learn," I said, and my pride swelled in anticipation of the learning we would do together in geography, history, literature, the arts.

"I want to learn how to cook, how to do my own money, how to take care myself," she said, taking a pin to my puffed-up thoughts. "So I can live on my own," she added. I took in a sharp breath and looked around the room as if I would find my ego on the floor somewhere, wrinkled and deflated like a punctured balloon. "So, you'll help me?" Her voice brought my eyes back to her face, her confident beautiful face.

"Yes, I'll help you," I said, and she smiled and turned and left the room.

But she stuck her head around the corner before disappearing down the stairs. "And I want to learn how to sing better," she said through a Cheshire-cat grin.

THE DELTA COUNTY SCHOOL District had a program called Vision Home and Community Program, which provided structured support for families educating their own children. This support included a salaried mentor/liaison who helped families draft reasonable education goals, troubleshoot and stay on track. It also included financial resources for approved purchases related to meeting students' educational goals, and a graduation ceremony and school district diploma upon the successful completion of one's studies.

When Brittany and I had our first meeting with Don Pyle, our Vision HCP resource expert, we had already drafted a set of goals Brittany wanted to achieve for graduation. He helped us break the goals down into a semester-by-semester plan, and to write a budget for the first semester that he would submit on our behalf for approval. Brittany's goals included several things that had been on the life map she had made three years earlier: physical fitness, health, and singing. Her new goals she expressed as: manage my own money; spend time with my family; take care of myself and do my own cooking.

With Mr. Pyle's help, the breakdown for the first semester became: Health/Fitness—work out two hours a week in Special Olympics and two hours a week weightlifting at the gym; Singing—take a weekly voice lesson with a private tutor and complete whatever the tutor assigns for practices; Family--keep track of family birthdays and purchase and mail a birthday card for each person in time for their birthday, and contact Tim by telephone every Saturday unless already visiting him; Money—work at least two hours a week at a job using a time sheet to track hours; Personal Care—make own bed daily and do all own laundry; Cooking—using a microwave, cook own meals for breakfast and lunch.

We submitted a budget request for funding for the gym membership, mileage to and from fitness practices, weekly voice lessons and mileage to and from the tutor's house, a small microwave oven, an electronic can opener, various kitchen utensils and some basic school supplies. Our request was accepted without modification, and we were good to go.

Within the first week Brittany made one change to her list of goals. When she found out that Mr. Pyle had been a Spanish teacher, she asked him to include a Spanish lesson in the once-a-week trips he made to our house, and he agreed. "Spanish" became another bullet point on Brittany's master list of things-she-wanted-to-do.

Finding a job turned out to be the most difficult thing for Brittany to accomplish: few employers would even consider hiring a first-time worker, let alone one who needed a lot of coaching. I had only just begun the process of applying for Social Security Disability benefits for Brittany, which would include some sort of vocational training, but the process would take months to complete. It was important for Brittany to understand the relationship between work and reward, to commit to a regular work schedule and to track her hours, however, so we came up with a plan that satisfied Brittany, me and Mr. Pyle: Brittany would volunteer two days a week at the animal shelter, she would record her volunteer hours on a time sheet and every two weeks she would turn the sheet in to me. Bo and I would compensate her for her time.

Brittany later wrote:

> I worked at the animal shelter. I cleaned the cages of the cats and gave them fresh water and food. And I would hold them, especially the kittens. The feral cats downstairs I can't hold them because they're wild; they might scratch me. After I'm done working there I have to wash my hands, and when I get home I have to put the clothes I was wearing in the laundry basket.

> I worked with Rich. He was awesome and so smart, an awesome boss. Then Rich quit the job because he wasn't making enough money and someone new started. So I quit, because I didn't want to work there any more.

> Then I worked at the community center for awhile, helping to get lunches ready for the elders. I had to wear a hair wrap. Ugh. That was boring. I had to stand up for a long time, and I can't stand that long. It hurt my feet. So I left that job.

> Then I worked at the Community Methodist Church. The boss there was Kathy Shelby. I loved her so much, because she was a good friend, and I liked their church. I folded the church bulletins for Kathy so she could get them ready for Sunday. I worked there for almost a year. On the 28th of September I had to work on my birthday. After I got all my work done, Kathy said, 'There's someone coming over and bringing something, but I can't tell you what it is.' It was a birthday celebration; our friend Merriam brought a Sonic chili cheese dog, and chili cheese fries, and a soda and a dessert on my birthday. And Pastor Deb was there, and somebody bought me flowers with a balloon. It was a great day!

Brittany and I opened a joint checking account, which we used for her educational expenses and the compensation we received from the school district. After Brittany turned in her biweekly time sheet, Bo or I wrote her a check drawn on our account, and she and I walked to the bank, where she would use her new, state-issued ID to cash her checks. She quickly earned a reputation as a connoisseur of one dollar bills, and after the third time cashing her check, the tellers knew to pay her in ones, which, Brittany said, made her feel "richer." We did not require her to leave money in the bank for savings, knowing it would be too hard for her visualize, but she did have a jar at home where she kept money, often for several paychecks at a time, until she had enough to buy the things she wanted.

DORAN HAD SAVED ENOUGH money to buy a used car and now had a new job, working as a librarian for the Delta County Library System in the Delta branch. He had been tasked with developing programs to bring youth into the library and was sponsoring an event on a Saturday when Jason and Keeley were visiting. We were all sitting on the front porch enjoying the last shade of a summer morning when Doran suggested that Bo and I bring all the kids to the library for his program. Jason and Keeley perked up immediately. "Can we ride with you?" Jason asked.

"Well, yes, on the way, but you'll be leaving before I get off," Doran said.

"I know," Jason said. "Cool."

"Why don't we take swim stuff and go to the Rec center afterwards," I suggested, and it was Keeley's turn to say "Cool." She and Jason jumped to their feet and went inside to pack their swimming things.

"Can I invite Dave?" Brittany asked.

Doran, Bo and I exchanged glances. There was a name we hadn't heard in a while.

"You still seeing him, Sis?" Doran asked.

"Well, not really," she answered. "But can I invite him?"

I shrugged and looked at Bo, who also shrugged. "Okay," I said. "We'll be leaving soon, though."

"I know," Brittany said, and she got up and went inside. We listened in silence as the creaking of floor assured us of Brittany's retreat from the front of the house.

"Whatever happened with him?" Doran asked.

"I have no idea. She just stopped calling him finally," I said.

"It was a real surprise to me," Bo said. "Surprised the hell out of me that she would want to be home-schooled when all she could talk about every day was Dave this, Dave that. I mean the fact that he was on the school bus every day was a real plus for getting her on that bus on time."

"I know," I said. "She still sees him at Special Olympics practices," I said, looking at Doran. "But he dropped off her radar for everything else until…just now," I finished quickly, hearing Brittany's footsteps approaching the door.

"So, is he coming, Sis?" Doran asked.

"No, nobody answered the phone," she said. "He's just a big jerk!"

Years later as Brittany and I worked on this book together I told Brittany I had reached the point where I would be writing about Dave. "Ugh, don't," she said.

"Why?"

"He's way beyond history," she said. "I don't want to think about him."

"Well, what about the parts I've already written and the parts you wrote in the green notebook? Can we keep those?" I asked.

"Okay, we keep those. But no more!"

I smiled. "I understand," I said. "I had a very hard time writing about my divorce." She looked into my face. "I didn't want to write about it at all."

She smiled. "Why don't we just leave them out, both of them!" she suggested. "It's our book."

"It's a book about our life, though, and they were parts of our life."

"Okay, but just a little bit," she said, holding her forefinger and thumb together to show me that Dave and Tim merited a half inch at the most. "But I want Dave's photograph to go in the corner," she added. "And the caption should say (air quote) Ex-boyfriend in the corner, where he belongs! (air quote)"

> My ex-boyfriend Dave, he always was a selfish jerk to me and other girls. He blamed me for his bus ticket; I did nothing wrong. Also, he would never call me, and he didn't answer the phone when I called him. Also, he promises a girl out on a date, then suddenly he would say (at the bowling alley): I'm gonna dump you for Dawn. And Dawn is more good-looking than you. To me, it felt like Dave didn't like a girl with Down Syndrome.

> Then suddenly, he dumped Dawn and was going out with Ailene. Then he dumped her for another girl named Shannon. It means that Dave will always do this to girls: just date you, then cheat on you and dump you. That's one jealousy way!!!

> Charles was so cute, and he loved me a lot. At Dave's graduation Dawn and I were talking where we were sitting, and Dawn asked Charles: Are you someday going to marry Brittany? And Charles said: Uh, yeah. But I say I'd rather not; I think I'll find another guy.

> Charles didn't talk very much, he could say my name and talk to me for a while, but mostly he was very shy and spent his time alone or with Dave. Charles will never be independent; he can't do much for himself. But he sure was cute.

> Tommy used to be kind of my best friend until he hangs around with Dave, then I have to leave his friendship. And Tommy was with Dave all the time.

As I typed Brittany's entry into the computer, I puzzled over her words "blamed me for his bus ticket," and I called her upstairs to explain it to me.

Ex-boyfriends in the corner, where they belong.

"Dave got in trouble on the school bus. Tafney (the driver) gave him a ticket," she said.

"What's a ticket?"

"Like a bad thing. It says you can't ride on the bus the rest of the week."

"Ah. Then what happened?"

"Dave blamed me. When I got to school he told the others and they blame me. After school I walk around the corner and Dawn and Dave and Tommy and Jacob were there and they jumped me and they holded my arms behind my back and they hurt me!"

I was speechless. How could this have happened? How could she have not told me?

"Dave's a stupid Super-jerk," Brittany said. "I did not go to that school any longer!"

IN THE FALL OF 2006 an extraordinary thing happened: the Internet finally reached our house! I had been writing my articles at home on my personal computer, copying them to a floppy disk and then driving to the library where I would wait in line to use a computer to access the Internet and file my stories. With the World Wide Web right there on my dining room table, my writing career would be transformed! I could send my stories right after I wrote them! I could attach photos! I could do research without driving to town!

I was spending more time at home helping Brittany take progressively more challenging steps toward meeting her educational goals, and the ability to do research at home dramatically improved my productivity. The Internet also helped me develop new ideas for freelance stories, and I successfully pitched these ideas to several of my publishers. It was an awesome tool, and a welcome one.

Brittany watched as I worked my way across the web, and within days of seeing the Internet's potential for me, she learned how to tap into it for herself—to find song lyrics, Disney movie trailers, and web sites devoted to the child actors that had become, for her, like not-so-distant cousins. On the Internet, she discovered, she could learn the important stuff: when each actor was born (including the year, month, day and, often, the time); the actors' middle names; where they lived; what they ate; and whether they had pets.

She did this research with permission and always at the dining room table with me in the room. One day she typed "Judith Barsi" into the search box and pushed enter. Barsi had done the voice-overs for many of Brittany's favorite movies, including *All Dogs Go to Heaven* and *Land Before Time*. Brittany wanted to know more about her; have a face to associate with the voice. Within cyber seconds, Brittany found herself on a site dedicated to the memory of Judith Barsi and two other child actresses, Jon Benet Ramsey and Heather O'Rourke. Each actress had met a tragic end—Barsi had been murdered by her father in Hollywood, Ramsey's unsolved murder had taken place on Christmas, and O'Rourke had died from complications of Crohn's disease. There was nothing I could do about it: Brittany's web search had brought her face-to-face with horrid details of each young girl's death.

For the next few days, Brittany talked about nothing except the deaths of these girls. When I left the house to go for a walk or to run an errand I would find her on the computer when I got home, scrolling down the screen to read every horrible detail and transcribing the text on a sheet of paper. I would disable the computer when I left the house, only to find her up in the middle of the night sneaking peaks when she thought everyone was asleep. At a friend's house or at work she would ask to use the computer and she would find the web site and, if it was possible, she would print the terrible text, which she would then conceal in her bedroom. And she would write the details over and over again, on lined sheets of paper, as if she was trying to engrave the words on her memory.

I called these writings "Brittany's Barsi papers," and I did random searches of Brittany's room to find them. "Why are you writing this stuff?" I would demand.

"I don't know. I just want to know what happened," she would answer.

"Well, you know what happened. It isn't good for you to keep writing about it over and over," I would say, and I would wad her papers up and throw them in a garbage bag. "You need to stop writing about this stuff."

"I will, I will," she would answer, furious that I was invading her room and messing with her stuff. But the next day I would find the awful details written on another sheet of paper in Brittany's small, neat script.

After several months of the same scene—the tragic stories in her handwriting, my outbursts, her anger—she finally took her writing in a new direction. She invented several fictional characters and started writing stories about them. Chapter One always involved travel: a ten- or twelve-year-old hero ready for adventure, his family, their suitcases, a taxi taking them to the airport. Promising material, except that Brittany's hero was always brutally murdered in Chapter Two, usually in a basement wine cellar, the place Ramsey's body had been found. I would read these, feel my blood boil and not be able to control myself: "Murdered, again?!"

"Mom! You hate my writing!"

"I hate that everyone gets murdered."

It was obvious that Brittany was struggling to deal with death, and I knew this struggle had a lot to do with her experiences with her dad. When she was younger she worked through some of her feelings with toys—she had even convinced me to knit a funeral shroud for her Ken doll—but Brittany's obsession with writing about murders was more threatening to me than the play therapy of her childhood. Like music, the written word has a powerful influence on the soul, and it concerned me that Brittany's literary fixation would be, ultimately, harmful to her and not cathartic. But I wasn't a psychologist, and I couldn't afford to hire one so I dealt with the situation as best I could. One day as she sat down at the computer and started a new Chapter One, I told her, "I understand your character is probably going to die." She looked at me defensively.

"That's okay," I said, and her look changed to one of suspicion. "But before he dies, I want you to write five chapters about his life."

"What do you mean?"

"Where he lives. Where he goes to school. What kinds of things he likes. His family. Let him live for five chapters, and then you can kill him. Deal?"

"Deal," she said, smiling and sticking out a hand to shake mine.

Chapter Thirteen

Showtime

Brittany was on target to complete her education goals and graduate with other Vision HCP students in May, 2007. Through each of her three semesters in the home school program we had adapted her "independent living" curriculum, challenging her to achieve higher levels of proficiency in managing her time, being a responsible employee, developing and cooking an appropriate menu, sticking to her gluten-free diet, planning an evening hosting guests at home, developing a grocery list and taking care of herself at home when Bo and I were working. We adapted her physical fitness curriculum, too, switching from weight lifting to ice skating and then bike riding, to keep her interested and active in the fitness goal. She continued to learn basic Spanish vocabulary words with Mr. Pyle, and even got his assistance writing the lyrics of the hymn "Silent Night" in Spanish, so that it became "Noche de Paz."

She continued taking weekly voice lessons with the tutor in Delta, and received permission to add her new Spanish Christmas song to the repertoire she practiced there. The tutor met her students at her home, a 1920s-era bungalow, facing a large city park in Delta. When the weather permitted, I sat on the front steps while I waited for Brittany, and I watched people play in the park with their kids and dogs. If the weather was bad, I *waited in the tutor's sitting room, where I could watch Brittany practice while the tutor coached her and accompanied her on the piano.*

After three semesters in choir classes at the high school and three semesters in private lessons, Brittany had improved various aspects of her performance ability. She maintained a professional posture, engaged her audience appropriately and introduced herself and her performance piece with grace. She could tap her foot or snap her fingers in tempo with the rhythm of the music, memorize lyrics, get enough breath to vocalize and even recognize that the musical notes on a page hold clues about the melody. After eighteen months of individual lessons, she even had managed to increase her range and now comfortably sang in a mezzo-soprano voice, a surprise to me, given the depth of her speaking voice.

But with our time in private lessons coming to an end, Brittany still couldn't read music, couldn't translate the notes from the page into appropriate sounds vocally or on the piano and couldn't imitate a melody she heard. Nor could she control the pitch or vibration of her voice, or hear when she was singing too softly or too loud.

She was completely unbothered by these limitations. She was going to become a child star, she was sure of it—just like Charlotte Church and Billy Gilman and the other child prodigies she researched on the Internet.

BRITTANY SAT AT THE computer working on Chapter One of a book about a boy named Jonathan. She had kept her end of our bargain, and was writing a life for her characters before killing them. She had written several scenes in Jonathan's life, with each scene constituting its own chapter. She had never been much of a fiction reader, and as a consequence, she had difficulty describing the scenes she envisioned. Her chapters resembled movie scripts more than they did books, with their central dramas emerging through dialog and action. She was dissatisfied with her writings about Jonathan, however, and she had dragged all of her chapters about his life into the computer's recycle bin. His story was beginning anew.

I sat across the room at another computer. I was finishing a five-part series about my grandfather, a trail rider and nature photographer. I had inherited several boxes containing his photographs, negatives, slides and log books. One night when all four children were home I had shown the family some of the artifacts and told stories about how my grandfather had lugged his cameras into remote areas on horseback and how the Forest Service later used his photographs to make maps and catalog Rocky Mountain flora. Bo convinced me to develop a series of articles about my grandfather's life. I had pitched the idea to one of my publishers, and to my delight, the publisher agreed to print the entire series in five consecutive journals. After months of research and writing, I was nearly done with the project.

"Mom?" Brittany said. She had stopped typing and had turned in her chair to look at me.

"Hmmm?"

"What's that weird name, your weird name on your articles?"

"You mean my pen name?" I asked, and she nodded. I smiled. "Why do you call it 'weird'? You helped me choose it."

"I don't know. It's just—weird," she said.

"Hunter Lee." I answered. She stared at her computer screen, rubbed her chin with her hand and whispered my pen name several times. Then she turned to face me again.

"I've got it!" she said, beaming. "I've got a pen name."

"Oh, what is it?" I asked.

"Junior," she said. "Junior Lee."

"That's funny," I said, laughing.

"I know it is," she said, giggling. "Junior Lee. Junior Lee. Junior Lee. Junior Lee."

WORKING WITH MR. PYLE, Brittany submitted a list of people who would be good candidates to serve on her graduation committee, which would evaluate Brittany's progress in relation to the standards she had established for herself. Through the Vision

HCP, the committee would recommend either that Brittany continue another year in home school or that the school district award her a high school diploma certifying completion of an accredited program of study. After Brittany's list was approved, she had to complete another requirement of her degree: a "public demonstration" of her educational prowess.

Mr. Pyle told us about the demonstrations other students were doing. One student, who had been studying mechanics in home school, was going to dismantle the engine of a motorcycle and reassemble it within the span of hour—with his graduation committee as his audience. Another student had emphasized art in her studies; a local gallery would feature an exhibit of her work and a meet-the-artist session in which she would answer questions. For Brittany's public demonstration she decided she would host a luncheon in mid-December for which she would do the planning, shopping, cooking, decorating and cleaning. During the luncheon she would do a demonstration of her cooking skills and answer questions about her goals for independent living.

She and I sat at the dining room table one day and began brainstorming the guest list. As she suggested names we decided it would be best to draft two lists: one list of people she would invite to her graduation ceremony and party and a second, smaller, list of people who would come for the demonstration.

"I want everybody to see," she initially had protested.

"Yes, but we have to do it inside our house, and our house is tiny," I reminded her.

"Oh, yeah," she said, and we were able to whittle the list down to fifteen people: the three members of her graduation committee, Mr. Pyle, the voice tutor, the people who had been Brittany's supervisors at work, several teachers from Delta School District's Special Education Department, and Bo and I.

As Brittany and I printed the invitations, it occurred to me to ask one more person. "Is it okay if we invite Pat?" I asked Brittany.

"Pat? You mean your editor at the DCI?" she asked.

I nodded. "If Pat writes an article about you, other people can learn about becoming independent."

"Okay," Brittany said, and she coaxed the computer to print another invitation, which she handed to me. "Take one to Pat."

I EMPTIED A LOAD OF dirty laundry into the washer downstairs and stopped in Brittany's room to have a look. The room was a wreck: papers piled everywhere, CDs and DVDs in heaps, clothes on the floor. The bed, at least, was made.

I picked a piece of lined paper off the floor and looked at it. Brittany had drawn three shapes that looked like Us with a bar across the top. Each one had a symbol on it; one looked like an H; the other two were the same but were meaningless to me. I rotated the paper so the Us looked like Ds, but that didn't help clarify things. I rotated it again. Oh. I took a heavy breath. Tombstones with the initials: "H," "J," and "J"—Heather, Judith and Jon Benet.

"You're still obsessing over this?" I said, startling Brittany, who was sitting at the computer.

"Mom! What are you doing in my room!?"

"Finding tombstones!" I said, holding out the drawing. "Why are you doing this?"

"You should learn to stay out of my room!" Her face was red with anger.

"Why, Brittany?" I was calmer now, but still upset.

"I don't know." She looked away from me. "I'm sorry. I'll stop."

Silence hung between us as we both allowed our hurt to subside. Finally, I sank down into the chair next to hers at the computer table.

"Mom? What is Crohn's disease, anyway?" she asked. I could feel the blank look on my face. "Crohn's disease," she repeated. "What Heather O'Rourke died from."

"Oh, um…hmmm…I'm not really sure what it is," I said. "I had a student who had it once and he almost never could come to school. I always put work in a box for his mom to pick up and take

Brittany chose this photograph, taken in the front yard of the Cedaredge house, for her graduation announcements.

home to him. I think he was sick to his stomach all the time. The last time I saw him he was very, very thin and pale."

"Poor thing!" she said, and I felt sad thinking about him. I had spent an entire semester as his teacher and saw him in class only three times. Never really talked to him or learned much about him. None of the teachers had. What had become of him, I wondered to myself.

"No more of these," I said as I grabbed the tombstone paper and stood. "I need to finish dinner, and you," I said, pointing at her, "you need to go tend to your room." She started to protest, but thought better of it and headed immediately for the stairs, a sure sign that she had more tombstones down there.

BRITTANY CARRIED GROCERY bags into the house and set them on the dining room table while Bo and I unpacked our purchases, putting the family food in the pantry, the food for Brittany's demonstration on one end of the counter and the food Brittany would use to cook her own meals in the plastic bins reserved for that use in the refrigerator and under the microwave cabinet.

We had done our shopping in Delta, stopped at the bank and picked up a package at the post office. It was only three in the afternoon, but we were already weary from a long day. Doran's girlfriend Ashley would be joining us for dinner, and I was anxious to get the house tidied up and dinner started. I needed a second wind. "I'll put the tea on," I told Bo, "that'll put the lifeblood back in us."

"Good idea," he said, and he took a grocery bag of toiletries to the bathroom to put away.

I stood in the kitchen, listening to the rattle of the water in the tea kettle and humming to myself. It was a tune from an old Irish ballad. I never learned the name of the song, but somehow it always came to mind when I was waiting for tea. The kettle whistled and I set it on the back burner while I put the tea bags in our mugs and spooned out sugar. I placed the mugs on a tray, singing my song absent-mindedly, humming again where the notes were too high or where I had forgotten the lyrics.

"Stop singing," Brittany said as she rounded the corner with the last grocery bag. "It's annoying."

"That isn't very nice!" I said, facing her.

"I don't...just stop," she said. "I don't like it."

Bo stepped into kitchen. "Your mother has a beautiful voice. I love to hear her sing," he said.

Brittany made a talk-to-the-hand gesture, looked down at the bag she was carrying, and said, "It bugs me."

"That's rude!" Bo said. Brittany set the bag on the counter and walked toward the hallway to go to her room. "You always want people to listen to your singing," he called after her. "It's rude to tell other people that they can't sing!

"And it's rude to turn your back and walk away!" he added down the stairs after her.

BRITTANY WANTED TO DRESS up for her public demonstration, so we went to the secondhand store in Delta and found a black and red dress that made her look professional and sophisticated. She balked at my suggestion to wear panty hose, but let me talk her out of wearing athletic shoes and chose instead a pair of black slip-on dress shoes we had found at a yard sale. She had moved a small desk from her room into the living room, set a chair to one side of the table and "Voila!" had a "reception desk," where she had blank name tags, a black marker and a sign-up sheet ready for her guests.

She laid out the snacks attractively on the dining room table with disposable napkins, plates and cups in blue with a white snowflake motif, the same theme she had used on the invitations to the event. She had the materials for a cooking demonstration set up in the kitchen, along with a notebook she had kept to help her track family birthdays and mail out birthday cards. At 11:45 a.m. her first guest arrived—Marcy Peterson, an adult friend Brittany had requested to be on her graduation committee. When Brittany saw Marcy walking on the path out front, she dispensed with the formality of the reception desk and ran outside to greet her friend.

"Get a photo," I heard her yell as the screen door slammed shut, so I grabbed the camera and joined the two of them on the front porch. "A photo," Brittany said to Marcy, and they posed, arms around each other, broad smiles on their faces.

A tan SUV pulled into our driveway, followed by a small pick-up truck. I tapped Brittany lightly on the shoulder and pointed them out to her. "It's showtime," I said, and she grabbed Marcy's hand and pulled her into the house. She slipped behind the reception desk and handed Marcy the marker, "Name tag," she said curtly and then she pointed to the sign-up sheet, "Sign in, please."

Marcy smiled and teased, "Name tag! You know who I am."

"The other peoples don't!" Brittany said. Marcy concealed a smile as she, obediently, filled out the tag, peeled off the backing and attached it to her blouse.

Bo had to work, and the people who had been Brittany's job supervisors were likewise unable to attend, so a small but suitably name-tagged group of people gathered around our dining room table for snacks and then in our tiny kitchen for the demonstration. I gave a brief introduction to Brittany's home school program, deferring to Mr. Pyle where it seemed appropriate. I also introduced the group to the concept of Celiac disease and explained why Brittany's ability to cook gluten-free meals for herself was a critical element in her ability to manage her disease and to live independently.

From there, Brittany took over, making a Rocky Road Pudding recipe she had selected. She showed the audience how using color-coded recipes and measuring cups helped her overcome her inability to understand the math involved in cooking. She demonstrated how her recipes all featured a picture of a white measuring cup to indicate "one cup," a picture of a blue measuring cup to indicate "1/2 cup," and a picture of a red measuring cup to indicate "1/4 cup." Then she successfully measured ingredients into a bowl, using a white cup two times for 2 cups of milk; a blue measuring cup for 1/2 cup marshmallows, and a red measuring cup for 1/4 cup nuts. After she vigorously stirred her creation, she set it in the refrigerator and asked if there were any questions.

A lively question-and-answer session followed, and Brittany performed beautifully. I could see that she was getting tired, though, so I diverted the group's attention to Brittany's birthday notebook. I held up the notebook open and showed everyone that Brittany had made a list of the months with each family member's birthday listed under the appropriate month.*

"I don't need the list, though," Brittany piped in.

"No, she does not. She remembers everybody's birthday," I said. I pointed out that each individual family member had his or her own pocket divider in the notebook and that the pocket

*The kitchen system and birthday notebook were programs developed by Nancy Baesman of Littleton, Colorado, and sold through her company, Visions for Independent Living.

contained labels with the person's mailing address pre-printed on them.

"So, when some peoples have a birthday, I get money from my money bag and ride my bike to the store and buy a card," Brittany said. "I leave a note on the table telling my parents where I am. When I come back I get the people's mailing address and stick it on the ventilope, then I write my name in the card and put it in, then I put on the stamps that are here, see," she said, taking the notebook in her own hands and pointing out the sheet of stamps in the front. "Then, voila, I mail it!"

"And you just get on your bike and go to the store?" someone asked.

"Yep. I leave a note," she answered confidently.

"What's that like, Mom?" Pat, the newspaper editor, asked.

"It was scary at first," I said, surprised by the question. "My heart always skips a beat if I'm away from home and I call and she doesn't answer."

"But she knows what she's doing," I said, and I meant it.

Brittany wrapped up the demonstration at 1:30, showed her guests to the door and thanked everyone for coming. "I'm exhausted," she said. "I'm going to bed."

"Uh-uh," I said. "This is the part where we clean up and talk about all the fun we had. C'mon, there's not much to do. Your guests didn't leave many leftovers!"

"Ooo-kaaaay," she said and she walked stiff-legged to the table. "How come Rich didn't come, or Kathy?" she asked.

"Probably had to work," I said. "Don't worry about it. Look who all came."

Brittany stacked all the unused paper products on top of each other and carried the bundle to the kitchen. "Do you think Pat will write an article?" she asked, as she returned for the last few items remaining on the table.

"I think she will," I said. I gave her a hug and patted her on the bum. "You can go rest now. You did well."

Bo, Suzanne, and Brittany walking with Charley in Cedaredge.
(Photo by Bob Borchardt.)

Pat's article appeared several weeks later, a full-page, four-color feature she had titled "The Quest for Independence." I was reading the article for the second time when Bo pulled into the driveway. He joined me on the front porch and smiled when I handed him the paper.

"Well, I guess this qualifies as a 'public' demonstration," he said, putting on his glasses to read.

"No kidding," I said. I smiled at my husband. "She's modified her goals," I said.

He looked at me. "What do you mean?"

"Read it."

"Brittany Tregarthen has clear-cut goals for her future. She's even written them down, with marriage topping the list....Uh-oh," Bo said.

"Uh-oh," I repeated.

DURING THE HOME-SCHOOL months the green notebook got very little attention. But one special day stood out for Brittany and she asked me one afternoon to write an entry she wanted to call "Graduation Day."

GRADUATION DAY

I was so nervous on my graduation day. When they called my name I was nervous. I stood there until the speaker—the one who introduced me—was done. Then I went back to my seat. My Daddy Bo was the speaker; his name is Don Edward Bobo. He is a good speaker.

After they called everyone's names we went to the party. The party was awesome.

I cut the cake—a cake I could have. I cut a big piece for myself!

I saw my best friends there and my parents and family members.

Then everybody went home, well, not exactly because my mom and me, my Aunt Bonnie, my little cousin Emily, my Grandma Flo and my dad were there cleaning up from the party.

THE DAY AFTER BRITTANY'S graduation Bo and I sat on the front porch sipping tea and recounting the previous day's highlights. It had been a brilliant party; we had rented the community center, cooked a huge dinner and baked a graduation cake. Jason and Keeley had helped with the decorating, and Doran with the cooking. A DJ played fabulous music and teased and encouraged Brittany as she danced with her family, her friends and her young cousin Emily. Her grandparents had come from California and from Rifle; Tim had come from Colorado Springs, assisted by David who once had been his home-care nurse. Ashley had been there, stealing kisses from Doran in the kitchen, gifts had been opened, stories shared, congratulations extended.

"Two done," I said to Bo. "Two more to go."

"Yep. But a wedding between now and then," he said, reaching for my hand. "Boy, I tell you what, once that boy makes up his mind about something there's no stopping him."

"No kidding," I said. "Doran's always been that way. He loves Ashley. Come hell or high water, he'll marry her *soon*, mark my words."

"Yes he will," Bo said. He took a sip of tea; then he shifted his weight in his chair and cleared his throat. "Now that Brittany's done with her schooling, I sure would like to see you get back to that project you were doing with her...the green notebook."

"We kind of let that fall by the wayside," I said. "But this summer we'll pick it up again, I promise. I have some ideas for how I'll write my parts of the book; I'm ready to get them in some kind of order."

He smiled and squeezed my hand. "Whatever it takes," he said. "You two need to get that done."

Chapter Fourteen

Time Doesn't Work

Bo was in the bathroom shaving while I was taking a shower. It had been a pleasant evening, cooler than normal for August with a light breeze. We had stopped at a roadside produce stand and bought a grocery bag stuffed with fresh-picked Olathe sweet corn. We shucked and steamed the corn immediately after we got home and ate it on the front porch, where we laughed as salty butter dripped down our forearms. Doran and Ashley joined us for a while and we chatted and watched a mule deer doe and her two fawns munching on apples that had fallen from a tree across the street. Brittany excused herself from our company and sat at the dining room table, where she was got busy copying song lyrics from sheets printed off the computer to her own lined notebook paper. She worked on her songs while the rest of us took a walk around the neighborhood, conversing happily as the long summer day slowly came to a close. We walked at a slower pace than normal for my sake, because the pain in my lower back had returned with a vengeance. It helped to stretch it out by walking, but I was in no mood to hurry, and neither was anybody else.

Now I was bent over in the shower, letting the hot water work its magic, adjusting my position to target the water on the spot that hurt the most.

"Looks like you're in exercise class," Bo said, chuckling.

"Yeah, well at least I can still touch my toes!" I said playfully.

"Yeah, well, we won't discuss whether I can," he said.

Bo fell asleep as soon as his head hit the pillow, but I could not find a position that gave me any comfort. It ached if I lay sideways, throbbed if I lay on my back, stabbed if I lay on my stomach. I felt an urgency to use the bathroom several times, thinking I would have a bowel movement, but each time I just sat on the toilet until I got too cold or too sleepy to sit up any longer, and then I went back to bed. Several hours into the night I got extremely hot and kicked off the covers, sweat now adding to my discomfort. Soon after, I felt a chill. I wrapped myself in the blanket and lay there, shivering, pushing my body against Bo's for warmth.

I WOKE TO THE SOUND of Bo puttering in the kitchen, and I knew that he must have the coffee ready. I sat upright on the bed and reached for my robe, which I had left on the bedpost. I felt a stabbing pain in my lower right abdomen and thought that I would cry from the shock of it. I took in a shallow breath, slipped on my robe and got to my feet.

"You up?" I heard Bo yell from the kitchen. "It's 9:00. I didn't think you were ever—what's wrong?" He stood in the doorway and saw me, hunched over, making slow progress to the dining room table. He set the coffee cups on the table and came to my side, supporting me as I lowered myself into a chair. I put my elbow on the table and rested my head in my hand.

"It hurts so bad," I said. I was shaking from the effort of speech. "I was awake all night."

"Where does it hurt the most?" he asked, and I pointed to lower right abdomen, then my back.

"It feels like I swallowed a wheelbarrow," I said, trying to make a joke.

"We need to get you to the doctor," Bo said. "Now."

I called my physician's office and told them I thought I might have a raging bladder infection, but the receptionist told me Dr.

Wade was leaving at noon and wouldn't be back until Monday. He had no openings until then. I asked about his partner and was told she no longer worked with him. "Dr. Craig now works with Dr. Smith in Delta," she said.

I thanked her and rang up Dr. Smith's office. "I'm afraid it may be my appendix," I said, looking for the words that would get me seen today.

"Dr. Craig can see you as soon as you can get in," the receptionist told me.

Bo helped me get dressed and wrote a note to Brittany, who was still sleeping. I was concerned about leaving her but knew how terrified she would be if we woke her now. "We probably won't be very long," I said out loud, trying to convince myself. "How long does it take to pee in a cup?"

But Dr. Craig didn't give me a cup. She asked questions, pushed on my belly and put on her stethoscope to listen to my abdomen. Then she straightened up and said. "Here's what I am going to do. I am calling the ER, and you're going to go right over there. They'll be expecting you. Please don't make any detours."

"'Kay," I said. I looked at the worried expression on my husband's face and hot tears streamed down my cheeks.

The ER nurse asked if I thought I would be capable of giving a urine sample, and I said I would. She handed me a cup and gestured toward the bathroom. When I returned she walked me to an ER bay, gave me a gown and pulled the curtain closed as she walked away. When the lab tech opened the curtain, I was resting on my back on the bed, with the blankets around me, holding tightly to Bo's strong hand. The nurse entered the room with pain medication, which I refused, because I didn't want to be doped up if the kids came to see me. Still, I faded in and out of consciousness as the minutes in the ER turned into hours and numerous tests were performed.

Bo called Doran at the library and a friend in Cedaredge who agreed to pick up Brittany and bring her to the hospital. He held my hand as the fevers came and went, answered the doctors' questions when I faltered, and demanded the attention of a nurse when an IV needle collapsed the vein in my right arm. When Doran and Brittany arrived he soothed them, and I could hear him on his cell phone, calling my mother, sister and brother in Rifle.

After Bo took Brittany home that night I accepted a dose of pain medication, but I was unable to sleep. The doctors had given me foul-tasting stuff for what they called a "bowel prep," a horrible experience that resulted in me sitting on the toilet for the first half of the night. The awful prospect of the colonoscopy I knew was awaiting me in the morning weighed heavy on my nerves. When I finally went to bed I couldn't sleep because I kept experiencing "night sweats." Three times I drenched the bed with sweat and sat up waiting for the staff to bring me a change of nightclothes and dry bed linens.

Bo and Brittany sat beside me the next morning when the hospital surgeon came to my room and leaned against the foot of my bed. "It looks like you'll be in here for a while," she said. "The results from your colonoscopy are virtually conclusive. We are waiting for results from a biopsy, but we're virtually certain you have Crohn's disease."

"What!" Brittany said. "Crohn's disease? What Heather O'Rourke died from?" She looked at the surgeon and then at Bo, but neither one seemed to hear her. I heard her, but I avoided looking at her. Her words hung heavy in the air; I couldn't bear the weight of them or the fear I knew was lurking behind them.

AS THE SURGEON HAD predicted, I stayed in the hospital for a long time. One friend checked in for a knee replacement and another had triple-bypass heart surgery and both were admitted and released while I sat in my hospital room waiting for my intestines to "rest." I was allowed to drink clear liquids, but all other nourishment had to go through my IV.

Bo brought Brittany to see me every day, and on the long weekend he had Jason and Keeley he brought them to see me, too. It was the day before his 58th birthday, and he grumbled that he didn't need to celebrate it, but I made the girls promise they would do right by him. Brittany called Marcy, who helped her make a chocolate raspberry cake—Bo's favorite—with gluten-free flour, and Keeley talked Doran into giving them all a ride to a shop where they found some presents they thought Bo would like. Our neighbor friend Verity came to the house to bring birthday candles and to help them sing happy birthday, and Doran teased Bo by bringing a fire extinguisher to the table. Bo called me from the house, to include me in the celebration. He started to ask me if I wanted him to bring me some cake; then remembered I still wasn't allowed to have any real food.

Finally, I was given permission to reintroduce solid foods into my diet, put on a prescription combination (prednisone, an antibiotic and sulfasalazine), scheduled for an appointment with a gastroenterologist in Grand Junction and sent home. I was weak and sore, but the prednisone duped me into thinking I was capable, and I tried to catch up on all the chores I had left undone and the stories I had left unwritten. Every day around 1:00 p.m., though, my system seemed to shut down and I felt like I spent the rest of the day dragging my body around like some unwieldy sack of potatoes.

"You're just going to have to learn to slow down," Bo told me one day. I had carried the remote phone to the south side of the house, where I was transferring watermelon-sized rocks from the edge of the property closer to the house to make a border for a flower garden. Using a wheelbarrow, I had moved eight of the rocks; I needed about twenty more. But it was hot, and my head hurt; I felt fuzzy, so incredibly weak. So I had sat down on the flat top of one of the rocks and was busying myself pulling weeds when Bo called.

"I can't do it," I said. "I don't understand; it's not a difficult thing to finish, but I just can't."

"Get yourself in the house out of the heat. Direct sunlight's not good for you anyway with those meds," he said. "Please. Get yourself inside, and put on the kettle for tea." I promised I would go inside, and, slowly, I got to my feet, but it was starting to dawn on me that I was sick, really sick, and that all the tea in China couldn't restore me.

I started surfing the Internet for information about Crohn's disease, getting up at night and reading the dreadful information while everyone else was asleep. I started with the site Brittany had found—the web shrine devoted to the dead child actresses—and I educated myself about the peculiar circumstances that had led to Heather O'Rourke's sudden death from the disease. From there I pored over postings made by the Mayo Clinic and other medical agencies and read the depressing postings in medical chat rooms.

I was horrified by the stuff I saw on the computer, and I wanted to close my eyes to it, but I couldn't tear myself away from it. These were important things I needed to know, but the knowledge of them was making me heartsick. When I closed the computer and went to bed, instead of drifting into soft, healing sleep, I would lay awake, fretful and worried and sweating heavily. I was anxious to see the specialist, certain he would say I had been wrongfully diagnosed, but just as certain he would tell me to brace myself for life with Crohn's.

As the days passed, I began making a list of things to ask the doctor. Already I knew quite a bit, I told myself. Crohn's disease is an autoimmune disorder, a phenomenon I had already studied at length. Multiple sclerosis, the disease my ex-husband had, was classified as an autoimmune disorder, as was Celiac disease, Brittany's intestinal condition. With this knowledge in my mental toolbox, I began to understand why I felt so tired and why stress had been causing me to experience physical symptoms. But I still couldn't understand where the illness had come from, nor why it had seemed to attack out of nowhere, nor why, when most Crohn's patients complain of terrible diarrhea, I could never ever recall being troubled by that particular symptom.

"Of course, everyone experiences illness differently," the specialist, Dr. Prosser, said. "Some people with Crohn's don't have diarrhea, but that is rare." As he talked with me about my particular symptoms, my health history and the circumstances leading to my sudden diagnosis with Crohn's disease, Dr. Prosser did seem skeptical that the diagnosis was correct. But after excusing himself to review the pictures from the colonoscopy and the reports from the pathology lab, he returned to the examination room and said, "There is no doubt. It's unequivocal," he looked sorry to be delivering the verdict. "The only thing that puzzles me, after looking at the condition of the terminal ileum especially, is how, with that much scarring and inflammation, you were able to walk into this office at all."

DESPITE THE DIAGNOSIS—OR, perhaps, because of it—Bo and I continued to talk about moving to Alaska. Brittany had graduated high school; Doran and Ashley were getting married and needed a place to live; Jason and Keeley were both in middle school, and the every-other-weekend-visitation schedule was becoming increasingly inconvenient and awkward for them; and a full-time position as a news reporter had become available in the very town where we wanted to move. I had emailed my resume to the editor and had already done an interview over the telephone.

Doran seemed intrigued by the idea of starting his married life in our house, and even if he decided against it, we knew we could find a local real estate company to manage the property as a rental. I had met again with my specialist in Grand Junction and had decided to continue to treat my disease with the prescription combination, since it seemed to be working. As long as the area where we moved had a hospital and surgeons qualified to treat me in an emergency, the specialist thought, there was no reason I couldn't move there and check in with him every six months or so.

Going to Alaska again—this time to stay.

"At my age," I said to Bo one day, "and with this diagnosis, I might have only one more great adventure left in me. I'd like to go before it's too late."

ON OCTOBER 3, 2007, Brittany and I lugged four suitcases, two backpacks and two additional carry-on bags into Denver International Airport and boarded an 8:00 a.m. flight for Seattle, then another for Anchorage, then one for Kodiak Island, Alaska, where we arrived at 3:30 p.m. We loaded our bags and ourselves into a taxi and whooped and hollered as the van rounded Deadman's Curve bringing St. Paul Harbor into view. I took a deep breath as I took in the view of the glassy emerald waters, the fishing vessels as big as buildings swaying on the water; the tall, skinny warehouses where the fishermen store their nets, the kittiwakes and crows swooping and squawking for attention, and the blue domes and the three-bar crosses on the top of the Orthodox Church.

"The Russian Heritage Inn," I reminded the driver when he asked again where we were staying, and he turned left as we pulled into town and deposited us at the aged motel, no more than a five-minute's walk from the harbor and its spectacular, sparkling water.

The next morning, Brittany told the hotel managers our life story. "And my Daddy Bo is coming in two weeks, and my mom and I going to find a 'partment, and my mom going to work at the newspaper, and I going to be a writer, too, and did you know I graduated already and I'm 20 years old," she told Neil and Diane, as they smiled and waited patiently to get a word in edgewise. They gave us directions to the public assistance office and to the newspaper, put us in contact with several landlords and offered us rides to places when they could get away from the desk. They hooked us up to the Internet in the motel office and chatted companionably with Bo and my mother if they happened to call when Brittany and I were gone.

By the end of our first week at the hotel, we had enrolled Brittany in Alaska's public welfare system, including Medicaid and Adult Public Assistance; transferred her Social Security Disability address to a post office box in Kodiak; got her established as a client with Hope Community Resources, a local provider of services for disabled persons; found a promising, sunny apartment that would be available in two weeks; enrolled Brittany in Kodiak Special Olympics and attended her first bowling practice, and attended a service at Holy Resurrection Orthodox Cathedral. After church we ran to the motel, splashing through a downpour in our skirts and dress shoes, and laughing at the bald eagles perched on streetlights with their wings cocked out at funny angles, a position that helps them slough the water off their bodies but makes them look very undistinguished.

By the middle of the following week I began to get nervous about the newspaper job. I had been to the office for a face-to-face interview, and the editor seemed impressed by my qualifications and abilities, but I had not received an offer. When another position opened at a local title company, I applied for it and almost immediately was offered the job. I called the newspaper and got a noncommittal reply, so I accepted the job at the title company and started work on my eighth day in Alaska. Brittany stayed at the motel, entertaining Neil and Diane, busying herself with coloring books and making arrangements to participate in recreation activities sponsored by Hope Community Resources, including "Burgers and Bowling" at the Coast Guard base, swimming at a local pool and a three-day trip to the village of Port Lions, located on the northwest side of the island and to which she would travel by boat. While she was gone, I bought a stack of postcards and wrote to our friends and family in Colorado. On each one I wrote: "Brittany is running the island."

In the green spiral notebook she wrote an entry she called:

MY TOWN

Kodiak is a wonderful place to live and go places. You can go on boats. I like going to places to eat and to play in the park. Everything is close together, not that far walking distance or riding my bike (when my dad brings it from Colorado!). Kodiak is a better place to live because I can find better friends that don't tell lies or betray you or hurt your feelings or break your heart. In Kodiak, there's more to do.

Justin Wood at Hope Community Resources is a great person to hang around with and give us nice activities, like bowling and swimming and things like that. In Colorado I was sitting around a lot and that gave me too much fat on me.

Suddenly my parents decided to move to Kodiak. I was not that worried to move, because I wanted to get those old high school friendships out of my mind.

I'm getting more meat on my bones, more muscles back and losing my fat. I am getting more stronger and buff!"

BO ARRIVED IN KODIAK on October 20, a sunny, unseasonably dry day. My supervisor Mary Lee suggested I take the day off to move our things from the motel to the apartment, do some shopping for household items and generally get settled. I thought it was a little silly to take a day off of work already and told Mary Lee the weekend would be soon enough. "Trust me. When you get a dry day, use it," she said. Two solid weeks of rain following that one brilliant day of sunshine underscored the wisdom of her words.

We wouldn't have our vehicle until the following spring, so for seven months we used our feet to get where we needed to be, except on Saturdays when we hired a taxi for our grocery shopping. Unlike our home in Colorado, where our activities had been spread over a 1,150 square-mile county, life in Kodiak was compact: all the buildings, activities and events clustered near the shore. From our apartment, it was a one-mile walk to work, a three-quarter-mile walk to church, the bowling alley or the movie theatre, a half-mile walk to the auditorium at the high school. And for Alaska, the weather was relatively warm. Warmed by the trade winds of the Pacific Ocean, Kodiak's climate resembles that of northern Scotland more than it does that of Anchorage. We wore heavy rain gear and rubber boots to stay dry; staying warm was easier in Kodiak than it had been in Colorado. The long hours of darkness were difficult to get used to. We walked in the dark for Sunday morning services, carrying flashlights to see the path. By the middle of November, it was pitch dark when I walked to work in the morning and when I walked home from work at night.

"Brittany seems to be adjusting to the climate well," Mary Lee said at work one day, when she was faxing a lengthy loan document from the copy machine outside my office.

"She is. She loves it here," I said.

"Only, she has trouble understanding time relative to all the darkness," I added. "When she gets out of bed and it's still dark, she gets mad because she thinks we woke her up too early."

I got up from my chair and stood by my colleague. "You know what Brittany told me the other day?" I said. Mary Lee looked up at me. "She said 'Time doesn't work in Alaska!'"

Mary Lee laughed. "That girl!" She smiled and shook her head. "That girl is going to open doors for you all over this town."

It struck me as an odd thing to say. Hadn't I always been the one opening doors for Brittany? And the past few months, when I dashed hither-and-thither around the island, signing Brittany up for this and for that — wasn't I still the one opening doors, or at least knocking on them? But she was 20 years old, a high school graduate, a young woman; not a girl. She can knock on doors herself, I thought. Maybe she will knock on a few for my sake.

"Yes, I think you may be right," I said to Mary Lee. "You may be right."

WE WERE MAKING PLANS for attending Doran and Ashley's wedding, which would take place in April. I found some dresses on ebay and got them delivered to Kodiak in March, with plenty of time to make alterations if necessary before we flew to Colorado. Mine was a classic mother-of-the-groom ensemble — a beaded periwinkle, floor-length gown, with a matching jacket and purse. It fitted perfectly. I even was able to find periwinkle shoes on ebay to match. Brittany had chosen a black, off-the-shoulder, floor-length dress that was sashed with white satin at the waist. It made her feel very sophisticated when she modeled it around the apartment, wearing her black slip-on shoes for height. Though it was a petite size, still Brittany had to gather the dress up in her hands when she walked, so we took it downtown to an alterations shop to have about eight inches cut off the length.

WE HAD THE RED-EYE flight to Denver. My brother had business to do there, so he volunteered to pick us up at the airport, and was waiting for us early in the morning. We got something to eat and headed west across the mountains dividing the eastern

Brittany with the newlyweds, Doran and Ashley.

plains from the western slope. I slept the entire way, waking occasionally to the sound of conversation in the truck, but too tired and cozy to take notice of what was being said.

In the eight months since my diagnosis with Crohn's disease I had lost thirty pounds, most of it while living in Alaska. The drug regime, particularly the prednisone, had given me the energy to maintain my work schedule and to run all my errands on foot, but the drug hadn't stopped the progress of the disease. My intestines were unable to process nutrients; despite the fact that I was eating—or trying to eat—I gained very little from the calories in my food. And, unlike many people whose appetites increase while they are taking prednisone, I experienced the opposite effect. I was caught in an unhealthy cycle: I needed prednisone to reduce inflammation so that my intestines could absorb nutrition, but when I was taking prednisone I could not tolerate food. I had caught a glimpse of myself in the mirror at the alterations shop when we had picked up Brittany's dress, and I had been shocked by my own reflection. Now that we were back in Colorado, the worried faces of my family reflected a similar shock. I told everybody I had been working out a lot, but Doran, especially, could not be fooled. He reached out his long arms to hug me, and then, while I was in his embrace, he asked, "Where are you, Mom? Mom?"

BRITTANY WROTE IN THE green notebook:

THE WEDDING OF DORAN AND ASHLEY

I was nervous about part of the wedding. I carried the communion wine, and I wasn't sure when to go. I was afraid I would spill it. There were so many people there, a thousand of people, people I didn't even know. And my family were there, all of them!

My brother Doran was way beyond very nervous. He was so nervous because he wanted Ashley to say I do. Before the wedding started Doran was sitting by his father, Tim, and he was clenching his hands tight; he was so scared. When it was time for the wedding to start we did the procession and Doran had to stand right there up front, and Ashley's father took her up the aisle and gave her to Doran's hand.

When I was watching I felt for my brother Doran love and joy, kindness and so proud of my big brother Doran.

After the wedding, we took photos first and said goodbye to part of our family. Some of the family came to Cedaredge for the reception. There was food and dancing, and they played tricks on Doran, and I was laughing my head off.

Since we were young, Doran never danced with me, I asked him but he would never budge. At the wedding reception, now that he was grown up, he danced with his wife first and friends and Grandma, and my mom and aunt, and he finally danced with me!

Doran and Ashley are married because they want to be together because they are in love. Doran and Ashley are a very beautiful good couple, married that day April 19; they have wonderful hearts together and they will have a wonderful life.

WE TOOK CARE OF THE house while Doran and Ashley spent their honeymoon in a warm location. Brittany reviewed the wedding photographs in the digital camera, cooing over the photos from the rehearsal and laughing out loud every time she saw the photos that reminded her of the tricks Ashley's brother played on Doran at the reception.

"There's a picture of Doran and Ashley with her parents at the church," she said after a while. "But the picture of Doran and Ashley and you doesn't have Daddy Bo in it. Why?"

"Let me see," I reached for the camera and thumbed through the images.

"You're right. Why didn't Bo get in this picture?"

"Oh, I remember!" Brittany said. "Daddy Tim had to leave to go to the hotel to get some rest. Daddy Bo went out to help David get Daddy Tim into the van."

"He did?"

"Yep," she said, and she reached up for the camera.

"I think I look pretty," she said, pointing to the thumbnail of her posing alone on a pew inside the church. She panned in on the image so it tightened around her face. "I think I look old enough to get married."

"No more weddings, we told you. Not another wedding for ten years," I teased. "Not in this family."

Chapter Fifteen

Heartbeep

Brittany wrote: "I met Michael in Anchorage at Special Olympics State tournament for 2008 Summer Games. I did swimming and he did power lifting. He was on my Kodiak team but I never really noticed him until this trip. I looked behind my seat on the bus, and I saw him and I was love-struck! He told me what his name was and how he pronounces it.

"I was love-struck because Michael took care of things, like he was taking care of Andy. When Andy was crying and Michael was sitting next to him trying to calm him down. I don't know what Andy was crying about.

"I noticed that Michael was love-struck too, and he was staring at me also and he wanted to ask me out. I was dreaming and wishing he would ask me out on a date. He had a girlfriend before me, but she had moved away and I told him he had to leave that in the past.

"Michael is very big, like strong big, and very handsome. I like his laugh. I like his smile and his grin when he looks at me.

"After the Summer Games I saw him again, and he asked me out. He asked what is my name and I told him and he said, 'Brittany, can I go out with you some time?' And I said 'Yes, I would love to.'

"I saw him at summer recreation program stuff that summer, like swimming and picnics. I loved him very much for a boyfriend and someday

I will love him for a husband. He always has my heart. He can keep my heart always when I'm not with him. He takes care of me when I'm hurt.

"Michael is a good friend because he thinks straight and puts things together and takes care of people, like he takes care of his mother and his family. He works at a grocery store. He stocks shelves.

"He likes to hang out with his friends, he likes to watch DVDs, he likes lots of sports like floor hockey, power lifting, basketball, bowling and golf."

INCLUDING DORAN AND ASHLEY, eight couples in our circle of family and friends had wed in the previous three years; three more couples planned nuptials before the end of the year. This trend, combined with an overindulgence of Disney princess movies, had given Brittany a serious case of what Bo and I called "bridal-brain." After Brittany met Michael on the Special Olympics bus, it seemed like she processed every incoming stimulus through a wedding filter. If we drove past a grove of trees, she saw a backdrop for her wedding photo. A song on the radio inspired her to comment that it would make a great song for their wedding dance. She kept asking me to spell the word "tuxedo."

When Brittany was not daydreaming about her wedding, she was strategizing. She asked the clerk at a department store to measure her ring size, and she wrote the number on a piece of paper for Michael. Then, she had the clerk measure Michael's finger. She called Ashley several times asking advice for getting Michael to propose. She informed me that she had asked all of our parish priests (during confession) to pray that the proposal would be forthcoming. When I petitioned the State of Alaska to have my guardianship of her transferred from Colorado, Brittany told her court-appointed lawyer that she wanted Michael's parents to be her guardians so that she could live in their house. At night Bo and I could hear her praying aloud to the saints in her bedroom, begging them to put a marriage bug in Michael's ear.

Two more weddings did occur in the immediate family. In December 2008 Brittany received a form Christmas letter from

Auntie Brittany
and Connor

Tim in which he announced that we would soon marry Dinora,
a nurse with whom he had fallen in love during his visit to California in 1999. He would move to California with her in early
January, and they would be married in a private ceremony at
the end of that month.

And Father Innocent, our parish priest in Kodiak, took me and
Bo aside one day after Christmas and gently suggested that we
have our marriage blessed by the church. "It is time," he said, "to
live your lives fully."

I felt a tremendous wave of relief as he spoke. Since my childhood the church had been so important to me, and my life as a
Christian a fundamental part of my being. Yet, for reasons now
beyond my understanding, I had neglected to seek the blessing of
the church on my marital life. Tim and I had been married in an

outdoor ceremony by a non-denominational minister. Bo and I had married in a courthouse. By inviting me to marry in the Church, Father Innocent acknowledged my heartfelt desire for a marriage that was salvific—strengthened for my sake, Bo's sake and the sake of our children, by the power of the Holy Spirit. "All the issues of anger, guilt, resentment," Fr. Innocent said—all those feelings I had stored up in 19 years of marriage to Tim—"you've worked through those, completely."

He was right. Even Tim's public admission that he had fallen in love with another woman five years before our marriage ended, even that didn't upset or derail me. I was ready to bring my marriage to the Church and so happy, with Bo, to be offered that blessing.

There was only one Sunday the cathedral would be available between then and the beginning of Lent, however. On that day, January 18, Father Innocent celebrated the service of Holy Matrimony for Bo and me, with Brittany and three other people in attendance. As Bo and I snuggled close on the couch that night, watching a movie and warming our legs under a fleece blanket, Brittany looked at us and smiled. "When I see you sitting like that, so happy, I just want to have the same thing, too."

WE ENROLLED BRITTANY in another season of Special Olympics bowling and learned that they needed some additional partners on the team, so Bo and I agreed to participate. I had never bowled, save for one time in junior high, so I was pretty clumsy. At practice one day Brittany scolded me to quit messing around; then she realized I simply didn't know how to do any better, so she got her ball, told me to "focus" and demonstrated how I ought to be playing. Over the season my game improved, my "unified" team won some medals at the state bowling tournament, and I was hooked on bowling. When the Special Olympics season ended and the city bowling leagues started, Brittany and I formed a mixed doubles team with Bo and one of the male bowlers we knew from

Special O—and we discovered how looking forward to Wednesday night bowling could help us get through the long Alaska winter.

Michael also competed on one of the mixed doubles teams, so our involvement in Wednesday night league gave Brittany a regular opportunity to socialize with her boyfriend. There were so many pitfalls, it seemed, on Brittany's road to romance. Neither she nor Michael could fully master the concept of time, so it was difficult for them to plan outings with one another. Neither could drive, so their planning always had to include making arrangements for transportation. Money was another problem. Both Michael and Brittany had spending money, but neither had any real concept of how much they needed relative to the plans they wanted to make. Finally, while there were some events, such as those sponsored by Hope Community Resources, where I was comfortable Brittany would have adequate supervision, for most activities she and Michael planned, I felt a chaperone was necessary. Brittany and Michael had to plan around that requirement as well.

Bo and I wanted to help Brittany spend quality time with Michael, so we were thrilled to enroll our family in the bowling league, and we all made new friends through our involvement in it. There was another advantage: Brittany's excitement gave Bo and me excellent leverage for getting her to clean her room at least once a week, as a clean room became a requirement for going to the bowling alley.

WE TRAVELLED TWICE A year to Colorado for lengthy visits with the family, but now that she had a boyfriend, Brittany was the most reluctant traveler in all Christendom. She resisted packing her suitcase. She muttered at the ticket agents at the airport. She grumbled as she passed through security. She talked about Michael incessantly for the first full flight, wondering out loud what he was having for breakfast or what he was wearing to work. She called him from her cell phone every time she had an opportunity. She made rough drafts of her wedding invitations in her notebooks. She worried that Michael would find a new girlfriend while she was gone.

After we landed in Denver and crossed by car over the mountain passes, Brittany would get her bearings, gradually becoming less consumed by her thoughts about Michael. In Cedaredge we would pack ourselves happily into the tiny house we now called "Doran and Ashley's place," Bo would make the long drive to pick up Jason and Keeley and Brittany would participate fully in the life of the family, joining the rest of us as we cooked and shared huge meals, sat on the front porch, played board games and laughed, sharing our highlights and most-embarrassing moments with one another.

In the fall of 2009 we joined the rest of the family in Cedaredge to celebrate the birth of Connor, Doran and Ashley's baby boy. Brittany was eager to help Ashley with the baby. She held his head so he could learn to latch on to Ashley's breast, she offered to change his diapers, she asked if she could babysit while Ashley took showers. She wanted no part of the midnight duties, however. Doran had a job in an underground coal mine and was working the overnight shifts, so Bo and I helped out at night, hoping Ashley could get some rest and we could get long turns holding the baby.

Just looking at little Connor was enough to take my breath away. The facial expressions, his large hands, the cleft in his chin, it was like my Doran all over again. Nothing I had ever done or could ever do made me worthy to experience the joy of having held Doran so near; now here I was receiving the gift again, that blessed joy in the form of a grandson. As Bo and I sat on the couch, snuggling close and watching a movie, I held Connor asleep on my chest and wondered, is this little house big enough to contain my happiness?

Brittany came upstairs to go the bathroom and saw us sitting on the couch. She squeezed between Bo and me, rubbed Connor's back, and said, "You really love him, don't you?"

"Oh, yes. Now maybe you can see how much a baby is loved, how much you were loved," I said.

"By some," she said. "I was gived up by my birthparents, remember?"

So there it was. Since Connor's birth, Brittany had seemed distracted even though she had been so actively involved in Connor's care. I had wondered if Connor's birth had caused her to reflect upon her own, and here was the proof that it had. In fact, since my diagnosis with Crohn's disease, Brittany had become increasingly more interested in her birthparents. She riffled through the strongbox where I kept the photos and letters the couple had sent to her shortly after her adoption was finalized. She asked if I could help her locate her birthparents. She had learned that her birthparents had divorced and she had grieved over this. She wrote a letter to her birthparents. She asked me to explain to her why they had given her up and kept her older sister. Now that we all gathered in joy to celebrate Connor's birth, Brittany's distress over her own birth circumstances deepened.

Bo wrapped his arm around her and pulled her close to his chest. "No one could have loved you more than the mother sitting right next to you," he said. She closed her eyes drowsily and snuggled in closer to him.

"I like the sound of your nice, strong heartbeep," she said, and she fell asleep.

By the time we returned to Kodiak Brittany and I had filled the green spiral notebook, and I was typing her essays directly into the laptop. Several days after we got home she asked me to help her write:

BROTHERS AND SISTERS

Jason has changed a lot. He used to be very mean around me. If he picked fights with me then I fought back. He could start it and I could finish it. Now he gets along with me and talks to me nicely with nice words. I say kind things to him, like: You're a great brother—younger brother. And I ask before I look at his stuff. I changed a lot with him, too. In Colorado Jason went with us to this amusement park called Bananas, and he showed me everything, how to play it—like Laser Tag, and he shared his tickets with me. I think he changed a lot, even more than me, but I did change a lot, too.

Keeley is changing. She helped me to write my first song about October leaves and she helped me to hold Connor and put the pillow around my waist, so I can hold Connor better. Keeley did nice things, sticking with me and playing with me. Keeley went on the boat with us and went fishing. She helped me to reel in my big cod. And Keeley shared her things and I shared my things.

Keeley is now a teenager. She just turned 13. She is nice and tall and thin, has nice brown hair and brown eyes. She's got her mother's eyes and her father's spirit. PS: I wish I was taller than Keeley, so I can call her Shorty.

Doran got married in April 2008. He got married to a wonderful, perfect wife named Ashley Tregarthen. Doran changed a lot. Like I asked him if he would play on the Wii with me and he helped me with that; he helped me to finish this game.

Doran always called me, Sissy, or Britt, or Bren-Ditty (when he was younger), and Gracie. I don't like it when he calls me those names. It's very irritating.

When Doran and Ashley got pregnant and lost their first baby, I felt very sad. But they got pregnant again, and now they have a baby boy named Connor Doran Tregarthen. I could tell my brother Doran was very, very worried that the baby would make it out. And Ashley had to have a C-Section. That scared my brother, but I heard a couple of cries later and it was baby Connor. That meant that Doran had a son!

I love my first brother Doran, I love him very much because he was my first brother. Jason, I love him too, also. I miss him dearly. And Keeley, I miss her lovely face and voice when she talks—the horse lover!

I VISITED MY SPECIALIST and learned that the Crohn's was getting worse. We adapted my treatment, starting the more aggressive immunosuppressants that would work, theoretically, by shutting down my immune system in order to keep it from attacking my own body. All along we had hoped to avoid having to surgically remove the most diseased section of my ileum; gradually we all had to accept that even surgery wasn't an option given the severity of disease throughout my bowels. I had asked for a reduction in my hours at work, shifting to half-days, so I could get more rest. Finally, Bo appealed to me to leave my job altogether, a decision Brittany resisted.

"No!" she said, when he brought it up at the supper table. "It was so, so, so hard for Mom to find a job in the first place!" she said. "Besides, I like them at the office."

"I do, too, Honey, but I need more rest," I told her.

"There is one other thing," Bo said, and Brittany and I turned our heads to look at him. "You haven't done any writing since you got here. You need to get back to your writing." Brittany realized that Bo was referring only to me—she had done plenty of writing!—so she kept uncharacteristically quiet while Bo and I continued our conversation.

"You mean our book?" I said, and I winked at Brittany.

"Your book, all those other things you wanted to do. It's time." His voice was firm.

"We can't do…" I started to say, but he cut me off.

"You tell me what I have to do," Bo said, laying his hand on my arm. "Tell me what I have to do to make it happen. I will do it. I want you to get back to your writing. It's who you are."

I looked across the table at Brittany, who was trying to suppress a smile. "I think I'll just…clear the table," she said, grabbing her dish and fork and making a mad dash for the kitchen sink.

Several days later, Brittany asked me to help her type this essay into the computer.

Brittany and Bo (Photo by Vic Downing.)

WHO I AM

The reason I want to be a writer is because I want to be just like my mother. Because when I see her in her study when she is writing her articles, I want to do it also.

I like to write about love and marriage and having kids—write about pretending I have kids. I write stories about life, like how the trees live so long and how to make the grass so dark green and the sky, how to make it blue.

When I get frustrated about my writing I get anger. I get frustrated when my words don't make sense to me at all. I go to my mother and ask her to help me, and my father too—so I won't get frustrated. My mother helps me stay on one task. My father helps me do that too. I also need help with spelling.

I want to make my own book—just me—about Michael and me falling in love. I also like to make picture movie DVDs. They are awesome to make to give to people. They're so cool. You can make them every day.

It's part of my life to make things. That's who I am.

THE DIRECTOR OF THE Kodiak-area Special Olympics program asked me if I could join the Community Management Team as a public relations specialist, and I agreed. I began submitting articles about the program to the local newspaper and developed a newsletter we would mail to athletes and local supporters of Special Olympics. I also drafted community service announcements for the Orthodox Cathedral and the seminary. I drove to the office of the Kodiak Daily Mirror one day to drop off some press releases, and I asked to see the new editor, hoping I could convince him to make space for an article about an upcoming event. I had met him when I had interviewed at the newspaper previously—when he was the special features editor—and he took a few minutes to ask how things had been going for me. We chatted about Kodiak, about the weather, about his new position as editor, about his music and his boat. Finally, he asked if I would consider writing a column, every other week, for the Friday edition.

Bo had driven me to the newspaper office and was waiting in the truck. I sidled up next to him and smiled. "You're not going to believe this," I said.

He grinned. "I'd believe anything," he said. "Let's go get a cup!"

"MOM," BRITTANY SAID. "I need you to help me write my song." I was sitting at the dining room table, finishing the last few sips of my morning coffee.

"I can help for a minute, but it's almost time for me to go down in my catacomb," I said. Brittany rolled her eyes. It annoyed her that I withdrew into my study every morning at 8:00 a.m., pulled the door closed behind me and refused to engage in conversation until my first coffee break, two hours or so later. Her writing style was different. She liked to carry her work into the center of family activity, bounce ideas off of anyone who would listen, grasp at the words expressed by others and then wrestle with them until the words became her own.

"I'm writing about my sapphire eyes," she said. "I need help."

"Okay, I'll help you spell things. But the words have to be your own."

"But I don't understand how to write it in a song," she said.

"Well, I'm not a songwriter, either, so I can't help you there." I was hedging. I felt like she was setting me up, trying to stall my retreat into my cave, or to get me to write her song for her, so I was trying to set a boundary. "You're the one who studies song lyrics. But, anyway, I can tell you how to spell things."

"Here's what I say," she said, and she showed me her paper. It read: My blue eyes I don't understand why I have these colors in my eyes.

"That's nice," I said.

"But now I want to say that Michael loves the blue that rises like the waves in the ocean and the waves rising in my eyes and he loves it."

"Well, write that," I said, and she did, with my help spelling "ocean," "waves" and "rising."

"I think the idea with songwriting is to make your sentences shorter," I said.

"What do you mean?"

"Not so many words."

She gave me a surprised look and started to say something, then stopped herself. She pushed the paper toward me and said, "Show me."

"Okay. Here where you say '…the blue that rises like the waves in the ocean…'" I circled it with the pencil she handed me. "Here you can just say 'ocean blue.'" I wrote those words on the paper. "Like that. It tells the same idea in not so many words."

She looked at it. "Ocean blue. Rising," she said, and then she repeated it. "Ocean blue rising. Ocean blue rising.

"Okay," she said, dismissing me to my cave. "I get it."

Two days later she asked if she could use the computer to type her song. I showed her how to format it, using short lines like a poem, rather than the long, prose lines she had written on the paper. And I suggested one part of the song that looked like it would work for a chorus. She agreed the verse would make a good chorus and typed that part into the computer twice. After she finished typing the words, she played with the font style. Her finished song went like this:

MY SAPPHIRE EYES

My blue eyes
I don't understand why
I have these colors in my eyes

He loves to see
The blue in my eyes
Ocean blue rising
Waves so high

Don't make my blue eyes cry
When I'm all alone
And don't make my blue eyes dry
When I'm on my own

Now Tears building up
Like waves on the Ocean
My Sapphire will burn into flames

Like the beating of
My swollen heart
My Sapphire will fall in love

Don't make my blue eyes cry
When I'm all alone
And don't make my blue eyes dry
When I'm on my own

Bo put on his reading glasses and read the lyrics when Brittany handed him the paper at supper that night. "That's really good, Baby," he said, and he looked over his reading glasses at her. "Who's that copy for?" he asked, nodding to the sheet she held in her hand.

She sat upright in her chair. "It's for Father Innocent," she said. "He used to sing in a band. He said he would look at my songs."

Bo looked at me. "Oh?" he said, as if this was something I had already known.

Chapter Sixteen

The Road Going

We had the rare combination of money to spend and time to spend it, so before their summer visit to Alaska we took the children on a bona fide family vacation. Brittany and I already had spent a week in Southern California where Brittany visited Tim and his wife and some of their extended family. During that time, she and I stayed in a hotel in Pasadena, working on our book each day after she returned from her dad's. After we checked out of the hotel we picked up Bo, Jason and Keeley at the LAX airport and drove south to Dana Point to stay in a hotel near Brittany's grandparents.

It was a perfect trip. We all enjoyed several meals with Brittany's grandparents. We licked ice cream off our spoons as we strolled by the yachts moored at the harbor. We lounged at the hotel's outdoor pool and laughed at Jason's reaction when a dozen teen-age equestriennes joined him in the hot tub. Best of all, we played on the beach, a glorious expanse of white sand and rolling waves just a short walk away from our hotel. Jason and Keeley, new to the ocean's majesty, were slow to enter the water and timid in the face of the waves. Brittany dropped her towel on the shore and ran below the tide line. She dared the waves to hit her, then laughed as they pulled her down. It would frighten most parents to see the waves toss their child this way, but I knew this was just Brittany's way of greeting the water.

By our second day there I had found body boards for each of us. Brittany embraced her board and then showed her siblings how you swim out on your board, wait for a wave, paddle with your arms as the wave picks you up, and enjoy the ride to shore! Brittany and I went out again and again, pausing between trips to coax Jason and Keeley to try. After a while they did, but the grip of the Pacific Ocean's undercurrent spooked them, and they didn't see the fun in the whole enterprise.

On our last beach day Brittany and I took the body boards out while Jason buried Keeley in the sand and Bo struck up conversation with a man who was fishing from the shore. It was low tide and difficult to catch waves; we had to paddle farther out than normal. From my board I could see the shore filling up with fishermen. I started to worry that Brittany and I would get caught up in one of their lines, so I kept moving us to different areas to try to avoid a problem.

It became very frustrating after a while, and I was getting tired, so I told Brittany we needed to stop. I tried to point out the hazard with the fishing lines, but she balked. It was our last day riding waves, and she wanted to keep going. One more wave, I told her; then we needed to quit.

But it was a disappointing wave that fizzled before it took us to shore. Brittany headed out for another, and there was nothing I could do but follow her. She was too far away from me for conversation, and she refused to look at me. I felt marooned. I was very tired physically and even if I could get Bo's attention, there was nothing he could do for me. It was just me and Brittany, and she was in a mood to resist. God help me. It wasn't exactly a prayer; more like a lump in my throat.

Finally, the ocean began to swell, a huge roll appeared on the horizon. Brittany saw it, too, and positioned her body board to take advantage. She whooped as the wave picked up her and the board and surged them onto the shore. She sprang to her feet, grabbed the bow of her board and started to dash out again, but her board would not budge. I had a hold of the handle. She glared at me, then brushed the matted hair off her face and smiled. She turned and ran up the beach to hug Daddy and tell him how much fun she had, leaving me to carry her blasted body board.

IN LATE NOVEMBER 2009 Michael's mother Lydia was hospitalized. Diagnosed with pneumonia, physicians suspected also that she had the H1N1 influenza virus, but her underlying condition was cancer, which she had battled for seven years. The family had planned to take a vacation to Hawaii for Christmas, but we heard from Michael's dad Matthew that the nurses had decorated Lydia's hospital room in a luau theme, with the expectation that she would finish her earthly journey on the third floor of Providence Kodiak Island Medical Center.

Brittany asked if we would take her to the hospital to see Lydia; Michael and Matthew were there, along with Michael's older brother and Lydia's sister, who had both flown in from out of town. Brittany approached Lydia's bed and said hello, and then she sat in a chair next to Michael and rubbed his shoulder. Matthew, Bo and I talked softly while Brittany and Michael made faces at one another and giggled. As Bo and I got ready to leave, Brittany got serious, gave Michael and Matthew a hug and told Matthew how sorry she was that Lydia was ill. She and I held hands as we walked down the hallway, and as we passed the nurses' station, Brittany said, "Lydia is going to die. I can feel it. Poor Michael. Poor, poor Matthew."

I thought about Lydia. Poor Lydia. As her time draws near, does she agonize over Michael, how he will function in this world without her daily care? As she nurtured Michael during his 27 years had she anticipated a day when she would leave this earth and he would stay? How had she prepared herself for it? Heaven would have to be a very special place, I thought to myself, to comfort a woman whose death causes her to part from a child like Michael. I wondered how God would use the rest of us to watch over him.

Brittany's tug on my arm brought me back to earth. She remembered that Michael's brother had a birthday in two days. "We should get the cake for him," she said. "Lydia (would) want us to get a cake for him." I called Matthew that night and asked if he minded, and then Brittany and I drove to the bakery, where she selected a luau cake we would pick up and deliver to the family's house the next day.

Lydia died in early December, and our family attended her funeral service at the Roman Catholic Church four days later. Brittany sat with Michael's family and kept, as she called it, "a brave face," though she got irritated when Michael's neighbor asked her to scoot over so that she could sit next to Michael. "That wasn't right," Brittany complained later to me and Bo. "I was 'posed to sit next to Michael; not her."

"I know it hurt, Honey. But she's been a friend to Michael for a long, long time. Kind of like another mother to him."

"But it wasn't right. I'm his girl now," Brittany said, and she went to bed feeling conflicted: sad because of Lydia's death and angry because she had felt marginalized at the very moment she most wanted to feel included.

BRITTANY DECIDED SHE would produce a CD of her own songs. She had several ideas for new songs and asked me to write down the words she thought she would use to write them. She kept the lists in the same file folder she used for her songs, and referred to them as she worked, feverishly, on "Dancing Girl," and "Lights of Heaven," the two songs that had gelled most in her thoughts. She wanted to complete six songs, she said, record them on CDs and sell them at Wal-Mart.

True to his word, Father Innocent helped her, composing a melody for "October" and recording the melody onto a CD so Brittany could sing the lyrics along to it at home. He also composed a melody for "My Sapphire Eyes," and he recorded his own vocal rendition of that song on a separate CD, which he gave to her. He reviewed her draft of "Lights of Heaven" and suggested that she write more, as the lyrics could be improved, he said, with the addition of a chorus.

After playing the "October" melody repeatedly in her room, Brittany brought the CD upstairs and asked Bo and me to listen while she sang to the music. She stood next to the CD player, drew her shoulders back, closed her eyes and took a deep breath. Then she held the lyrics in front of her, adjusted her glasses and pressed the arrow button on the CD player. A piano softly played the "October" melody, and Brittany started to sing along: "When October changes colors/ With all the colors blending/ The angels sing in the choir—

"—Ugh." Even though Brittany's vocal abilities had shown dramatic improvement over the past few years, she was having trouble carrying the tune written for this song, and her timing was off. "Okay, stop." She punched the button on the CD. "I try again."

She closed her eyes and took a deep breath, and then she pressed the play button. "When October changes colors/ With all—

"—Ugh! Stop! I do it again."

She made several more attempts and then turned off the CD player and collapsed in a heap of discouragement on the couch. I let her sit there for a spell and then I asked her, "Why don't you let Fr. Innocent sing the lyrics?"

"I want it to be my voice singing," she said.

"It is your voice in the writing," I answered, but she wouldn't look at me.

"Look, you like how 'My Sapphire Eyes' sounds with Father singing, don't you?"

"Yeah! That sounds awesome!" she said. "But it's not my voice."

"But it is your writing! Father Innocent can't write lyrics like you write them, but he can sing, and you like his singing." I paused, hoping for a response, which did not come. "You do the writing; he does the singing, what's wrong with that?"

Still no response. "Look, think about me and Victor," I said, diverting her attention to a friend we had at church. "I take good photos, right?" Brittany nodded. "But Victor takes even better photos. If Victor and I did a book together, who should do the writing?" I asked.

"You," she said. "You're a better writer—I think."

"And who should take the photographs?" I asked.

"Victor," she said in a monotone. "I get it!" She got up from the couch, went to the CD player and retrieved her CD. "You know what I think?" she said, looking at me. "I think you hate my singing!" She turned around and left the room; stomping down the stairs for emphasis.

"I hate it when she does that," Bo said. "That is so rude."

BO WAS RETIRED NOW. Hunting season was over. It was too cold to fish. So Bo spent most of his time at home. Brittany and I both worked at home. Windy, wet weather prohibited us from spending much time out of doors, and there was precious little daylight to cheer us. As the winter equinox neared, and the days grew progressively shorter, our tempers grew shorter as well.

Just as Brittany and Jason had once butted heads, now Brittany and Bo argued over everything. Bo resented Brittany's "hissy-fits"; Brittany hated it when Bo "said swear words." When Brittany rolled her eyes and scoffed, Bo told her she was being rude. When he lost his cool, she accused him of shouting.

We were living in a two-storey house and we had built a small studio apartment for Brittany in the basement. She had a bedroom and a cooking and dining area where she usually ate her breakfasts and lunches at her own leisure. We insisted that she join us for supper each night, and she came upstairs for company often during the day, sometimes just to "check-in," sometimes to do her writing in the center of all the upstairs action. Inevitably, she would get into an argument with Bo and then stomp downstairs in a huff. One night, after hearing her slam the door to her apartment, Bo went downstairs and told her he would remove the door from its hinges if she ever did that again.

At supper one night, I told them both that I had had enough. Bo had set the table, and Brittany was complaining that he had given her a "too-big fork." He started to get agitated, but I stopped him. "Sit down, both of you! This is the supper table," I said. "I want peace at this table. No shouting." Bo and Brittany sat down, and the three of us joined hands, said the Lord's Prayer in unison, and then began eating in deafening silence.

"You can talk," I said finally. "Just not fight."

"We're not really fighting," Bo said, looking at Brittany. "It's just how we relate to each other."

Brittany's eyes got big and she nodded. "It's not fighting, Mom. We're friends," she said.

"Well, it drives me crazy," I said, putting on my worst Mom-face and looking from one of them to the other. "There are other ways to relate to each other." They looked at each other and smiled, and I knew I was outnumbered.

AFTER REVIEWING THE results of my last colonoscopy and consulting with my specialist and primary care physician, I had decided to undergo a chemotherapy treatment for the Crohn's disease. It was another immune suppressant, but it worked in a different way than the previous medications had. While the risks associated with it were worrisome, it seemed like I had no other real alternative except giving up, which I wasn't ready to do. By December of 2009, I had received three infusions of the drug, and I felt confident that the infusions were helping. As the weeks stretched out between infusions, however, I would experience an exacerbation in my Crohn's-related symptoms, starting with a dramatic loss of energy.

A fellowship meal always followed the Sunday service at our church, and it was my team's turn to cook the meal the Sunday before Christmas. It had been seven weeks since my last infusion, and I felt tired, I told Bo, "clear down to my bone marrow." I was relieved when I could get home from church and rest. I sat in a recliner near our large picture window, covered myself with a fleece blanket and for a few moments I watched the seagulls play over the channel that flows between our house on Kodiak Island and Near Island, some five hundred feet away. I leaned back in my chair, feeling a strong urge to sleep, and heard Brittany padding softly up the stairs.

"It's okay," I said. "I'm awake."

"What are you doing?" she asked as she came into the room.

I pointed out the window. "Look at that. Watch the gulls. Do you see how they fly up, up, up and then...Look! See how they dive headlong toward the water! Doesn't it look like they're going to crash?"

"Wow!" she said.

"But, look, they never crash. See how the wind catches them every time, how it tosses them around—makes them do somersaults over the water, but doesn't let them fall?"

"It looks like fun," she said, and she sat on the couch, facing me. She watched Bo as he came into the living room and settled in his chair, where he, too, would take a nap.

"Mom? Dad?" she said tentatively. "I decided I going to give up the Orthodox Church, be a Catholic. Doran did it. I do it, too."

WE TALKED FOR OVER an hour, her words sounding like they had come from a prepared script, her arguments like they had been drafted by scholars. I had never heard such formal logic from her, and the impact of it was sobering. We had been so happy to move to a place where our church was understood and appreciated within the culture. And Brittany had seemed happy at church, eager to learn the hymns, asking good questions about church practices, busy with the friendships she had made there. Now here she was, a junior Martin Luther with her 95 theses, and I felt like the wooden door she was hanging them on. Each blow with the hammer struck deep into the grain of my being.

Doran had converted to Roman Catholicism; that was true, and when it had happened, Brittany had been furious with him. I, on the other hand, had not experienced reservations or hard feelings. It was obvious he was committed to raising his family in the love of God. He and his wife Ashley attended church regularly, served others readily and were making preparations for their son Connor to receive the sacrament of Holy Baptism. And Doran's great mind had always been capable of separating the wheat from the chaff in any literary work, system of thought or religious dogma. More capable, indeed, than my own. How could I feel bad about his choice?

With Brittany it was different.

She talked about having a family and had made a list of the first and middle names of all of her seven future children, the way I had when I was in fifth grade. She talked incessantly about her future wedding with Michael. She had made it a personal goal to live independently, and she worked—hard—to learn the things she needed to learn to accomplish that goal. She had all the right ideas. But she had tried holding a job outside the home, even getting help from the vocational rehab office in Kodiak, but could never really focus on a task (other than writing) that lasted more than an hour a day. Her boyfriend seemed content to live with his dad and had no apparent interest in marriage. When Brittany and Michael went on a "date," their time together usually became a time for burping contests, not for conversation.

Was it reasonable to think that Brittany's future would include marriage, child-rearing and a place of her own? Were we preparing Brittany for adulthood in the same way we had prepared Doran and hoped to help prepare Jason and Keeley? Were we preparing her for a life that was independent, or just independent of us, a life that would continue after we were gone but in which she was still dependent on someone else to help her cope with the demands of everyday life? For all her talents, strengths and abilities, she still needed help understanding she should expect change when she used a twenty-dollar bill to pay for a four-dollar item. She still screamed out "Mommy" when she woke in the middle of the night with a nightmare or a toothache.

As tough as her younger years were, they seemed so much simpler. Back when she was small and so very ill—and I was young and strong and healthy—I thought it was my job just to love her

Brittany and her boyfriend comparing bowling scores.

and keep her alive and safe. So many times I feared I would lose her, but even then I comforted myself with the thought that if I did outlive her, at least she would never be alone in this world—and defenseless. Now, I understood that she would probably outlive me, and I had prepared her the best I knew how for her own life, but had I done enough? I had built a net for her, a support system within our church, our family and our circle of friends. What if Brittany refused to respond to the system in place for her? What if she chose a completely different path?

As Brittany, Bo and I discussed her motives for wanting to leave our church, we reminded her of the many friendships she had made in the parish, that the priest helped her with her music, the parish nurse helped her learn healthy habits and various parishioners enjoyed taking her out for movies, bowling and lunch dates. Our church had become for her just as we had hoped it would: a large network—a family—of people concerned about her and willing to help her grow spiritually and emotionally.

"I know," she said. "But when I see you and Daddy, so happy together, I want that." She held her fists tight to her chest for emphasis.

"So, this is really about Michael," I said.

She nodded and squeezed her eyes together to press out tears. "I asked him over and over to come to church," she said. "I been to his church. I been to Catholic Church. Why he never comes to mine?"

"I don't know, Honey. But even if you did get married, you can still get married in the Church even if you're Orthodox, and he's Catholic. Remember, you asked Father Innocent; he said sometimes mixed marriages happen in the Church."

"In our Church," Brittany said, without skipping a beat. "Only in our Church. What if Michael wants to get married in his Church? If we get married in Catholic Church I have to be Catholic."

"Aren't you getting a little ahead of yourself?" Bo asked. "You're ready to leave the Church for a wedding that isn't even taking place. That's what this is about, right, or am I missing something?"

Neither Brittany nor I answered. Instead, I asked Brittany to let us think about her words and resume the conversation another day. "'SOkay," she said. "I'm tired anyways." She pushed herself off the couch, gave me a kiss and headed for the stairs. Halfway across the room, she straightened her body dramatically, screeched "Ooooo," and said, "my movie. I gonna watch my movie now!" And she skipped the rest of the way to the stairs, dropped to her bottom and slid down, making "Uh" noises as she hit each step. She grunted at the base of the stairs as she pulled herself to her feet. Bo and I looked at each other as we listened to her run down the hall, close her apartment door behind her, and shout "Whoopee!"

Bo held his hands up as if to say, "I don't get it." I smiled at him.

"She's trying to define herself apart from us," I said, finally answering the question I had ignored moments ago. "But it's also about Michael and marriage..."

Bo shook his head.

"I want her to have what we have, companionship and love, someone to share her ups and downs with," I said to my husband. "If I truly believe that marriage is a sacrament—and I do—why wouldn't I want Brittany to participate? I just don't think we do her any favors," I said, "by letting her live in a fantasy world. That boy has no interest whatsoever in marriage. Not that I can see. Not yet."

"No," said Bo. "I don't believe he does, but how do we convince her?"

Bo and I mulled things over for several days and finally struck this comprise with our daughter: we would make it possible for her to spend more time with Michael, so that the two of them could develop a better understanding of one another. We would also help her socialize more often with other people her age, including some of the younger adults from our church who had just become respite providers at Hope Community Resources. We would encourage some of these providers to chaperone Brittany's outings with Michael, so that the lovebirds didn't always have her parents around. In exchange, she had to drop all talk—all talk—of weddings and marriages and conversions to Catholicism until Michael himself brought up the subject. Brittany drew her fingers across her mouth to show us her lips were sealed.

I asked her also if she wanted me to help her make an entry in her journal about her views about the Church. Her song writing consumed more and more of her time, and she hadn't shown an interest in the journal for months. She stood over my shoulder at the computer and started to reformulate her thoughts. But her heart wasn't in it. She was a lyricist now, not a prose writer, and she was more interested in composing the song she was calling "I Believe" than the essay she had entitled "Saints." I suggested that we work on the song instead, and she raced to her room to get her notes.

I BELIEVE HYMN
I believe in you, my Lord
You give me your life
I hear the angels' voices
Beautiful hymns
And rhythms resound
And what was lost is found
I believe in love

When you
Open the door
You reach your hand to hold mine
My heart opens with joy
I believe in you, my Lord
You give me your life
I hear the saints
Colorful Lights

When you
Open the door
You reach your hand to hold mine
My heart opens with joy
I believe in you, my Lord
You give me your life
I hear you call my name
Mary Magdalene*
Tower of strength.

*Mary Magdalene is the saint for whom Brittany is named; Magdala is translated "tower of strength."

When she finished typing her finished lyrics Brittany printed a copy and slipped it into her file folder, snapped the folder shut and said, "That's it! That's the sixth song. That's my whole album CD." She told me her ideas for the CD jacket, asking if I thought a photo of October leaves would be best or a photo of fireworks.

"I guess you have to decide," I said. "Do you want me to take some photos for you?"

"No, thanks," she said curtly. "I'll get Victor."

BRITTANY WAITED UNTIL we were on the very edge of sleep before she tiptoed up the stairs and stood quietly outside our bedroom door, which was open. "Are you decent?" she finally called.

"No," Bo grumbled. "Go to bed." Brittany came in and walked to my side of the bed. In the darkness I could barely make her out, but I could tell she was bending over the bed, looking for my face.

"Just one more kiss," she said.

I moaned and reached up for her. "We were almost asleep," I said. "Here." I pulled her close to me and hugged her tight. "Good night..."

"...for the fourth time!" Bo added, but he couldn't foil Brittany, who was making her way to other side of the bed for one more kiss from him. He hugged her, and she turned to leave. "Now, get your ass in bed!" Bo said, and he reached out to give her a playful smack. Brittany screeched and ran across the room, through the doorway and to the stairs, whooping and laughing. At the top of the stairs, she paused.

"Kiss my grits!" she shouted to Bo and then she dropped to her bottom, laughing as she slid down the stairs. She jumped to her feet at the bottom of the stairs and ran down the hallway. "Whoo-hoo!" she yelled from her room. "Whoo-hoo!"

Epilogue

I sit at the computer with a cup of tea and a copy of our manuscript, which is riddled with both red marks and encouraging comments from editors. Today my plan is to make all the corrections that will make the book ready to take to press. But I am distracted by telephone calls and urgent emails, all having to do with Brittany's music. She and Father Innocent decided to call their band Ocean Blue Rising, a phrase that came from one of Brittany's songs. I helped Brittany to complete the paperwork necessary to register Ocean Blue Rising as a business in the State of Alaska. Father Innocent registered the band's first single, "October," with the United States copyright office. An attorney in Anchorage wrote and registered a (d)(4)(A) trust which will enable Brittany to earn royalties from her music without losing control of her copyrights or jeopardizing her eligibility for Medicaid and other sources of federal and state benefits. By the end of the day, one urgent email tells me, "October" will be uploaded to the web. A voice on the telephone asks if Brittany and I can take some time now to review both the music video and the video teaser that will appear on Brittany's Facebook page.

Brittany and Suzanne sledding down the steep driveway of the Kodiak house.

I will work on the manuscript later.

My mind is on the book as I review the video, however. I am thinking particularly of one comment about our title. "*The Road Going* is a great title," Gen had said, "and it begs the question, What will you name the sequel?"

That is a good question. Brittany blossoms in her new career as a lyricist. It fills me with satisfaction and pride to watch her work. I am her financial adviser, driver and chief spelling assistant as she crafts songs, but I keep my distance when creative and business decisions evolve. Father Innocent is Brittany's partner in Ocean Blue Rising, not I; I try to remember my proper place.

As for *The Road Going*, Brittany is anxious to see the book to completion. She hovers over my shoulder as I place photographs and she makes suggestions for captions and throws up her arms and says, "Finish it, for Pete's sake!"

"I'm going as fast as I can," I tell her. "I only have two eyes and one pair of hands!" She winks and tells me I'd better hurry, because she has an idea for another book.

The sequel to *The Road Going*, perhaps? And there is my answer for Gen. There may very well be a second book about our journey, but if there is, it will be Brittany, not I, who is in charge of it.

Index

A

adoption 23, 26-28, 237
Adult Public Assistance 223
amniocentesis 25-26
Anitra Circle 39, 41, 48, 53-54, 73, 87, 141
antiobiotics 30-31

B

Baclofen 63-65
Baesman, Nancy 209
baptism 23, 30, 61
Barsi, Judith 198, 205
birthparents 13, 237
body image 59, 77, 94, 103, 115-119, 146-47, 150, 152, 196, 224, 229, 243
bunions/bunionectomy 59

C

Cedaredge, Colorado 138-140, 144, 160, 163, 186, 206, 211, 217, 228, 236
Celiac disease 104, 111-118, 146, 209, 220
central auditory processing delay 45
Children's Hospital (Denver) 32-33, 59-60
Colorado College 42, 48, 55, 134
Colorado Springs, Colorado 12-13, 28, 38, 42, 53, 60, 75, 87, 93, 95, 96, 108, 128-129, 136-141, 153-154, 161, 164-165, 212
Colorado Supreme Court 35
Craig, Colorado 167-169
Craig, Dr. Jennifer 217
Crohn's disease 198, 205, 218-221, 227, 237, 239, 251

D

Delta, Colorado 144, 146-156, 160-161, 168-169, 173, 176, 179-183, 190, 194, 201, 204, 207-208, 217
Delta County Independent 180, 204
divorce 132, 134, 140, 195
Down Syndrome 10-11, 16-20, 25-26, 29, 104-105, 113, 152, 196
Dresdow, Fr. Innocent 233, 244, 249, 255, 259-261
drug overdose 62-65

M

O

P

R

S

Reflect and Discuss
"The Road Going"

By Kitty L. Deal, MS, CRC

1. In Chapter One, Suzanne shares her parenting philosophy of allowing Brittany to try—and perhaps fail—in order to facilitate her child's learning. What are the advantages and challenges with this philosophy? How might a parent's philosophy differ when parenting a child with special needs versus a child who is typically developing?

2. Compare and contrast a biological and adoptive family's emotional response to the diagnosis of a child with disabilities. Do you think the cycle of grief and acceptance is different for these families?

3. Tim, Suzanne and Bo are faced with situations where people express the view that individuals with special needs have less than full human value. Faced with the same scenarios as described on pages 16, 22, 28-29, and 184, how would you react? As advocates for individuals with special needs, how do we educate the general public on full acceptance for individuals with differing abilities?

4. What roles do faith and religion play in the Tregarthen family? In the Bobo family? For Brittany?

5. Suzanne, who has an affinity for research and lifelong learning, became a lay "expert" in specific medical conditions, dietary issues, special education, behavior management and navigating the complex landscape of social services agencies. For parents and advocates less proficient in personal education and research, what resources and/or services need to be

available to provide essential information? Who is responsible for providing the resources and/or services for children with special needs? Does the responsibility change as the child transitions to adulthood?

6. Reflect on the contrast between Brittany's public school (Chapter 12) and home school experience. How did the right to a Free Appropriate Public Education (FAPE) for Students with Disabilities under Section 504 of the Rehabilitation Act of 1973 fail for Brittany?

7. Brittany's fascination with maps facilitated the development of her "life map." How was this exercise in person-centered planning a crucial turning point in her education?

8. Reflect on the transition plan developed by Brittany, Suzanne, and Mr. Pyle in Chapter Twelve . How did these goals help Brittany bridge her secondary education to post-secondary activities? How is the value of self-determination exemplified with Brittney's plan?

9. Brittany developed social skills which allowed her to "work the crowd." How can individuals with disabilities move beyond surface social skills to the authentic friendships described by Suzanne on pages 152-153.

10. Brittany not only becomes interested in the idea of marriage, but progresses to having "bridal brain." Discuss the rights of adults with disabilities to marry and/or engage in sexual relationships. What unique considerations must be explored when individuals with disabilities contemplate marriage (i.e. independent living, eligibility for social services, guardianship, etc.)? What are the parameters for determining informed consent for adults with disabilities?

11. What role do Suzanne and Bo play in Brittany's literary, athletic and musical aspirations? How do Brittany's accomplishments as a writer, athlete, and lyricist build her self confidence?

12. Like many families, Brittany's family encounters life changes such as divorce, relocation, chronic illness, financial strain, and blending due to remarriage. How are family dynamics impacted when one or more member has special needs?

Kitty Deal has spent her lifetime as an advocate for individuals with special needs. As a natural outgrowth of her family of origin experiences, Kitty became a certified special education teacher in 1983 and a certified rehabilitation counselor in 1993. She worked in public and private education (birth through grade twelve) and counseling for 24 years before moving to higher education in 2007. Kitty currently works as an Assistant Professor in the College of Education for The University of Alaska Anchorage, at Kodiak College.

Drezolutions Productions Introduces

OCEAN BLUE RISING

www.oceanbluerising.com

A Kodiak band featuring the songs of Brittany Tregarthen and Daniel Dresdow. Brittany is a Special Olympics athlete and author. Daniel is a musician and an Orthodox Christian priest (Father Innocent). Together they compose inspirational, jazzy songs against a magnificent background of ocean, mountains and sky. Listen to their music on www.oceanbluerising.com.